Convenience Food Facts

Help for the Healthy Meal Planner

Arlene Monk, R.D. and Marion J. Franz, R.D., M.S.

2nd Edition

Wellness and Nutrition Library
from
Diabetes Center, Inc.
Minneapolis, Minnesota

International Diabetes Center
© 1984, Revised 1985, Revised 1987

Library of Congress Cataloging-in-Publication Data

Monk, Arlene.
    Convenience food facts.

        1. Food—Composition—Tables. 2. Convenience foods—
Composition—Tables. 3. Brand name products—Composition
—Tables. 4. Diabetes—Nutritional aspects. I. Franz,
Marion J. II. Title.
TX551.M56   1987   641.1'0212   87-5379
ISBN 0-937721-20-4

Published by Diabetes Center, Inc.
P.O. Box #739
Wayzata, Minnesota 55391

Printed in the United States of America
10 9 8 7 6 5 4 3 2 1

Table of Contents

Convenient Nutrition for Everyone

In our busy, hustle-and-bustle society, convenience can be one of the biggest influences on how we order our lives. This is certainly true of our eating habits. If we're not grabbing a bite at a fast food restaurant, we're looking for a meal that is quick and easy to prepare so we can spend as much time as possible with interests other than cooking.

Convenience foods offer just that — convenience. They are the fastest growing processed food group because they give us what we demand — quick, easy to prepare, good tasting, and relatively inexpensive meals.

Consumers also are becoming more knowledgeable about nutrition and the effects different foods have on health. We eat not only for the energy that we need to fully enjoy our daily activities, but also to ensure our health throughout a long and productive life.

Unfortunately, the goals of convenience and good nutrition are not always easily achieved together. This is not to say that good nutrition is inconvenient. It is just that you need to know about the nutrients in the foods you buy, so you can plan a healthy diet which offers the convenience you appreciate. ***Convenience Food Facts*** will give you that information.

This book is designed to help convenience food users meet many different nutritional needs and desires. You may want to achieve one or more of the following goals, and the Convenience Foods product nutrition tables can help you.

Limit Calories to Reduce Weight

If you are trying to lose weight, a safe and reasonable weight loss goal is 1 to 2 pounds of fat per week. Each pound of fat contains approximately 3,500 calories. This means that you must increase you energy expenditure (exercise) and cut back on your calorie intake for a total of 3,500 to 7,000 calories per week (or 500 to 1,000 calories per day) less than the calorie intake at which you maintain your weight.

A weight control program that is nutritionally safe as well as low in calories should provide 1,200 to 1,500 calories per day. It is important to spread these calories throughout the day, rather than skip breakfast and lunch, thus consuming all 1,200 or 1,500 calories late in the day. About 400 to 500 calories, or one-third of the total, should be consumed at each meal.

For weight maintenance, adults usually require approximately 1,800 to 2,400 calories per day, or approximately 600 to 800 calories at each meal. Calorie values of convenience foods can help you decide on your portion sizes.

I

Foods that contain fewer than 20 calories per serving can be used as "free foods" up to two or three times per day, for a total of not more than 50 to 60 calories per day. These foods are good snacks to help curb hunger and reduce total calories.

Knowing the number of calories per serving will help you decide if and how a product might fit into your meal plan. The first column next to the product name in the nutrition tables contains the portion sizes on which the nutritional information is based. The next column indicates the number of calories contained in that portion size of the product.

Reduce Fat Content of Diet

A high fat diet, especially one high in saturated fats and cholesterol, is related to increased risk of heart disease, which is America's number one killer disease. Saturated fats and cholesterol are found in meats, dairy products, and eggs. The *Dietary Guidelines for Americans* recommend that the diet contain no more than 30 percent of total calories from fat, 50 to 60 percent of the total calories from carbohydrates ("naturally occurring" sugars and starches), and 15 to 20 percent from protein.

To the right of the calorie column are three columns that list the carbohydrate, protein, and fat content of the product. The column listing grams of fat can help you judge the amount of fat in the product. To achieve the goal of 30 percent or less of your calories from fat, follow these guidelines: On a weight loss diet, one meal should contain 15 to 18 grams of fat. On a weight maintenance diet, one meal should contain 20 to 28 grams of fat.

Fifteen grams of protein for women and 19 grams for men per meal will supply one-third of the day's requirements for protein.

Reduce Salt Content of Diet

Many convenience foods are high in salt. Salt is usually added not to preserve the food, but to satisfy the public's desire for salty tasting foods. It is wise to cut back on the salt in your diet, because salt is 40 percent sodium, and too much sodium has been linked to high blood pressure (hypertension). The average American eats 10 to 60 times the 200 milligrams of sodium the body needs per day. It has been recommended that Americans limit their daily sodium intake to approximately 1,000 to 3,300 milligrams. At one meal, sodium intake should not exceed 1,000 milligrams; people on sodium restricted diets should consume less than 700 milligrams per meal.

Sodium content in milligrams per serving is listed in the column second from the right.

Use Exchange Lists for Meal Planning

The column labeled "Exchange Values" is intended for people who use the exchange system of meal planning. This system was designed to take the guesswork and calorie counting out of meal planning.

Two other bits of information on the nutrition tables are intended specifically for people with diabetes. A † next to the exchange value indicates a recommendation that this product be used with caution in a diabetic meal plan because it contains a moderate amount of sugar. A ** in the exchange column indicates a recommendation that this product be avoided by people with diabetes because it contains a high amount of sugar. If you do not have diabetes but want to cut down your consumption of refined sugar, these recommendations will help you also.

This book was written by staff at the International Diabetes Center in Minneapolis, Minnesota. You may wonder why health professionals concerned with care and education for people with diabetes are distributing nutrition information to everyone else to use. The answer is that one of the most important ways to control diabetes and prevent the most common type of diabetes is to follow a well-balanced and nutritious meal plan. Many people who have diabetes also need to lose weight. So you see, the goals of people who have diabetes are goals that you may share.

The next brief section is specifically for people who have diabetes. If you do not have diabetes, you may wish to go to page IV for some helpful hints on wise shopping strategy.

If You Have Diabetes

All of the information in this book can be just as helpful to you as to everyone else. Of course, you will want to pay special attention to the exchange values and the recommendations to avoid or use certain products with caution.

If you do not have an individualized meal plan and do not know how to use the exchange system, we encourage you to see a dietitian or nutritionist who is familiar with diabetes nutritional management. Ask your doctor for a referral. The exchange system allows maximum flexibility and variety while helping you control your diabetes.

If you already have an individualized meal plan, become familiar with the foods you can eat. Then outline your weekly menu so when you shop, you can choose foods that fit into your planned exchanges for meals and snacks. High sugar foods often contain calories without many other valuable nutrients. It is wise to avoid them. If you do eat foods containing moderate amounts of sugar, eat them with a meal, when absorption of the sugar will not be as rapid. It also may help to eat them before exercise, because exercise can help lower blood glucose levels. For weight control, pay special attention to calorie values and avoid high fat, high sugar, and/or high calorie foods.

This book will help you learn the nutritional value of convenience food products. This information plus the exchange values will help you make wise food choices. Generally, nutritional adequacy can be ensured by eating a variety of foods throughout the day.

For products that are not contained in this book, the guide on page XII will help you compute exchange values from a product's nutritional label. Especially important are the sections on shopping strategy and product labeling.

Shopping Strategy

One of the hardest things about grocery shopping is to come home with only the foods you wanted to buy. Try the following general recommendations for food purchasing:

- **Plan Ahead!** The food you buy on your weekly shopping trip will determine your food choices throughout the week.

- **Outline Your Weekly Menu.** Occasional meals from convenience foods are not a problem, nor do they compromise the nutritional quality of your food intake. But overuse of any food, including convenience foods, can be a problem. Use the product nutrition tables to plan convenience meals that will not jeopardize your nutritional goals.

- **Make Your Grocery List from Your Menu Outline.** Your menu will help you avoid impulse eating, and your grocery list will help you avoid impulse buying.

- **Shop for Groceries When Your Stomach is Full.** You will be most likely to shop carelessly when you are hungry, and will tend to buy foods you don't need or shouldn't have. Purchase ONLY those items on your grocery list.

- **Avoid Buying Foods You Tend to Overeat.** Certain foods are just too tempting once they are in your cupboard. Avoid buying these and other foods you know are not appropriate for your nutritional goals.

- **Be Aware of Distractions.** Attractive displays and advertising can tempt you to buy without thinking. In addition, products the grocer is trying hardest to sell will often be placed at eye level. Remember—your grocer's choices are not always your best buy!

- **Keep Costs Down.** Good nutrition is not expensive. In fact, making wise food choices can help you eat better and save money. The most dramatic savings will occur when you cut back on simple sugar items, such as soft drinks, candy, sweet baked goods, and presweetened cereals. Lean cuts of beef, chicken, or turkey are usually less expensive than high fat meats, such as prime beef or processed luncheon meats. Margarine is less expensive than butter. Reducing your use of salad dressing, catsup, and sauces can also cut expenses. And remember, home-prepared meals are often less expensive than meals of convenience foods. Decide when convenience foods can help you without ruining your budget and nutritional goals.

- **Learn to Read Labels.** Lists of ingredients and nutritional labeling can help you make wise food choices. However, food labels frequently do not tell the whole story. Many of the terms used on labels have not been regulated and can be misleading, while other terms are regulated and can be helpful. You need to know what labels really tell you in order to be able to use them. The next section will help you do just that.

What Is REALLY in the Food You Are Buying?

There are several specific regulations regarding food labeling. For example, ingredients must be listed in descending order according to the percentage of weight they contribute to the total weight of the product. If a manufacturer makes a nutrition claim or adds nutrients to a food, the package must contain a complete nutrition label substantiating the claim. Misleading photographs are unlawful. And a few terms, such as "low sodium" or "low calorie," are specifically defined by federal regulations.

However, there still is a considerable amount of information manufacturers do not tell us: Many of the almost 3,000 additives in current use do not need to be specifically named; a so-called natural food can still contain artificial ingredients; foods "with no salt" can still contain a lot of sodium; "light" may refer to a product's color or density, not necessarily its calorie or fat content; "sugar-free" products need not contain fewer calories than their counterparts with sugar.

Let's take a closer look at food labeling terms and regulations and how they can help you purchase nutritious products.

Food Labeling Terms Can Be
Both Helpful and Misleading

Two federal agencies are responsible for food labels. The Food and Drug Administration (FDA) is responsible for all food labeling except meat and poultry. The U.S. Department of Agriculture (USDA) regulates meat and poultry products. Some terms such as "light" or "leaner" may be regulated by one agency but not by the other.

Below are some common terms used on food labels with the FDA and USDA regulations that apply to them. Some food labeling terms are well regulated, while others can be confusing or misleading to the consumer.

Low Calorie: These foods may contain no more than 40 calories per serving or no more than .4 calorie per gram. (Serving size can, however, vary.) Foods naturally low in calories, such as vegetables, cannot be called "low calorie," but they may be labeled "vegetables, a low-calorie food."

Reduced Calorie: These foods must have one-third fewer calories than the standard product and must include on the label a comparison of calorie content of the standard and reduced-calorie versions. USDA regulations, on the other hand, require that "reduced calorie" foods have a 25 percent reduction in calories.

Diet or Dietetic: These foods must meet the same requirements as "low calorie" or "reduced calorie" foods. They must contain no more than 40 calories per serving or have at least one-third fewer calories than the regular product. However, this does not always mean that they will be truly low in calories, just lower than the regular product. In addition, "diet" or "dietetic" may mean that a product is lower in sodium, but not calories. In this case, it will still be labeled "diet," but the product does not need to meet the requirements of "low calorie" or "reduced calorie" foods.

Sodium Free: Foods must have less than 5 milligrams of sodium per serving.

Very Low Sodium: Foods that have no more than 35 milligrams of sodium per serving.

Low Sodium: Foods that contain no more than 140 milligrams of sodium per serving.

Reduced Sodium: Sodium levels of these products have been reduced by at least 75 percent. The label must compare the sodium level of the "reduced sodium" product with the regular product.

Low Fat: Dairy products (low-fat milk, yogurt, cottage cheese) must, according to the USDA regulations, contain between .5 and 2 percent milk fat. Low-fat meat will have no more than 10 percent fat by weight (same as "lean" meat).

Lean: When lean refers to meat and poultry products, the USDA regulations state that it will have no more than 10 percent fat by weight. "Extra lean" meats must have no more than 5 percent fat. "Leaner" may be used if a meat product has at least 25 percent less fat in comparison with USDA standards. Actual fat content must appear on the label, along with a comparison of the fat content of the product and the standard. However, if "lean" or "light" is part of the brand name of a frozen dinner used to suggest that the product may help promote weight loss, the only requirement is that the product have a nutrition label.

Enriched or Fortified: These products contain added vitamins, minerals, or protein. The label must include full nutritional disclosure; "per serving" amounts of nutrients must be given.

Imitation: These products are nutritionally inferior—that is, lower in protein, vitamins, or minerals—to the standard product. Foods that are lower in calories, fat, or cholesterol are the exception; they are not considered imitation.

The following terms are not regulated, and they can be misleading as you read labels:

Light or Lite: These terms can mean anything from a lighter color or texture than the regular product to less sodium, calories, or fat. The FDA has not defined "light" food products. The USDA, on the other hand, which regulates meat and poultry products, defines "light" (also "leaner" and "lower fat") as meat with at least 25 percent less fat than regular products. "Light" may also mean 25 percent less sodium, calories, or breading. The label must indicate what nutrient has been reduced to earn the claim "light." These restrictions do not apply to frozen dinners.

Sugar-free or Sugarless: Although these foods cannot contain sucrose (table sugar), they can include other sweeteners such as honey, corn syrup, fructose, sorbitol, or mannitol. If a food labeled "sugar-free" is not low in calories, the label must tell the consumer that it is not a reduced-calorie food.

Be wary of ice cream, candy bars, and cakes that are labeled "sugar-free" or "sugarless." Many of these products can be higher in calories than the products they are replacing. They are often made with sorbitol, which is the alcohol form of glucose. It contains four calories per gram, just as any other carbohydrate. Because sorbitol is not soluble in water, the fat content of these products is usually higher in order to dissolve the sorbitol. Products containing sorbitol can also cause diarrhea.

Sugar-free products that might be useful are artificial sweeteners, diet soda pop, dietetic gelatin or pudding, and fruit canned without added sugar. Products that may be useful as free foods (a free food contains less than 20 calories per serving) include diet syrup, diet jam or jelly, diet hard candy, and sugar-free gum.

Low Salt: Since salt is not the only ingredient that contains sodium, a food that is low in salt is not necessarily low in sodium. Terms such as "unsalted," "salt-free," "no salt," "no salt added," "without added salt," or "no salt added during processing" refer to salt, but the food could still contain significant levels of sodium, either naturally or from substances added for preservation, leavening, palatability, or other purposes.

No Cholesterol: These food products do not contain cholesterol. Remember, however, that only foods from animal sources contain cholesterol. Vegetable sources never contain cholesterol. In addition, "no cholesterol" does not mean that the food is low in fat or in saturated fat.

Natural: This term provides no guarantees unless the product is meat or poultry, because the FDA does not regulate the word "natural." The USDA does, and "natural" on meat and poultry means there are no artificial flavors, colors, preservatives, or synthetic ingredients of any kind, and the food and its ingredients are not more than "minimally processed." For any other food, such as baked goods, beverages, or processed foods that do not contain meat or poultry, the term means anything the manufacturer wishes it to mean.

Organic: This term has no legal meaning and can be used without any guides. The USDA, however, does not allow its use on meat or poultry products.

Ingredients List Is the Second Clue

An important part of your shopping strategy should involve looking at the ingredients list on the foods you buy. Of course, you can't look at every label, but if you are considering a new product or just want to familiarize yourself with foods you eat regularly, take the time to read and understand the ingredients list.

Ingredients are listed in descending order according to the percentage of weight they contribute to the weight of the product. For example, if sugar is the first, second, or third ingredient on the label, the product probably contains a large amount of sugar. When sugar is near the end of a list of four or more ingredients, the amount of sugar is probably not significant.

Sometimes the manufacturer will list on the label all the ingredients that are similar to sugar, but the word "sugar" may never appear. If these ingredients were grouped together and labeled as sugar, they might be the first ingredient on the list. Check to see how many items on the label are similar to sugar, and then notice their position in the ingredients listing. Words ending in "ose" are generally a form of sugar. Table and baking sugar is sucrose. Other sugars include dextrose, fructose, levulose, lactose, and glucose.

Another phrase used for sugar-type ingredients is "nutritive sweetener." This identifies a sweetener that contains calories. Examples of nutritive sweeteners besides sugar are invert sugar, corn syrup, corn sugar, dextrin, molasses, sorghum, honey, and maple or brown sugar.

Especially if you have diabetes, remember the sources of sugar:

brown sugar	corn syrup	dextrose	invert sugar
fructose	glucose	honey	
lactose	levulose	mannitol	
maple syrup	molasses	sorbitol	
sorghum	sucrose	xylitol	

The phrase "non-nutritive sweetener" identifies a sweetener that contains few or no calories. Examples are saccharin and aspartame. (You may know aspartame by the brand names Equal® or NutraSweet™.)

In addition to sugar, you should be aware of ingredients that are high in saturated fat. High fat items that may appear on food labels are:

animal fat	lard
bacon fat	meat fat
beef fat	milk chocolate
butter	palm or palm kernel oil
chicken fat	pork fat
cocoa butter	shortening
coconut	turkey fat
coconut oil	vegetable fat or ⎤ often will be palm
cream and cream sauces	vegetable oil ⎦ or coconut oil
egg and egg-yolk solids	vegetable shortening
hardened fat or oil	whole milk solids
hydrogenated fat or oil	

If you have been advised to or want to limit your sodium intake, watch out for the following high sodium ingredients:

broth	salt (sodium chloride)
baking soda (sodium bicarbonate)	brine (salt and water)
monosodium glutamate or MSG	soy sauce
bouillon	

In summary, note the following as you check the ingredients list:

1. The order of ingredients.

2. Ingredients — by any name — that you want to limit or avoid.

Clue Three: Take Advantage of Nutritional Labeling

In addition to food labeling terms and the list of ingredients, many food labels include "nutrition information per serving." This information can help you fit the product into your meal plan. It can also help you meet the nutritional goals of controlling fat, sugar, and sodium intake.

Nutritional labeling is voluntary for most food products, but it is required on any product for which special nutritive claims are made or to which extra nutrients are added. Manufacturers making any nutritional claim for their product must by law include the following information:

1. Serving size. The amount of food for which nutrition information is given, such as 1 slice, 1 cup, or 3 ounces. The number of servings per container is also given.

2. The amount of food energy in total calories.

3. The grams of protein, carbohydrate, and fat furnished by one serving of the food as it comes from the container. (One gram of carbohydrate or protein supplies four calories; one gram of fat supplies nine calories.)

4. Milligrams of sodium per serving.

5. Percentages of the U.S. Recommended Daily Allowances (RDA) for protein, vitamin A, vitamin C, three B vitamins (thiamin, niacin, and riboflavin), calcium, and iron in a serving of the food as it comes from the container.

6. Other nutrient information, such as amounts of cholesterol or grams of saturated or polyunsaturated fat, is optional. This information is usually included only if a specific nutritional claim has been made, such as "low cholesterol product."

The following nutrition labeling format is currently being used:

NUTRITION INFORMATION
(per serving)
Serving size=1 cup
Servings per container=2
Calories 110
Protein. . . . . .1 gram
Carbohydrate . . . . .25 grams
Fat. . . . . .1 gram
Sodium . . . . .275 milligrams

Percentage of U.S.
Recommended Daily
Allowances (U.S. RDA)
Protein 2
Vitamin A 25
Vitamin C 25
Thiamin 25
Riboflavin 25
Niacin 25
Calcium 4
Iron 4

The following are examples of nutritional labeling on specific products:

ENRICHED HARD ROLLS

Nutrition Information
(per serving)

Serving=1 roll
Servings per container=6
Calories .160
Protein . . . . .5 gms.
Carbohydrate . . . . .30 gms.
Fat . . . . .2 gms.
Sodium . . . . .155 mg.

Percentage of U.S. Recommended
Daily Allowances (U.S. RDA)

Protein. 8	Niacin 8
Vitamin A 0	Calcium 2
Vitamin C 0	Iron 6
Thiamin (B_1). 10	
Riboflavin (B_2) 6	

DRY ROASTED PEANUTS

Nutrition Information
(per serving)

Serving size=1 ounce
Servings per container=8

Calories 160
Protein ....7 gms.
Carbohydrate ....6 gms.
Fat (71% of calories)
from fat ....14 gms.
   Polyunsaturated......5 gms.
   Saturated.............2 gms.
   Cholesterol............0 mg.
Sodium ....250 mg.

Percentage of U.S. Recommended
Daily Allowances (U.S. RDA)

Protein 10	Niacin 20
Vitamin A................0	Calcium 0
Vitamin C................0	Iron 2
Thiamin (B_1) 0	
Riboflavin (B_2) 2	

If you do not use exchange lists for meal planning, go on to page XIV for an introduction to the convenience food nutrition tables.

Using Nutritional Labeling in Diabetic Meal Planning

Nutritional labeling is especially valuable if you have diabetes. But in order to effectively use the information on product labels, you must first understand the basis for grouping foods into exchange lists. Each list is comprised of a group of foods in amounts that all contain approximately the same number of calories and grams of carbohydrate, protein, and fat per serving.

By looking at the nutritional label on a food product, you can estimate how many exchanges are in a serving of that food. This will help you decide if and how you can include it in your meal plan. Exchange conversions have already been done for all of the convenience foods in the tables starting on page 1. But for other foods, you can use the table below to convert nutritional labeling information to the exchange system. (It is important to correctly convert calories and grams of carbohydrate, protein, and fat into exchanges, but don't worry about variations of a few calories or grams.)

Exchange	Calories	Carbohydrate	Protein	Fat
1 starch/bread	80	15 gms.	3 gms.	trace
1 lean meat	55	0	7 gms.	3 gms.
1 med.fat meat	75	0	7 gms.	5 gms.
1 high fat meat	100	0	7 gms.	8 gms.
1 vegetable	25	5 gms.	2 gms.	0
1 fruit	60	15 gms.	0	0
1 milk (skim)	90	12 gms.	8 gms.	trace
1 fat	45	0	0	5 gms.

Steps for Converting Nutritional Labeling to Exchanges. The following information is from a 10-ounce box of frozen pizza.

Nutrition Information Per Serving

Serving size .... ½ pizza (5 oz.)
Servings per container 2
Calories 350
Protein .... 18 gms.
Carbohydrate .... 33 gms.
Fat .... 16 gms.

To convert label information into the exchange system, follow these steps:

1. Check the label for the information you need to convert to the exchange system. You need:
   serving size: ½ pizza   protein: 18 grams
   calories: 350   fat: 16 grams
   carbohydrate: 33 grams

2. Check for serving size. Is this a reasonable size for your use?

3. Compare the label information with the carbohydrate, protein, fat, and calories on the exchange table. First, convert grams of carbohdyrate in your serving size to exchanges. In this case, 33 grams of carbohydrate would be 2 starch exchanges:

	Carbohydrate	Protein	Fat
½ pizza	33 gms.	18 gms.	16 gms.
2 starch exchanges	30 gms.	6 gms.	—

4. Next subtract the grams of protein you used in converting the carbohydrate to exchanges. Then convert the remaining grams of protein to meat exchanges. Use the medium fat meat exchange values.

	Carbohydrate	Protein	Fat
½ pizza	33 gms.	18 gms.	16 gms.
2 starch exchanges	30 gms.	–6 gms.	—
		12 gms.	16 gms.
2 med. fat meat exchanges		14 gms.	10 gms.

5. Next, subtract the grams of fat in the meat exchanges from the fat contained in the serving size. Then convert the remaining grams of fat to fat exchanges.

	Carbohydrate	Protein	Fat
½ pizza	33 gms.	18 gms.	16 gms.
2 starch exchanges	30 gms.	–6 gms.	—
		12 gms.	16 gms.
2 med. fat meat exchanges		14 gms.	–10 gms.
			6 gms.
1 fat exchange			5 gms.

6. If you eat ½ of this 10-ounce pizza, you use the following exchanges from your meal plan: 2 starch, 2 medium fat meat, 1 fat

7. Final check:

	Carbohydrate	Protein	Fat	Calories
½ pizza Exchanges: 2 starch, 2 med.	33 gms.	18 gms.	16 gms.	350
fat meat, 1 fat	30 gms.	20 gms.	15 gms.	355

Once again, do not worry about small discrepancies in the final figures. These calculations are accurate enough to use in your meal plan.

8. If the difference between the grams per serving and the grams accounted for by the exchange system is less than one-half an exchange, you do not need to count those extra grams.

How Everyone Can Use the Convenience Foods Nutrition Tables

The nutrition information contained in the following tables was solicited and received in 1987 from a wide variety of food processing companies. The convenience food products are grouped according to major food categories that represent the way you would be most likely to use the product. Within each food category, brand names are in alphabetical order, with the parent company shown in parentheses after the brand name. Products are then listed alphabetically under the brand name.

In the tables themselves, each product is listed in a suggested serving size along with the number of calories and grams of carbohydrate, protein, and fat. Milligrams of sodium per serving are listed if such information was available. The exchange value column is for people who use the exchange system of meal planning, and is based on the 1986 revision of the exchange lists. Foods listed with a † have a moderate amount of sugar and foods with ** have a large amount of sugar. This information is intended for people who have diabetes, but is may be useful to anyone who wants to cut back on the amount of simple sugar in favor of starches and fiber in the diet. An "S" symbol in the left margin is another indicator that a product contains too much sugar. An "F" symbol in the left margin indicates that the product contains a large amount of fat. You may want to limit products which contain large amounts of sugar or fat.

This information will help you fit convenience foods into a nutritious, well-balanced diet. You cannot rely on these foods for all your meals, just as you cannot rely on any single type of food. It is true that the best consumer is an informed consumer, but we hope you will also act on this information to meet the nutrition goals that can mean a much happier and healthier life!

How to Use the Convenience Foods
Nutrition Tables if You Have Diabetes

All of the information in this book can be used by anyone. People with diabetes have just as much to gain from cutting back on simple sugars, saturated fats, and sodium as everyone else does. In fact, if you have diabetes, you have even more to gain, because you can use the information to plan a nutritious diet as well as to help control diabetes.

The exchange values in the tables were calculated using data on food values that were current in 1987. Product formulations will change from time to time. It is a good idea to check the information in the tables with current data as you happen to come across it. The nutrition information on the actual product label will be the most current.

The exchange values are only suggested exchanges. You may decide to use the calories and grams of carbohydrate, protein, and fat as other exchanges. Exchange values are largely a matter of personal preference, used for fitting foods into most meal plans. The method for calculating exchanges was based on ***Exchange Lists for Meal Planning—1986.***

You may find that many of the foods in the tables may not fit into your meal plan. They may contain too many calories or be too high in fat. As a result, the exchange values may be greater than the number you have available in your meal plan. Because of this, not all of the food items in the tables are recommended for your use. Check YOUR allowance.

Specific products are recommended for "occasional use only" or "not recommended for use." Products that contain moderate amounts of simple sugars are marked by † and are to be used with caution by people who have diabetes. Products with large amounts of simple sugars are marked with ** and are not recommended for use. No exchange values are given for this latter category. An "S" symbol in the left margin indicates that a product contains moderate to high amounts of simple sugars. An "F" symbol in the left margin denotes products that contain more than two fat exchanges.

In summary, use the information in these tables and the ingredients listed on products to decide if these convenience foods will fit into your meal plan. By doing this knowledgeably you can control your diabetes and your weight. And best of all, you can enjoy added variety and flexibility in the planning of your meals and snacks.

Acknowledgements

The authors wish to thank Neysa C.M. Jensen, editor. We would also like to thank the many food processing companies that responded to our requests for nutrition information about their products.

Marion Franz, M.S., R.D.
Director of Nutrition
International Diabetes Center

Accompaniments, Side Dishes

NUTRIENT VALUE

PRODUCTS	SERVING SIZE	CALORIES	CARBO-HYDRATE (g.)	PROTEIN (g.)	FAT (g.)	SODIUM (mg.)	EXCHANGES
CHOW MEIN NOODLES							
LA CHOY® (Beatrice Companies, Inc.)							
Chow Mein Noodles	½ cup	150	17	3	8	210	1 starch, 1½ fat
PASTA, PASTA SIDE DISHES							
BANQUET® (ConAgra® Frozen Foods Co.)							
Parsleyed Noodles, frozen	4 oz.	186	19	5	10	568	1 starch, 2 fat
BETTY CROCKER® (General Mills, Inc.)							
International Noodle Mixes							
Fettucine Alfredo (as prepared)	1 serving	230	25	8	11	590	1½ starch, ½ meat, 1½ fat
Romanoff (as prepared)	1 serving	220	24	7	11	630	1½ starch, ½ meat, 1½ fat
BETTY CROCKER® SUDDENLY SALADS® (General Mills, Inc.)							
Macaroni Salad, Creamy (as prepared)	⅙ package	200	20	4	11	260	1 starch, 2 fat
Pasta Salad, Classic (as prepared)	⅙ package	150	19	4	6	330	1 starch, 1 fat

†For Occasional Use   **Not Recommended For Use   *Not Available   Ⓕ More Than 2 Fat Exchanges   Ⓢ Moderate To High Sugar Content

NUTRIENT VALUE

PRODUCTS	SERVING SIZE	CALORIES	CARBO-HYDRATE (g.)	PROTEIN (g.)	FAT (g.)	SODIUM (mg.)	EXCHANGES
Pasta Salad, Italian (as prepared)	⅙ package	160	20	5	7	350	1 starch, ½ meat, 1 fat
CREAMETTE® (The Creamette Co.)							
Egg Noodles	2 oz. uncooked (1 cup cooked)	220	40	8	3	*	2½ starch
Macaroni, Spaghetti, Miscellaneous Pasta	2 oz. uncooked (1 cup cooked)	210	41	7	1	*	2½ starch
GOLDEN GRAIN® (Golden Grain Macaroni Co.)							
Noodle Roni® Parmesano® (as prepared)	½ cup	130	21	5	3	*	1½ starch, ½ fat
LA CHOY® (Beatrice Companies, Inc.)							
Ramen Noodles, all flavors (as prepared) (average)	½ package	190	28	5	7	740-1155	2 starch, 1 fat
LIPTON® (Thomas J. Lipton, Inc.) Noodles and Sauce							
Beef Flavor (as prepared)	½ cup	190	26	5	7	595	2 starch, 1 fat
Butter (as prepared)	½ cup	190	24	5	9	565	1½ starch, 1½ fat
Butter and Herb (as prepared)	½ cup	180	23	5	9	525	1½ starch, 1½ fat
Cheese (as prepared)	½ cup	200	24	5	9	540	1½ starch, 1½ fat
Chicken Flavor (as prepared)	½ cup	190	25	5	9	465	1½ starch, 1½ fat
Sour Cream and Chive (as prepared)	½ cup	190	23	5	9	455	1½ starch, 1½ fat
Noodles and Sauce, Deluxe							
Alfredo (as prepared)	½ cup	220	22	7	11	560	1½ starch, 2 fat
Chicken Bombay (as prepared)	½ cup	190	22	6	9	515	1½ starch, 1½ fat

†For Occasional Use   **Not Recommended For Use   *Not Available   Ⓕ More Than 2 Fat Exchanges   Ⓢ Moderate To High Sugar Content

NUTRIENT VALUE

PRODUCTS	SERVING SIZE	CALORIES	CARBO-HYDRATE (g.)	PROTEIN (g.)	FAT (g.)	SODIUM (mg.)	EXCHANGES
Parmesano (as prepared)	½ cup	210	22	6	11	445	1½ starch, 2 fat
Stroganoff (as prepared)	½ cup	200	22	6	10	510	1½ starch, 2 fat
Shells and Sauce Creamy Garlic (as prepared)	½ cup	200	27	5	9	535	2 starch, 1½ fat
Herb Tomato (as prepared)	½ cup	170	25	5	6	435	1½ starch, 1 fat

STOUFFER'S® (Stouffer Foods Corp.)

PRODUCTS	SERVING SIZE	CALORIES	CARBO-HYDRATE (g.)	PROTEIN (g.)	FAT (g.)	SODIUM (mg.)	EXCHANGES
F Fettucini Alfredo	½ of 10 oz. package	280	17	8	20	570	1 starch, 1 meat, 3 fat
F Fettucini Primavera	½ of 10⅝ oz. package	270	12	7	21	520	1 starch, ½ meat, 3½ fat
Linguini with Pesto Sauce	½ of 8¼ oz. package	210	20	9	10	250	1 starch, 1 meat, 1 fat
Noodles Romanoff	⅓ of 12 oz. package	170	15	8	9	700	1 starch, 1 meat, ½ fat

POTATOES
BANQUET® (ConAgra® Frozen Foods Co.)

PRODUCTS	SERVING SIZE	CALORIES	CARBO-HYDRATE (g.)	PROTEIN (g.)	FAT (g.)	SODIUM (mg.)	EXCHANGES
AuGratin Potatoes, frozen	4 oz.	98	17	2	2	472	1 starch

BETTY CROCKER® (General Mills, Inc.)

PRODUCTS	SERVING SIZE	CALORIES	CARBO-HYDRATE (g.)	PROTEIN (g.)	FAT (g.)	SODIUM (mg.)	EXCHANGES
Potato Mixes							
Au Gratin Potatoes (as prepared)	½ cup	150	21	3	6	605	1½ starch, 1 fat
Chicken 'n Herb Potatoes (as prepared)	½ cup	120	19	3	4	600	1 starch, 1 fat
Hash Browns with Onions (as prepared)	½ cup	160	24	2	6	460	1½ starch, 1 fat
Julienne Potatoes (as prepared)	½ cup	140	19	3	6	600	1 starch, 1 fat

†For Occasional Use   **Not Recommended For Use   *Not Available   F More Than 2 Fat Exchanges   S Moderate To High Sugar Content

NUTRIENT VALUE

PRODUCTS	SERVING SIZE	CALORIES	CARBO-HYDRATE (g.)	PROTEIN (g.)	FAT (g.)	SODIUM (mg.)	EXCHANGES
Parsley Creamed Potatoes, oven or saucepan method (as prepared)	½ cup	180	22	4	8	420	1½ starch, 1½ fat
Scalloped Potatoes (as prepared)	½ cup	140	19	3	6	570	1 starch, 1 fat
Smokey Cheddar Potatoes (as prepared)	½ cup	150	22	3	6	700	1½ starch, 1 fat
Sour Cream 'n Chive Potatoes (as prepared)	½ cup	160	21	3	7	530	1½ starch, 1 fat
Twice Baked Potatoes Bacon and Cheese, Family Style (as prepared)	1 serving	210	21	6	11	600	1½ starch, ½ meat, 1½ fat
Herbed Butter, Family Style (as prepared)	1 serving	220	20	5	13	540	1 starch, ½ meat, 2 fat
Mild Cheddar with Onion (as prepared)	½ cup	190	19	5	11	640	1 starch, ½ meat, 1½ fat
Sour Cream 'n Chive (as prepared)	½ cup	200	19	5	11	540	1 starch, ½ meat, 1½ fat

BETTY CROCKER® SUDDENLY SALADS® (General Mills, Inc.)

PRODUCTS	SERVING SIZE	CALORIES	CARBO-HYDRATE (g.)	PROTEIN (g.)	FAT (g.)	SODIUM (mg.)	EXCHANGES
F Potato Salad, Traditional	⅙ package	250	21	4	17	420	1½ starch, 3 fat

FRENCH'S® (The Pillsbury Co.)

PRODUCTS	SERVING SIZE	CALORIES	CARBO-HYDRATE (g.)	PROTEIN (g.)	FAT (g.)	SODIUM (mg.)	EXCHANGES
Au-Gratin Potatoes, Tangy (as prepared)	½ cup	140	19	4	6	470	1 starch, 1 fat
Creamy Italian-Style Potatoes with Parmesan Sauce (as prepared)	½ cup	130	21	3	4	430	1½ starch, ½ fat
Dinner Potato Pancakes (as prepared)	½ cup	80	16	3	1	410	1 starch
Scalloped Potatoes, Crispy Top with Savory Onion (as prepared)	½ cup	140	20	3	5	420	1 starch, 1 fat

†For Occasional Use   **Not Recommended For Use   *Not Available   F More Than 2 Fat Exchanges   S Moderate To High Sugar Content

NUTRIENT VALUE

PRODUCTS	SERVING SIZE	CALORIES	CARBO-HYDRATE (g.)	PROTEIN (g.)	FAT (g.)	SODIUM (mg.)	EXCHANGES
Scalloped Potatoes, Real Cheese (as prepared)	½ cup	140	20	3	5	370	1 starch, 1 fat
Sour Cream and Chives Potatoes (as prepared)	½ cup	150	20	3	6	560	1 starch, 1 fat
Stroganoff Potatoes, Creamy (as prepared)	½ cup	130	20	3	4	520	1 starch, 1 fat
FRENCH'S® IDAHO® (The Pillsbury Co.)							
Mashed Potatoes (as prepared)	½ cup	130	16	2	6	340	1 starch, 1 fat
Spuds Mashed Potatoes (as prepared)	½ cup	140	16	2	7	370	1 starch, 1 fat
GREEN GIANT® (The Pillsbury Co.)							
Stuffed Baked Potato with Cheese Flavored Topping	½ package	200	33	4	6	520	2 starch, 1 fat
Stuffed Baked Potato with Sour Cream and Chives	½ package	230	31	5	10	580	2 starch, 2 fat
HUNGRY JACK® (The Pillsbury Co.)							
Mashed Potato Flakes (as prepared)	½ cup	140	17	3	7	380	1 starch, 1 fat
ORE-IDA® (Ore-Ida Foods, Inc.)							
Cheddar Browns™ (as purchased)	3 oz.	70	14	2	2	310	1 starch
Cottage Fries (as purchased)	3 oz.	110	18	2	5	25	1 starch, 1 fat
Country Style Dinner Fries® (as purchased)	3 oz.	120	18	1	5	45	1 starch, 1 fat
F Crispers!® (as purchased)	3 oz.	240	24	1	16	540	1½ starch, 3 fat
Crispy Crowns® (as purchased)	3 oz.	150	19	1	9	540	1 starch, 1½ fat
Crispy Crowns® with Onions (as purchased)	3 oz.	160	19	1	10	580	1 starch, 2 fat
Golden Crinkles® (as purchased)	3 oz.	110	18	1	4	40	1 starch, ½ fat

†For Occasional Use   **Not Recommended For Use   *Not Available   F More Than 2 Fat Exchanges   S Moderate To High Sugar Content

NUTRIENT VALUE

PRODUCTS	SERVING SIZE	CALORIES	CARBO-HYDRATE (g.)	PROTEIN (g.)	FAT (g.)	SODIUM (mg.)	EXCHANGES
Golden Fries® (as purchased)	3 oz.	110	18	1	5	45	1 starch, 1 fat
Golden Patties® (as purchased)	2½ oz.	130	15	1	9	290	1 starch, 1½ fat
Hash Browns, Shredded (as purchased)	3 oz.	60	14	1	0	60	1 starch
Hash Browns, Southern Style (as purchased)	3 oz.	70	17	<1	0	45	1 starch
Home Style Potato Wedges™ (as purchased)	3 oz.	90	17	1	3	45	1 starch, ½ fat
Lites (as purchased)							
Crinkle Cuts	3 oz.	80	16	1	2	35	1 starch
French Fries	3 oz.	80	15	1	3	30	1 starch
Shoestrings	3 oz.	90	17	<1	4	45	1 starch, ½ fat
Microwave (as purchased)							
Crinkle Cuts	3½ oz.	170	26	1	8	45	1½ starch, 1½ fat
Tater Tots®	4 oz.	170	26	2	8	655	1½ starch, 1½ fat
Pixie Crinkles® (as purchased)	3 oz.	130	20	1	6	40	1 starch, 1 fat
Potatoes O'Brien (as purchased)	3 oz.	60	14	1	0	20	1 starch
Shoestrings (as purchased)	3 oz.	130	20	1	7	45	1 starch, 1 fat
Tater Tots,® plain and varieties (as purchased) (average)	3 oz.	130	18	1	7	560-740	1 starch, 1 fat
POTATO BUDS® (General Mills, Inc.)							
Mashed Potatoes (as prepared)	½ cup	130	17	3	6	360	1 starch, 1 fat
STOUFFER'S® (Stouffer Foods Corp.)							
Potatoes au Gratin (as prepared)	⅓ of 11½ oz. package	120	13	3	6	480	1 starch, 1 fat

†For Occasional Use   **Not Recommended For Use   *Not Available   F More Than 2 Fat Exchanges   S Moderate To High Sugar Content

NUTRIENT VALUE

PRODUCTS	SERVING SIZE	CALORIES	CARBO-HYDRATE (g.)	PROTEIN (g.)	FAT (g.)	SODIUM (mg.)	EXCHANGES
Scalloped Potatoes (as prepared)	1/3 of 12 oz. package	110	11	3	6	410	1 starch, 1 fat

RICE, RICE SIDE DISHES
BANQUET® (ConAgra® Frozen Foods Co.)

Vegetables and Rice with Butter, frozen	4 oz.	183	23	3	9	650	1½ starch, 1½ fat

FEATHERWEIGHT® (Sandoz Nutrition)

Spanish Rice, Low Sodium	7½ oz.	140	30	4	0	32	2 starch

GOLDEN GRAIN® (Golden Grain Macaroni Co.)

Beef Rice-A-Roni® (as prepared)	½ cup	130	26	4	1	770	2 starch
Chicken Rice-A-Roni® (as prepared)	½ cup	130	27	4	1	800	2 starch
Spanish Rice-A-Roni® (as prepared)	½ cup	110	22	3	1	720	1½ starch

GREEN GIANT® RICE ORIGINALS® (The Pillsbury Co.)

Italian Blend Rice and Spinach in Cheese Sauce	½ cup	170	23	4	7	400	1½ starch, 1 fat
Rice and Broccoli in Flavored Cheese Sauce	½ cup	120	18	3	4	510	1 starch, 1 fat
Rice Jubilee	½ cup	150	22	2	6	340	1½ starch, 1 fat
Rice Medley	½ cup	120	21	3	3	260	1½ starch
Rice Pilaf	½ cup	120	23	3	2	520	1½ starch
Rice with Herb Butter Sauce	½ cup	150	22	3	5	390	1½ starch, ½ fat
White and Wild Rice	½ cup	120	23	3	2	550	1½ starch

HEINZ® (H.J. Heinz Co.)

Spanish Rice	7¼ oz.	150	26	3	5	1045	2 starch, 1 fat

LA CHOY® (Beatrice Companies, Inc.)

Fried Rice, canned	¾ cup	190	41	4	1	820	2½ starch

†For Occasional Use   **Not Recommended For Use   *Not Available   Ⓕ More Than 2 Fat Exchanges   Ⓢ Moderate To High Sugar Content

7

NUTRIENT VALUE

PRODUCTS	SERVING SIZE	CALORIES	CARBO-HYDRATE (g.)	PROTEIN (g.)	FAT (g.)	SODIUM (mg.)	EXCHANGES
Rice Noodles	½ cup	130	22	2	5	380	1½ starch, ½ fat

LIPTON® (Thomas J. Lipton, Inc.)
Rice and Sauce

PRODUCTS	SERVING SIZE	CALORIES	CARBO-HYDRATE (g.)	PROTEIN (g.)	FAT (g.)	SODIUM (mg.)	EXCHANGES
Beef Flavor (as prepared)	½ cup	160	27	3	4	665	2 starch, ½ fat
Chicken Flavor (as prepared)	½ cup	150	26	3	4	525	2 starch, ½ fat
Herb and Butter (as prepared)	½ cup	160	25	3	5	510	1½ starch, 1 fat
Long Grain and Wild Rice, all varieties (as prepared) (average)	½ cup	160	27	4	3	400-590	2 starch
Mushroom (as prepared)	½ cup	140	26	3	3	560	2 starch
Oriental (as prepared)	½ cup	160	25	5	4	540	1½ starch, ½ fat
Spanish (as prepared)	½ cup	140	26	3	3	520	2 starch
Vegetables Florentine (as prepared)	½ cup	160	26	4	4	540	2 starch, ½ fat

Rice and Sauce Combinations

PRODUCTS	SERVING SIZE	CALORIES	CARBO-HYDRATE (g.)	PROTEIN (g.)	FAT (g.)	SODIUM (mg.)	EXCHANGES
Almondine (as prepared)	½ cup	170	25	4	6	470	1½ starch, 1 fat
Provencale (as prepared)	½ cup	150	25	4	4	460	1½ starch, ½ fat
Rice and Peas (as prepared)	½ cup	150	26	4	3	400	2 starch
Rice Italiano (as prepared)	½ cup	160	24	4	5	460	1½ starch, 1 fat
Rice Medley (as prepared)	½ cup	150	26	4	3	400	2 starch

MINUTE® RICE (General Foods Corp.)

PRODUCTS	SERVING SIZE	CALORIES	CARBO-HYDRATE (g.)	PROTEIN (g.)	FAT (g.)	SODIUM (mg.)	EXCHANGES
Regular (as prepared without salt or butter)	½ cup	90	20	2	0	0	1 starch

†For Occasional Use   **Not Recommended For Use   *Not Available   F More Than 2 Fat Exchanges   S Moderate To High Sugar Content

NUTRIENT VALUE

PRODUCTS	SERVING SIZE	CALORIES	CARBO-HYDRATE (g.)	PROTEIN (g.)	FAT (g.)	SODIUM (mg.)	EXCHANGES
Drumstick Rice Mix (as prepared with butter, salted)	½ cup	150	25	3	4	690	1½ starch, ½ fat
Fried Rice Mix (as prepared with oil)	½ cup	160	25	3	5	550	1½ starch, 1 fat
Long Grain and Wild Rice Mix (as prepared with butter, salted)	½ cup	150	25	3	4	570	1½ starch, ½ fat
Rib Roast Rice Mix (as prepared with butter, salted)	½ cup	150	25	3	4	720	1½ starch, ½ fat
STOUFFER'S® (Stouffer Foods Corp.)							
Apple Pecan Rice	½ of 5⅞ oz. package	130	22	2	4	200	1 starch, ½ fruit, ½ fat
Rice Medley	½ of 6 oz. package	110	20	2	2	340	1 starch, ½ fat
UNCLE BEN'S® (Uncle Ben's Foods)							
Brown and Wild Rice (as prepared)							
Without butter	½ cup	126	25	4	2	474	1½ starch
With butter	½ cup	150	25	4	4	506	1½ starch, ½ fat
Converted Brand Rice (as prepared)							
Without salt and butter	⅔ cup	129	29	3	0	2	2 starch
With salt and butter	⅔ cup	148	29	3	2	463	2 starch, ½ fat
Fast-Cooking, Long Grain and Wild Rice (as prepared)							
Without butter	½ cup	95	20	3	0	387	1 starch
With butter	½ cup	127	20	3	4	430	1 starch, ½ fat
Long Grain and Wild Rice (as prepared)							
Without butter	½ cup	97	21	3	0	420	1½ starch

†For Occasional Use   **Not Recommended For Use   *Not Available   Ⓕ More Than 2 Fat Exchanges   Ⓢ Moderate To High Sugar Content

NUTRIENT VALUE

PRODUCTS	SERVING SIZE	CALORIES	CARBO-HYDRATE (g.)	PROTEIN (g.)	FAT (g.)	SODIUM (mg.)	EXCHANGES
With butter	½ cup	113	21	3	2	442	1½ starch, ½ fat
Select Brown Rice (as prepared) Without salt and butter	⅔ cup	133	26	4	2	5	2 starch
With salt and butter	⅔ cup	152	26	4	4	458	2 starch, ½ fat

UNCLE BEN'S® COUNTRY INN® (Uncle Ben's Foods)

PRODUCTS	SERVING SIZE	CALORIES	CARBO-HYDRATE (g.)	PROTEIN (g.)	FAT (g.)	SODIUM (mg.)	EXCHANGES
Broccoli Rice Au Gratin (as prepared) Without butter	½ cup	130	22	4	3	350	1½ starch
With butter	½ cup	180	22	4	8	420	1½ starch, 1½ fat
Rice Florentine (as prepared) Without butter	½ cup	120	24	3	2	620	1½ starch
With butter	½ cup	150	24	3	4	650	1½ starch, ½ fat
Rice Oriental with Vegetables (as prepared) Without butter	½ cup	120	25	3	1	440	1½ starch
With butter	½ cup	140	25	3	4	480	1½ starch, ½ fat
Vegetable Rice Medley (as prepared) Without butter	½ cup	140	29	3	1	390	2 starch
With butter	½ cup	160	29	3	4	430	2 starch, ½ fat

VAN CAMP'S® (Quaker Oats Co.)

PRODUCTS	SERVING SIZE	CALORIES	CARBO-HYDRATE (g.)	PROTEIN (g.)	FAT (g.)	SODIUM (mg.)	EXCHANGES
Spanish Rice	½ cup	75	14	2	2	680	1 starch

STUFFING, STUFFING MIXES
BANQUET® (ConAgra® Frozen Foods Co.)

PRODUCTS	SERVING SIZE	CALORIES	CARBO-HYDRATE (g.)	PROTEIN (g.)	FAT (g.)	SODIUM (mg.)	EXCHANGES
Chicken Flavored Stuffing, frozen	4 oz.	281	44	8	8	693	3 starch, 1 fat

†For Occasional Use **Not Recommended For Use *Not Available Ⓕ More Than 2 Fat Exchanges Ⓢ Moderate To High Sugar Content

NUTRIENT VALUE

PRODUCTS	SERVING SIZE	CALORIES	CARBO-HYDRATE (g.)	PROTEIN (g.)	FAT (g.)	SODIUM (mg.)	EXCHANGES
BETTY CROCKER® (General Mills, Inc.)							
Stuffing Mixes							
Chicken (as prepared)	1 serving	180	21	4	9	620	1½ starch, 1½ fat
Corn Bread (as prepared)	1 serving	180	23	3	9	710	1½ starch, 1½ fat
Herb, Traditional (as prepared)	1 serving	190	22	4	9	640	1½ starch, 1½ fat
Pork (as prepared)	1 serving	190	22	4	9	640	1½ starch, 1½ fat
STOVETOP® (General Foods Corp.)							
Americana® New England Stuffing Mix							
As packaged	1 serving	110	21	4	1	560	1½ starch
As prepared with butter, salted	½ cup	180	21	4	9	630	1½ starch, 1½ fat
Americana® San Francisco Stuffing Mix							
As packaged	1 serving	110	20	4	1	560	1½ starch
As prepared with butter, salted	½ cup	170	20	4	9	640	1½ starch, 1½ fat
Beef Stuffing Mix							
As packaged	1 serving	110	21	4	1	500	1½ starch
As prepared with butter, salted	½ cup	180	21	4	9	580	1½ starch, 1½ fat
Chicken Flavor Stuffing Mix							
As packaged	1 serving	110	20	4	1	480	1½ starch
As prepared with butter, salted	½ cup	180	20	4	9	560	1½ starch, 1½ fat
Cornbread Stuffing Mix							
As packaged	1 serving	110	21	3	1	490	1½ starch
As prepared with butter, salted	½ cup	170	21	3	9	570	1½ starch, 1½ fat
Long Grain and Wild Rice Stuffing Mix							
As packaged	1 serving	120	22	4	1	470	1½ starch

†For Occasional Use   **Not Recommended For Use   *Not Available   F More Than 2 Fat Exchanges   S Moderate To High Sugar Content

NUTRIENT VALUE

PRODUCTS	SERVING SIZE	CALORIES	CARBO-HYDRATE (g.)	PROTEIN (g.)	FAT (g.)	SODIUM (mg.)	EXCHANGES
As prepared with butter, salted	½ cup	180	22	4	9	550	1½ starch, 1½ fat
Pork Stuffing Mix As packaged	1 serving	110	20	4	1	540	1½ starch
As prepared with butter, salted	½ cup	170	20	4	9	620	1½ starch, 1½ fat
Savory Herbs Stuffing Mix As packaged	1 serving	110	20	4	1	500	1½ starch
As prepared with butter, salted	½ cup	180	20	4	9	580	1½ starch, 1½ fat
Turkey Stuffing Mix As packaged	1 serving	110	21	4	1	550	1½ starch
As prepared with butter, salted	½ cup	170	21	4	9	630	1½ starch, 1½ fat
Wild Rice Stuffing Mix As packaged	1 serving	110	22	4	1	480	1½ starch
As prepared with butter, salted	½ cup	180	22	4	9	550	1½ starch, 1½ fat

STUFFING ORIGINALS™ (The Pillsbury Co.)

PRODUCTS	SERVING SIZE	CALORIES	CARBO-HYDRATE (g.)	PROTEIN (g.)	FAT (g.)	SODIUM (mg.)	EXCHANGES
Chicken (as prepared)	½ cup	170	21	4	7	670	1½ starch, 1 fat
Cornbread (as prepared)	½ cup	170	25	3	6	660	1½ starch, 1 fat
Mushroom (as prepared)	½ cup	150	19	4	7	780	1 starch, 1 fat
Wild Rice (as prepared)	½ cup	160	21	3	7	540	1½ starch, 1 fat

UNCLE BEN'S® (Uncle Ben's Foods)

Instant Stuffing Mix (as prepared)

PRODUCTS	SERVING SIZE	CALORIES	CARBO-HYDRATE (g.)	PROTEIN (g.)	FAT (g.)	SODIUM (mg.)	EXCHANGES
With margarine	½ cup	189	24	4	9	709	1½ starch, 1½ fat
Without margarine	½ cup	121	24	4	2	614	1½ starch

†For Occasional Use **Not Recommended For Use *Not Available F More Than 2 Fat Exchanges S Moderate To High Sugar Content

Appetizers

NUTRIENT VALUE

PRODUCTS	SERVING SIZE	CALORIES	CARBO-HYDRATE (g.)	PROTEIN (g.)	FAT (g.)	SODIUM (mg.)	EXCHANGES
BANQUET® (ConAgra® Frozen Foods Co.)							
Ⓕ Breaded Cheddar Cheese Nuggets	3 oz.	414	24	13	30	1015	1½ starch, 1 high fat meat, 4 fat
Breaded Mozzarella Cheese Nuggets	3 oz.	288	21	15	16	750	1½ starch, 1½ meat, 1½ fat
CHUN KING® (ConAgra® Frozen Foods Co.)							
Egg Rolls, small, frozen, all varieties (average)	2 rolls	85	14	3	3	208-278	1 starch, ½ fat
Meat and Shrimp Egg Rolls, large, frozen	1 roll (3.45 oz.)	207	33	6	6	589	2 starch, 1 fat
FARM RICH® (Rich-SeaPak Corp.)							
Ⓕ Cheddar Cheese Sticks	3 oz.	300	19	10	21	740	1 starch, 1 meat, 3 fat
Ⓕ Cheese with Bacon Sticks	3 oz.	300	21	11	19	790	1½ starch, 1 meat, 2½ fat
Ⓕ Fiesta Sticks	3 oz.	270	18	8	18	860	1 starch, ½ meat, 3 fat
Ⓕ Hot Pepper Cheese Sticks	3 oz.	260	20	8	17	700	1 starch, ½ meat, 3 fat
Mozzarella Cheese Sticks	3 oz.	240	19	10	13	570	1 starch, 1 meat, 2 fat
Vegetable Sticks	4 oz.	240	32	4	10	625	1½ starch, 1 veg., 2 fat

†For Occasional Use   **Not Recommended For Use   *Not Available   Ⓕ More Than 2 Fat Exchanges   Ⓢ Moderate To High Sugar Content

Beverages

Authors' Note: We have included a variety of convenience items in this section. This is not meant to imply that all are readily approved for general use or for use by people with diabetes. Many of these products contain large amounts of refined sugars. We recommend that these products be used in moderation, if at all. If you decide to use them, work the specific product into your meal plan, using the nutrition information supplied here. And if you have diabetes, remember that if you decide to drink a high sugar beverage, drink it with a meal, when it will be more slowly absorbed; or before exercise, so that it will be readily used for energy.

PRODUCTS	SERVING SIZE	NUTRIENT VALUE CALORIES	CARBO-HYDRATE (g.)	PROTEIN (g.)	FAT (g.)	SODIUM (mg.)	EXCHANGES
COFFEE, TEA							
INTERNATIONAL COFFEES® (General Foods Corp.)							
[S] International Coffees, all flavors (average)	6 oz.	50	8	0	2	15-105	½ fruit, ½ fat†
Sugar Free International Coffees, all flavors (average)	6 oz.	30	3	0	2	15-95	½ fat
LIPTON® (Thomas J. Lipton, Inc.)							
[S] Canned Tea, Lemon Flavored (average)	8 oz.	85	21	0	0	20	**
Canned Tea, Lemon Flavored, Sugar Free	8 oz.	2	0	0	0	25	Free
[S] Chilled Tea, Lemon Flavored	8 oz.	90	22	0	0	20	**

†For Occasional Use **Not Recommended For Use *Not Available [F] More Than 2 Fat Exchanges [S] Moderate To High Sugar Content

NUTRIENT VALUE

PRODUCTS	SERVING SIZE	CALORIES	CARBO-HYDRATE (g.)	PROTEIN (g.)	FAT (g.)	SODIUM (mg.)	EXCHANGES
Chilled Tea, Lemon Flavored, Sugar Free	8 oz.	2	0	0	0	25	Free
ⓢ Iced Tea Mix, Lemon Flavored, with Sugar (as prepared)	8 oz.	60	16	0	0	0	**
Iced Tea Mix, Sugar Free, Lemon Flavored (as prepared)	8 oz.	2	0	0	0	5	Free
Instant Tea, Regular or Lemon Flavored	8 oz.	2	0	0	0	0	Free

NESTEA® (Nestlé Foods Corp.)

PRODUCTS	SERVING SIZE	CALORIES	CARBO-HYDRATE (g.)	PROTEIN (g.)	FAT (g.)	SODIUM (mg.)	EXCHANGES
Free (as prepared)	1 serving	4	1	0	0	0	Free
ⓢ Iced Tea Mix, with Sugar and Lemon (as prepared)	1 serving	70	9	0	0	0	1 fruit†

FRUIT DRINKS, JUICES

BACARDI® (Coca-Cola Foods)

PRODUCTS	SERVING SIZE	CALORIES	CARBO-HYDRATE (g.)	PROTEIN (g.)	FAT (g.)	SODIUM (mg.)	EXCHANGES
ⓢ Tropical Fruit Mixers, frozen concentrated (as prepared)							
Daiquiri, all flavors, without rum (average)	8 oz.	140	35	0	0	0	**
Mai Tai, without rum	8 oz.	120	31	0	0	0	**
Pina Colada, without rum	8 oz.	190	34	0	6	30	**

BRIGHT AND EARLY® (Coca-Cola Foods)

PRODUCTS	SERVING SIZE	CALORIES	CARBO-HYDRATE (g.)	PROTEIN (g.)	FAT (g.)	SODIUM (mg.)	EXCHANGES
ⓢ Imitation Orange Beverage	4 oz.	60	15	0	0	10	1 fruit†

COUNTRY TIME® (General Foods Corp.)

PRODUCTS	SERVING SIZE	CALORIES	CARBO-HYDRATE (g.)	PROTEIN (g.)	FAT (g.)	SODIUM (mg.)	EXCHANGES
ⓢ Drink Mix, sugar sweetened, all flavors (average)	6 oz.	60	15	0	0	15	1 fruit†
Sugar Free Drink Mix, all flavors (average)	6 oz.	3	0	0	0	0	Free

†For Occasional Use   **Not Recommended For Use   *Not Available   Ⓕ More Than 2 Fat Exchanges   ⓢ Moderate To High Sugar Content

15

NUTRIENT VALUE

PRODUCTS	SERVING SIZE	CALORIES	CARBO-HYDRATE (g.)	PROTEIN (g.)	FAT (g.)	SODIUM (mg.)	EXCHANGES
CRYSTAL LIGHT® (General Foods Corp.)							
Fruit●Tea Sugar Free Drink Mix	8 oz.	4	0	0	0	0	Free
Sugar Free Drink Mix	8 oz.	4	1	0	0	0	Free
FEATHERWEIGHT® (Sandoz Nutrition)							
Tomato Juice, Low Sodium	6 oz.	35	8	1	0	20	1 vegetable **or** ½ fruit
FIVE ALIVE® (Coca-Cola Foods)							
Ⓢ All flavors (Chilled Products) (average)	4 oz.	60	15	0	0	11	1 fruit†
HEALTH VALLEY® (Health Valley Foods)							
Ⓢ Coolers, all varieties (average)	12 oz.	144	33	1	1	75	**
HI-C® (Coca-Cola Foods)							
Ⓢ Fruit Drinks, all flavors (average)	4 oz.	65	16	0	0	11-34	1 fruit†
KOOL-AID® (General Foods Corp.)							
Ⓢ Koolers® Juice Drink, all flavors (average)	8½ oz.	130	34	0	0	10	**
Soft Drink Mix, unsweetened, all flavors (as packaged) (average)	1 package, powder only	2	0	0	0	0-35	Free
Ⓢ Soft Drink Mix, unsweetened, all flavors (as prepared with sugar) (average)	8 oz.	100	25	0	0	0-35	**
Ⓢ Soft Drink Mix, sugar sweetened, all flavors (average)	8 oz.	80	20	0	0	0-25	**
Sugar Free Soft Drink Mix, all flavors (average)	8 oz.	4	0	0	0	0-35	Free
LAND O'LAKES® (Land O'Lakes, Inc.)							
Ⓢ Flavored Fruit Drinks, all flavors (average)	4 oz.	60	14	<1	0	5	1 fruit†

†For Occasional Use   **Not Recommended For Use   *Not Available   Ⓕ More Than 2 Fat Exchanges   Ⓢ Moderate To High Sugar Content

16

PRODUCTS	SERVING SIZE	NUTRIENT VALUE CALORIES	CARBO-HYDRATE (g.)	PROTEIN (g.)	FAT (g.)	SODIUM (mg.)	EXCHANGES
MAGIC TREE® (Kraft, Inc.)							
[S] Fruit Drinks, artificially flavored, all flavors (average)	4 oz.	67	17	0	0	0-20	1 fruit†
MINUTE MAID® (Coca-Cola Foods)							
[S] Crystals, all flavors (as prepared)	4 oz.	50	12	0	0	2-5	1 fruit†
Crystals, Lite, all flavors (as prepared) (average)	6 oz.	10	2	0	0	2-3	Free
[S] Fruit Punch	4 oz.	62	15	0	0	10	1 fruit†
[S] Lemonade and Pink Lemonade	4 oz.	55	15	0	0	11	1 fruit†
NUTRADIET® (S and W Fine Foods)							
Tomato Juice	6 oz.	35	8	1	0	20	1 vegetable **or** ½ fruit
Vegetable Juice Cocktail, Low Sodium	6 oz.	35	8	1	0	25	1 vegetable **or** ½ fruit
OCEAN SPRAY® (Ocean Spray Cranberries, Inc.)							
[S] Cranberry Juice Cocktail, sugar sweetened	4 oz. (½ cup)	70	17	0	0	<10	1 fruit†
Low Calorie Cranberry Juice Cocktail, sugar and artificially sweetened	6 oz. (¾ cup)	35	9	0	0	<10	½ fruit
Low Calorie Cranapple®, juice drink, artificially sweetened	6 oz. (¾ cup)	30	7	0	0	<10	½ fruit
[S] Cranapple®, juice drink	4 oz. (½ cup)	85	21	0	0	<10	1½ fruit†
[S] CranGrape®, juice drink	4 oz. (½ cup)	70	17	0	0	<10	1 fruit†
[S] Cranicot®, juice drink	4 oz. (½ cup)	70	17	0	0	<10	1 fruit†

†For Occasional Use **Not Recommended For Use *Not Available [F] More Than 2 Fat Exchanges [S] Moderate To High Sugar Content

PRODUCTS	SERVING SIZE	NUTRIENT VALUE CALORIES	CARBO-HYDRATE (g.)	PROTEIN (g.)	FAT (g.)	SODIUM (mg.)	EXCHANGES
[S] Cranraspberry® juice drink	4 oz. (½ cup)	70	17	0	0	<10	1 fruit†
[S] Crantastic®, blended juice drink	4 oz. (½ cup)	70	17	0	0	<10	1 fruit†
[S] Guava Drink	4 oz.	65	16	0	0	<10	1 fruit†
SUNKIST® (Thomas J. Lipton, Inc.)							
[S] Juice Drinks, all flavors (average)	8.45 oz.	140	34	0	0	0	**
Light Sugar Free Drink Crystals, all flavors (average)	8 oz.	6-8	2	0	0	20-70	Free
TANG® (General Foods Corp.)							
[S] Breakfast Beverage Crystals (as prepared)	6 oz.	90	22	0	0	0	1½ fruit†
Sugar Free Breakfast Beverage Crystals (as prepared)	6 oz.	6	1	0	0	0	Free
WELCH'S® (Welch Foods)							
[S] Cranberry Juice Cocktail, all flavors (average)	4 oz. (½ cup)	67	17	0	0	0	1 fruit†
Grape Juice, all varieties (average)	4 oz. (½ cup)	80	20	0	0	3-10	1 fruit
Tomato Juice	6 oz. (¾ cup)	35	7	1	0	550	1 veg. **or** ½ fruit
[S] Welchade Grape Drink	6 oz. (¾ cup)	90	23	0	0	20	1½ fruit†

†For Occasional Use **Not Recommended For Use *Not Available [F] More Than 2 Fat Exchanges [S] Moderate To High Sugar Content

Breads

PRODUCTS	SERVING SIZE	CALORIES	CARBO-HYDRATE (g.)	PROTEIN (g.)	FAT (g.)	SODIUM (mg.)	EXCHANGES
BISCUITS							
1869® (The Pillsbury Co.)							
Baking Powder or Buttermilk Biscuits	1	105	13	2	5	295	1 starch, 1 fat
BALLARD® (The Pillsbury Co.)							
Oven Ready® Biscuits	2	100	20	3	1	360	1 starch
HUNGRY JACK® (The Pillsbury Co.)							
Biscuits, all varieties except Extra Rich Buttermilk (average)	2	175	24	3	8	310-590	1½ starch, 1 fat
Extra Rich Buttermilk Biscuits	2	110	19	2	3	350	1 starch, ½ fat
PILLSBURY® (The Pillsbury Co.)							
Big Country® Buttermilk Biscuits	1	100	15	2	4	325	1 starch, ½ fat
Buttermilk and Country Style Biscuits (average)	2	100	20	3	1	340-360	1 starch
Heat 'n Eat Buttermilk Biscuits	1	85	13	2	3	265	1 starch, ½ fat

†For Occasional Use   **Not Recommended For Use   *Not Available   Ⓕ More Than 2 Fat Exchanges   Ⓢ Moderate To High Sugar Content

19

PRODUCTS	SERVING SIZE	CALORIES	CARBO-HYDRATE (g.)	PROTEIN (g.)	FAT (g.)	SODIUM (mg.)	EXCHANGES
Heat 'n Eat Deluxe Buttermilk Biscuits	1	130	16	3	8	305	1 starch, 1½ fat
Tenderflake Biscuits, all varieties (average)	2	110	14	2	5	340	1 starch, 1 fat

BREADS, DINNER ROLLS
HEALTH VALLEY® (Health Valley Foods)

Whole Wheat Amaranth Bread	1 oz.	80	13	4	1	150	1 starch

PEPPERIDGE FARM® (Campbell Soup Co.)

Bread, Sliced VeriThin, all varieties (average)	2 slices	80	16	2	1	150-170	1 starch
Butter Crescent Rolls	1	110	13	3	6	160	1 starch, 1 fat
Club Rolls, Brown 'n Serve	1	100	20	3	1	220	1 starch
French Style Rolls	1	110	19	4	1	250	1 starch
Golden Twist Rolls	1	110	14	2	6	160	1 starch, 1 fat
Parker House Rolls	2	100	18	4	2	180	1 starch
Party Rolls	3	90	15	3	3	150	1 starch, ½ fat
Sandwich Rolls with Sesame Seeds	1	130	23	5	3	210	1½ starch
Sourdough Style French Rolls	1	100	19	4	1	240	1 starch

PILLSBURY® (The Pillsbury Co.)

Butterflake Rolls	1	110	16	2	4	410	1 starch, ½ fat
Crescent Rolls	2	200	22	3	11	460	1½ starch, 2 fat
Crusty French Loaf	one 1" slice	60	11	2	1	120	1 starch
Hot Roll Mix (as prepared)	1 roll	120	21	4	2	215	1½ starch
Pipin' Hot™ Loaf	one 1" slice	80	13	2	2	170	1 starch
Soft Bread Sticks	1	100	17	3	2	230	1 starch

†For Occasional Use   **Not Recommended For Use   *Not Available   Ⓕ More Than 2 Fat Exchanges   Ⓢ Moderate To High Sugar Content

PRODUCTS	SERVING SIZE	CALORIES	CARBO-HYDRATE (g.)	PROTEIN (g.)	FAT (g.)	SODIUM (mg.)	EXCHANGES
SARA LEE® (Kitchens of Sara Lee)							
Bagel Time™ Bagels, all varieties (average)	1	240	45	9	2	260-560	3 starch
L'Original™ Croissants, all varieties except petite (average)	1	170	18	4	9	240-310	1 starch, 2 fat
L'Original™ Croissants, petite size	1	120	13	3	6	160	1 starch, 1 fat

BREAD AND CRACKER CRUMBS

PRODUCTS	SERVING SIZE	CALORIES	CARBO-HYDRATE (g.)	PROTEIN (g.)	FAT (g.)	SODIUM (mg.)	EXCHANGES
KEEBLER® (Keebler Co.)							
Graham Crumbs	1 cup	520	90	8	14	720	6 starch, 2 fat
Zesta Meal	1 cup	370	61	8	10	1000	4 starch, 1½ fat
KELLOGG'S® (Kellogg Co.)							
Corn Flake Crumbs	⅓ cup (1 oz.)	110	25	2	0	278	1½ starch
NABISCO® (Nabisco, Inc.)							
Cracker Meal	1 cup	440	95	11	1	*	6 starch
Graham Cracker Crumbs	for ⅛ pie (0.6 oz.)	70	12	1	2	*	1 starch

CORNBREAD, MUFFINS

PRODUCTS	SERVING SIZE	CALORIES	CARBO-HYDRATE (g.)	PROTEIN (g.)	FAT (g.)	SODIUM (mg.)	EXCHANGES
AUNT JEMIMA® (Quaker Oats Co.)							
Easy Mix Corn Bread (as prepared)	⅙ recipe	220	34	5	7	600	2 starch, 1 fat
BETTY CROCKER® (General Mills, Inc.)							
Corn Muffins (as prepared)	1 muffin (1/12 pkg.)	160	25	3	5	310	1½ starch, 1 fat
Muffins: Banana Nut, Blueberry, Apple, Cherry (as prepared) (average)	1 muffin (1/12 pkg.)	120	18	2	4	140-150	1 starch, 1 fat
Muffins: Carrot Nut, Oatmeal Raisin (average)	1 muffin (1/12 pkg.)	150	22	3	5	125-170	1½ starch, 1 fat

†For Occasional Use   **Not Recommended For Use   *Not Available   F More Than 2 Fat Exchanges   S Moderate To High Sugar Content

NUTRIENT VALUE

PRODUCTS	SERVING SIZE	CALORIES	CARBO-HYDRATE (g.)	PROTEIN (g.)	FAT (g.)	SODIUM (mg.)	EXCHANGES
DROMEDARY® (Nabisco, Inc.)							
Corn Bread Mix (as prepared)	2" square	130	20	3	3	480	1 starch, ½ fat
Corn Muffin Mix (as prepared)	1 muffin	120	20	3	4	270	1 starch, ½ fat
FLAKO® (Quaker Oats Co.)							
Corn Muffin Mix (as prepared)	1 muffin	140	23	3	4	370	1½ starch, ½ fat
Popover Mix (as prepared)	1 popover	170	25	7	5	360	1½ starch, 1 fat
PEPPERIDGE FARM® (Campbell Soup Co.)							
Cinnamon Raisin English Muffin	1	150	28	5	2	180	2 starch
English Muffin, plain	1	140	26	5	2	180	2 starch
Old Fashioned Muffins, all varieties (average)	1	180	27	3	7	170-300	2 starch, 1 fat
SARA LEE® (Kitchens of Sara Lee)							
Hearty Fruit™ Muffins, all varieties (average)	1	220	36	4	9	270-310	2 starch, 1½ fat

MISCELLANEOUS

PRODUCTS	SERVING SIZE	CALORIES	CARBO-HYDRATE (g.)	PROTEIN (g.)	FAT (g.)	SODIUM (mg.)	EXCHANGES
BISQUICK® (General Mills, Inc.)							
Bisquick® Mix (dry)	2 oz. (½ cup)	240	37	4	8	700	2½ starch, 1 fat
KEEBLER® (Keebler Co.)							
Breadstix, all varieties (average)	6	105	15	2	3	90-120	1 starch, ½ fat
Taco Shells	1	50	8	1	2	145	½ starch
KELLOGG'S® CROUTETTES® (Kellogg Co.)							
Croutons Dry Mix	⅔ cup	70	15	3	0	270	1 starch
As Prepared	⅔ cup	130	15	3	7	*	1 starch, 1 fat
MRS. PAUL'S® (Campbell Soup Co.)							
Apple Fritters	2 fritters (4 oz.)	270	36	3	13	610	1½ starch, 1 fruit, 2 fat

†For Occasional Use   **Not Recommended For Use   *Not Available   F More Than 2 Fat Exchanges   S Moderate To High Sugar Content

NUTRIENT VALUE

PRODUCTS	SERVING SIZE	CALORIES	CARBO-HYDRATE (g.)	PROTEIN (g.)	FAT (g.)	SODIUM (mg.)	EXCHANGES
Corn Fritters	2 fritters (4 oz.)	250	33	4	12	630	2 starch, 2 fat
PEPPERIDGE FARM® (Campbell Soup Co.)							
Croutons, all varieties (average)	½ oz.	70	9	2	3	160-210	½ starch, ½ fat
RAGÚ® (Chesebrough-Ponds, Inc.)							
Pizza Quick Mix for Homemade Pizza Crust (crust only)	1½ scoops	170	31	6	2	360	2 starch
SALAD CRISPINS® (The Clorox Company)							
Salad Crispins®, all varieties	2 heaping Tbsp.	60	8	2	2	*	½ starch, ½ fat
SHAKE 'N BAKE® (General Foods, Corp.)							
Seasoning Mixture, all varieties (average)	¼ pouch	80	15	2	1	410-840	1 starch
Oven Fry® Coating Homestyle	¼ pouch	80	15	1	2	950	1 starch
Extra Crispy Recipe (average)	¼ pouch	120	20	3	3	690-810	1 starch, ½ fat
WEINER WRAPS® (The Pillsbury Co.)							
Weiner Wrap, plain	1 wrap	60	10	1	2	430	½ starch, ½ fat

†For Occasional Use   **Not Recommended For Use   *Not Available   Ⓕ More Than 2 Fat Exchanges   Ⓢ Moderate To High Sugar Content

Breakfast Foods

PRODUCTS	SERVING SIZE	CALORIES	CARBO-HYDRATE (g.)	PROTEIN (g.)	FAT (g.)	SODIUM (mg.)	EXCHANGES
		NUTRIENT VALUE					
BREAKFAST BARS AND DRINKS							
CARNATION® (Calreco®, Inc.)							
[S] Breakfast Bar, all flavors (average)	1 bar	195	20	6	11	140-180	1 starch, ½ skim milk, 2 fat **or** 1 meat, 1½ fruit, 1 fat†
[S] Instant Breakfast, all flavors, dry mix (average)	1 packet	130	24	7	0	135-190	1 fruit, 1 skim milk **or** 1½ starch
[S] Instant Breakfast, all flavors, prepared with skim milk (average)	1 packet and 8 oz. skim milk	220	35	15	1	250-310	1½ starch, 1 skim milk†
CARNATION SLENDER® (Calreco®, Inc.)							
[F] [S] Carnation Slender, bar, all flavors (average)	2 bars	270	25	11	14	285-320	1 starch, 1 meat, 1 fruit, 2½ fat **or** 1 starch, 1 skim milk, 2½ fat†
[S] Carnation Slender, can, all flavors (average)	10 oz.	220	34	11	4	430-550	1½ starch, 1 skim milk, ½ fat†

†For Occasional Use **Not Recommended For Use *Not Available [F] More Than 2 Fat Exchanges [S] Moderate To High Sugar Content

NUTRIENT VALUE

	PRODUCTS	SERVING SIZE	CALORIES	CARBO-HYDRATE (g.)	PROTEIN (g.)	FAT (g.)	SODIUM (mg.)	EXCHANGES
Ⓢ	Carnation Slender, dry, all flavors (average)	1 packet	110	21	5	1	110	1½ starch†
Ⓢ	Carnation Slender, prepared with skim milk (average)	1 packet and 6 oz. skim milk	180	30	11	1	180	1 starch, 1 skim milk†
	FIGURINES® (The Pillsbury Co.)							
	Figurine® Diet Bars, all varieties (average)	1 bar	100	11	2	5	220-240	1 starch, 1 fat
	PILLSBURY® (The Pillsbury Co.)							
Ⓢ	Instant Breakfast, all flavors (as prepared) (average)	1 pouch and 8 oz. skim milk	210	39	14	1	300-330	2 starch, 1 skim milk†

CEREALS
COCO WHEATS® (Little Crow Foods)

	PRODUCTS	SERVING SIZE	CALORIES	CARBO-HYDRATE (g.)	PROTEIN (g.)	FAT (g.)	SODIUM (mg.)	EXCHANGES
	Coco Wheats, dry	3 Tbsp.	130	28	4	1	*	2 starch
	FEATHERWEIGHT® (Sandoz Nutrition)							
	Corn Flakes, Low Sodium	1 oz.	110	25	2	0	<10	1½ starch
	Crisp Rice, Low Sodium	1 oz.	110	26	2	0	<10	1½ starch
	GENERAL MILLS® CEREALS (General Mills, Inc.)							
	Body Buddies®, all varieties (average)	¾ cup	83	18	2	<1	210-218	1 starch
Ⓢ	BooBerry®	¾ cup	83	18	1	1	158	1 starch†
	Bran Muffin Crisp®	½ cup	98	22	2	1	188	1 starch
	Cheerios®	1 cup	83	15	3	2	218	1 starch
Ⓢ	Cheerios®, Honey Nut	½ cup	74	15	2	1	168	1 starch†
	Cinnamon Toast Crunch™	½ cup	80	15	1	2	147	1 starch
Ⓢ	Circus Fun®	¾ cup	83	18	1	1	120	1 starch†
Ⓢ	Cocoa Puffs®	¾ cup	83	19	1	1	150	1 starch†
	Corn Total®	¾ cup	83	18	2	1	233	1 starch

†For Occasional Use   **Not Recommended For Use   *Not Available   Ⓕ More Than 2 Fat Exchanges   Ⓢ Moderate To High Sugar Content

NUTRIENT VALUE

	PRODUCTS	SERVING SIZE	CALORIES	CARBO-HYDRATE (g.)	PROTEIN (g.)	FAT (g.)	SODIUM (mg.)	EXCHANGES
Ⓢ	Count Chocula®	¾ cup	83	18	2	1	158	1 starch†
	Country® Corn Flakes	¾ cup	83	19	2	<1	233	1 starch
	Crispy Wheats 'n Raisins®	½ cup	74	15	1	1	121	1 starch
	Fiber One®	⅔ cup	80	28	5	1	308	1 starch
Ⓢ	FrankenBerry®	¾ cup	83	18	1	1	158	1 starch†
Ⓢ	Golden Grahams®	½ cup	74	16	1	1	188	1 starch†
Ⓢ	Honey Buc★Wheat Crisp®	½ cup	74	16	1	<1	174	1 starch†
Ⓢ	Ice Cream Cones®, all varieties (average)	½ cup	74	15	1	1	127	1 starch†
	Kaboom®	¾ cup	83	17	2	1	218	1 starch
	Kix®	1 cup	74	16	1	<1	194	1 starch
Ⓢ	Lucky Charms®	¾ cup	83	18	2	1	135	1 starch†
Ⓢ	Pac-Man™	¾ cup	83	19	1	<1	150	1 starch†
	Raisin Nut Bran®	½ cup	110	20	3	3	140	1 starch, ½ fat
Ⓢ	Rocky Road®	½ cup	90	17	2	2	83	1 starch†
Ⓢ	S'Mores Crunch®	½ cup	80	16	1	1	168	1 starch†
	Total®	¾ cup	83	17	2	1	210	1 starch
Ⓢ	Trix®	¾ cup	83	19	1	1	128	1 starch†
	Wheaties®	¾ cup	83	17	2	1	203	1 starch

HEALTH VALLEY® (Health Valley Foods)

	PRODUCTS	SERVING SIZE	CALORIES	CARBO-HYDRATE (g.)	PROTEIN (g.)	FAT (g.)	SODIUM (mg.)	EXCHANGES
	Amaranth Cereal, all varieties (average)	1 oz.	110	20	4	2	10	1½ starch
	Amaranth Flakes	1 oz.	120	22	4	1	10	1½ starch
	Bran Cereal, all varieties (average)	1 oz.	100	21	3	1	10	1½ starch
	Healthy Crunch, all varieties (average)	1 oz.	120	20	4	3	10	1½ starch
	Hearts O'Bran, all varieties, (average)	1 oz.	110	19	3	1	10	1 starch

†For Occasional Use　　**Not Recommended For Use　　*Not Available　　Ⓕ More Than 2 Fat Exchanges　　Ⓢ Moderate To High Sugar Content

NUTRIENT VALUE

PRODUCTS	SERVING SIZE	CALORIES	CARBO-HYDRATE (g.)	PROTEIN (g.)	FAT (g.)	SODIUM (mg.)	EXCHANGES
Oat Bran Flakes	1 oz.	110	22	3	1	10	1½ starch
Orangeola Cereal, all varieties (average)	1 oz.	120	19	3	4	10	1 starch, ½ fat
Puffed Cereals: Corn, Rice, Wheat	¾ oz.	70	17	3	0	0	1 starch
Raisin Bran Flakes	1 oz.	110	24	3	0	1	1½ starch
Real Granola, all varieties (average)	1 oz.	120	20	4	3	10	1 starch, ½ fat
Sprouts 7, all varieties (average)	1 oz.	100	20	3	1	5	1 starch
Stoned Wheat Flakes	1 oz.	110	24	3	0	1	1½ starch
Swiss Breakfast, all varieties (average)	2 oz.	200	37	7	4	36	2½ starch
Wheat Germ/Fiber, all varieties (average)	1 oz.	100	20	3	1	15	1 starch

KELLOGG'S® (Kellogg Company)

PRODUCTS	SERVING SIZE	CALORIES	CARBO-HYDRATE (g.)	PROTEIN (g.)	FAT (g.)	SODIUM (mg.)	EXCHANGES
All Bran®	⅓ cup	70	22	4	1	260	1 starch
All Bran® with Extra Fiber	½ cup	60	22	3	1	270	1 starch
All Bran® Fruit and Almonds	⅔ cup	100	28	4	2	260	1 starch, ½ fat
Apple Cinnamon Squares™	½ cup	90	23	2	0	5	1 starch
Apple Jacks®	¾ cup	83	19	2	0	94	1 starch
Apple Raisin Crisp®	½ cup	91	22	1	0	161	1 starch
Bran Buds®	⅓ cup	70	22	3	1	150	1 starch
Bran Flakes	⅔ cup	90	23	3	0	220	1 starch
Ⓢ Cocoa Krispies®	½ cup	77	18	1	0	133	1 starch†
Corn Flakes®	¾ cup	83	19	1	0	218	1 starch
Ⓢ Corn Pops®	¾ cup	83	20	1	0	68	1 starch†
Cracklin' Oat Bran®	½ cup	110	20	3	4	150	1 starch, ½ fat
Crispix®	¾ cup	83	19	2	0	165	1 starch

†For Occasional Use   **Not Recommended For Use   *Not Available   Ⓕ More Than 2 Fat Exchanges   Ⓢ Moderate To High Sugar Content

NUTRIENT VALUE

	PRODUCTS	SERVING SIZE	CALORIES	CARBO-HYDRATE (g.)	PROTEIN (g.)	FAT (g.)	SODIUM (mg.)	EXCHANGES
Ⓢ	Froot Loops®	¾ cup	110	19	2	1	94	1 starch†
Ⓢ	Frosted Flakes®	½ cup	74	17	1	0	134	1 starch†
Ⓢ	Frosted Krispies®	½ cup	74	17	1	0	148	1 starch†
	Frosted Mini-Wheats®	3 biscuits	75	18	2	0	4	1 starch
	Fruitful Bran™	½ cup	84	21	2	0	161	1 starch
	Honey and Nut Corn Flakes®	½ cup	77	17	1	1	140	1 starch
Ⓢ	Honey Smacks®	½ cup	74	17	1	0	47	1 starch†
	Just Right™ All Grain	½ cup	70	17	2	0	140	1 starch
	Just Right™ with Fruit	½ cup	94	20	2	1	127	1 starch
Ⓢ	Marshmallow Krispies®	¾ cup	84	20	1	0	138	1 starch†
	Product 19®	¾ cup	83	18	2	0	240	1 starch
	Raisin Bran	½ cup	80	20	2	1	147	1 starch
	Raisin Squares™	½ cup	90	22	2	0	130	1 starch
	Rice Krispies®	¾ cup	83	19	2	0	218	1 starch
	Special K®	¾ cup	83	15	5	0	173	1 starch

LOMA LINDA® (Loma Linda Foods)

	PRODUCTS	SERVING SIZE	CALORIES	CARBO-HYDRATE (g.)	PROTEIN (g.)	FAT (g.)	SODIUM (mg.)	EXCHANGES
	Loma Linda® 7-Grain Cereal, Crunchy	⅓ cup	83	16	2	2	68	1 starch
	Loma Linda® 7-Grain Cereal, no sugar added	¾ cup	83	15	4	1	56	1 starch
	Ruskets Biscuits	2 biscuits	110	23	4	1	85	1½ starch

NABISCO® BRAND CEREALS (Nabisco, Inc.)

	PRODUCTS	SERVING SIZE	CALORIES	CARBO-HYDRATE (g.)	PROTEIN (g.)	FAT (g.)	SODIUM (mg.)	EXCHANGES
	Cream of Wheat®							
	Mix 'n Eat, Original (as prepared)	1 packet	100	21	3	0	180	1½ starch
	Mix 'n Eat, all other flavors (as prepared) (average)	1 packet	130	30	2	0	180-240	1 starch, 1 fruit
	Nabisco® 100% Bran	1 oz.	70	21	3	2	190	1 starch

†For Occasional Use   **Not Recommended For Use   *Not Available   Ⓕ More Than 2 Fat Exchanges   Ⓢ Moderate To High Sugar Content

PRODUCTS	SERVING SIZE	CALORIES	CARBO-HYDRATE (g.)	PROTEIN (g.)	FAT (g.)	SODIUM (mg.)	EXCHANGES
		NUTRIENT VALUE					
Shredded Wheat	1 biscuit	90	19	2	1	0	1 starch
Shredded Wheat 'n Bran	¾ oz.	83	17	2	1	0	1 starch
Toasted Wheat and Raisins®	¾ oz.	75	17	2	1	0	1 starch
Spoon Size® Shredded Wheat	¾ oz.	83	17	2	0	0	1 starch
Team® Flakes	¾ oz.	83	18	2	1	143	1 starch
NATURE VALLEY® (General Mills, Inc.)							
Granola, all varieties (average)	¼ cup	100	14	2	4	26	1 starch, ½ fat
NUTRI•GRAIN® (Kellogg Company)							
Almond Raisin	⅓ cup	75	16	2	1	110	1 starch
Corn	⅓ cup	70	17	1	1	119	1 starch
Wheat	½ cup	75	18	2	0	128	1 starch
Wheat and Raisins	scant ½ cup	88	21	2	0	114	1 starch
POST® (General Foods Corp.)							
Alpha-Bits®	¾ oz.	83	18	2	1	135	1 starch
C.W. Post® Hearty Granola Cereal, all varieties (average)	¾ oz.	94	16	2	3	60	1 starch
[S] Cocoa Pebbles®	¾ oz.	83	19	1	1	120	1 starch†
Fortified Oat Flakes	¾ oz.	83	15	5	1	188	1 starch
Fruit and Fibre®, all varieties (average)	1 oz.	90	22	2	1	180-190	1 starch
[S] Fruity Pebbles®	¾ oz.	83	19	1	1	120	1 starch†
Grape-Nuts®	¾ oz.	83	17	2	0	143	1 starch
Grape-Nuts® Flakes	¾ oz.	75	17	2	1	120	1 starch
[S] Honey Comb®	¾ oz.	83	20	1	0	120	1 starch†
Natural Bran Flakes	1 oz.	90	23	3	0	230	1 starch
Natural Raisin Bran	1 oz.	80	22	2	0	180	1 starch
Post Toasties® Corn Flakes	¾ oz.	83	18	2	0	210	1 starch
Raisin Grape Nuts®	¾ oz.	75	17	2	0	105	1 starch

†For Occasional Use **Not Recommended For Use *Not Available [F] More Than 2 Fat Exchanges [S] Moderate To High Sugar Content

NUTRIENT VALUE

	PRODUCTS	SERVING SIZE	CALORIES	CARBO-HYDRATE (g.)	PROTEIN (g.)	FAT (g.)	SODIUM (mg.)	EXCHANGES
[S]	Smurf-Berry Crunch®	¾ oz.	83	19	1	1	56	1 starch†
[S]	Super Golden Crisp®	¾ oz.	83	20	2	0	34	1 starch†
	QUAKER® (Quaker Oats Co.)							
	Hot Cereals							
	Enriched Corn Meal, White or Yellow (uncooked)	3 Tbsp.	100	22	2	1	0	1½ starch
	Grits							
	Instant Grits Product, plain	1 packet (0.8 oz.)	80	18	2	0	520	1 starch
	Instant Grits Product, all flavors (average)	1 packet (1 oz.)	100	22	3	1	700-900	1½ starch
	Masa Trigo® Wheat (uncooked)	⅓ cup	150	25	3	4	300	1½ starch, ½ fat
	Masa Harina®, De Maiz (uncooked)	⅓ cup	140	27	3	1	0	2 starch
	Oat Bran Cereal (uncooked)	⅓ cup	110	16	6	2	0	1 starch
	Oatmeal, Quick and Old Fashioned	⅓ cup, uncooked (⅔ cup, cooked)	110	18	5	2	0	1 starch
	Oatmeal, Instant							
	Regular Flavor	1 packet (¾ cup, cooked)	100	17	5	2	400	1 starch
	Apple and Cinnamon	1 packet (¾ cup, cooked)	130	26	4	2	260	2 starch
	Cinnamon and Spice	1 packet (¾ cup, cooked)	170	34	5	2	360	2 starch
	Fruit and Cream™, all varieties (average)	1 packet (1 ¼ oz.)	140	26	3	2	160-250	2 starch

†For Occasional Use **Not Recommended For Use *Not Available [F] More Than 2 Fat Exchanges [S] Moderate To High Sugar Content

NUTRIENT VALUE

PRODUCTS	SERVING SIZE	CALORIES	CARBO-HYDRATE (g.)	PROTEIN (g.)	FAT (g.)	SODIUM (mg.)	EXCHANGES
Maple and Brown Sugar, artificial flavor	1 packet (¾ cup, cooked)	160	31	5	2	330	2 starch
Raisins and Spice	1 packet (¾ cup, cooked)	160	31	5	2	310	2 starch
Raisins, Dates, and Walnuts	1 packet (¾ cup, cooked)	160	25	4	4	220	1½ starch, ½ fat
Real Honey and Graham	1 packet (¾ cup, cooked)	140	27	3	2	320	1 starch, 1 fruit
Wheat Farina, Quick	2½ Tbsp. (uncooked)	100	22	3	0	0	1½ starch
Whole Wheat Hot Natural Cereal	⅓ cup, uncooked (⅔ cup, cooked)	100	20	3	4	0	1 starch, ½ fat
Ready to Eat Cereals							
[S] Cap'n Crunch®, all varieties (average)	½ cup	84	16	1	1	134-168	1 starch†
Halfsies®	1½ cups	75	17	3	0	0	1 starch
King Vitamin®	1 cup	88	18	2	1	224	1 starch
Life®, Regular or Cinnamon, (average)	½ cup	90	14	4	2	135	1 starch
Life®, Raisin	⅓ cup	75	13	3	1	100	1 starch
Quaker®							
100% Natural Cereal, all varieties (average)	¼ cup	130	18	3	5	10-20	1 starch, 1 fat
Corn Bran	½ cup	90	18	2	1	225	1 starch
Puffed Rice	1½ cups	75	20	2	0	0	1 starch
Puffed Wheat	1½ cups	75	17	3	0	0	1 starch
Shredded Wheat	1 biscuit	80	16	3	1	0	1 starch
Unprocessed Bran	2 Tbsp.	20	4	1	0	0	Free
Quisp®	¾ cup	80	15	1	2	155	1 starch
Mr. T	⅔ cup	80	15	1	1	155	1 starch

†For Occasional Use **Not Recommended For Use *Not Available [F] More Than 2 Fat Exchanges [S] Moderate To High Sugar Content

NUTRIENT VALUE

PRODUCTS	SERVING SIZE	CALORIES	CARBO-HYDRATE (g.)	PROTEIN (g.)	FAT (g.)	SODIUM (mg.)	EXCHANGES
RALSTON PURINA CEREALS (Ralston Purina Company)							
Chex® Cereals							
Bran Chex®	½ cup	80	20	2	0	265	1 starch
Corn Chex®	¾ cup	80	18	1	0	226	1 starch
Crispy Oatmeal and Raisin Chex®	½ cup	84	19	2	1	144	1 starch
Rice Chex®	¾ cup	80	18	1	0	204	1 starch
Wheat Chex®	½ cup	80	18	2	0	160	1 starch
Wheat and Raisin Chex®	½ cup	85	19	2	1	140	1 starch
Ⓢ Cookie Crisp®, chocolate or vanilla flavors (average)	¾ cup	80	18	1	1	144	1 starch†
Ⓢ Donkey Kong and Donkey Kong Junior™ (average)	¾ cup	80	18	1	1	86-94	1 starch†
Ralston®							
Corn Flakes	¾ cup	80	18	2	0	195	1 starch
Crispy Rice	¾ cup	80	18	2	0	148	1 starch
40% Bran Flakes	⅔ cup	80	18	3	0	251	1 starch
Ⓢ Fruit Rings®	¾ cup	80	19	1	1	*	1 starch†
Raisin Bran	1 cup	80	20	2	0	208	1 starch
Ⓢ Sugar Frosted Flakes	½ cup	80	19	1	0	130	1 starch†
Ⓢ Sugar Frosted Rice	¾ cup	80	19	1	1	110	1 starch†
Tasteeos®	1 cup	80	16	3	1	151	1 starch

COFFEE CAKES, SWEET ROLLS, TOASTER PASTRIES

Authors' Note: We have included a variety of convenience items in this section. This is not meant to imply that all are readily approved for general use or for use by people with diabetes. Many of these products contain large amounts of fats and refined sugars. We recommend that these products be used in moderation, if at all. If you decide to use them, work the specific product into your meal plan, using the nutrition information supplied here. And if you have diabetes, remember that if you decide to eat a high sugar food, eat it with a meal, when it will be more slowly absorbed; or before exercise, so that it will be readily used for energy.

†For Occasional Use   **Not Recommended For Use   *Not Available   Ⓕ More Than 2 Fat Exchanges   Ⓢ Moderate To High Sugar Content

PRODUCTS	SERVING SIZE	NUTRIENT VALUE CALORIES	CARBO-HYDRATE (g.)	PROTEIN (g.)	FAT (g.)	SODIUM (mg.)	EXCHANGES
AUNT JEMIMA® (Quaker Oats Co.)							
[S] Easy Mix Coffee Cake (as prepared)	⅛ recipe	170	29	3	5	270	2 starch, 1 fat†
KELLOGG'S® (Kellogg Co.)							
[S] Pop Tarts®, nonfrosted, all varieties (average)	1	210	36	3	6	213-251	1 starch, 1½ fruit, 1 fat†
[S] Pop Tarts®, frosted, all varieties (average)	1	210	36	3	6	225-270	1 starch, 1½ fruit, 1 fat†
NABISCO® (Nabisco Brands, Inc.)							
[S] Toastettes® Pastries, all varieties (average)	1	200	36	2	5	170-210	1 starch, 1½ fruit, 1 fat†
PILLSBURY® (The Pillsbury Co.)							
[S] Apple Cinnamon Coffee Cake Mix	1/16 cake	120	20	2	4	80	1 starch, 1 fat†
[S] Danish Rolls with icing	1	145	20	2	7	225-245	1 starch, 1½ fat†
Fruit Turnovers, all varieties (average)	1	170	23	2	8	310-320	1 starch, ½ fruit, 1½ fat
Quick Bread Mixes, all varieties (as prepared) (average)	1/16 loaf	120	20	2	4	113-135	1 starch, 1 fat
[S] Sweet Rolls with icing (average)	1	100-115	15-17	1-2	5	130-260	1 starch, 1 fat†
Toaster Muffins,™ all varieties (average)	1	140	22	2	5	80-250	1 starch, ½ fruit, 1 fat
[S] Toaster Strudel™ Breakfast Pastries, all varieties (average)	1	190	27	2	8	190-200	1 starch, 1 fruit, 1½ fat†
SARA LEE® (Kitchens of Sara Lee)							
[S] Coffee Cakes, large, all varieties (average)	⅛ cake	170	22	3	8	160-180	1 starch, ½ fruit, 1½ fat†

†For Occasional Use **Not Recommended For Use *Not Available [F] More Than 2 Fat Exchanges [S] Moderate To High Sugar Content

NUTRIENT VALUE

	PRODUCTS	SERVING SIZE	CALORIES	CARBO-HYDRATE (g.)	PROTEIN (g.)	FAT (g.)	SODIUM (mg.)	EXCHANGES
Ⓢ	Coffee Rings, all varieties (average)	⅛ ring	135	18	2	6	120-135	1 starch, 1 fat†
Ⓢ	Country Danish, Apple or Cherry (average)	1	140	20	2	6	127-214	1 starch, ½ fruit, 1 fat†
Ⓢ	Country Danish, Cheese	1	150	14	3	9	166	1 starch, 2 fat†
Ⓢ	Individual Danish, all varieties (average)	1	130	16	2	7	120-140	1 starch, 1 fat†
Ⓢ	Le Pastrie™ Croissants Apple	1	260	36	4	11	400	1½ starch, 1 fruit, 2 fat†
Ⓕ Ⓢ	Chocolate	1	320	34	6	18	310	2 starch, 3½ fat†
Ⓕ Ⓢ	Cinnamon-Nut-Raisin	1	350	44	7	17	420	2 starch, 1 fruit, 3 fat†
Ⓕ Ⓢ	Strawberry	1	270	38	5	11	290	1½ starch, 1 fruit, 2 fat†
Ⓢ	Sweet Rolls: Apple Crunch, Cinnamon, Honey (average)	1 roll	105	14	2	5	*	1 starch, 1 fat†

EGG SUBSTITUTES
FLEISHMANN'S® (Nabisco Brands, Inc.)

	PRODUCTS	SERVING SIZE	CALORIES	CARBO-HYDRATE	PROTEIN	FAT	SODIUM	EXCHANGES
	Egg Beaters®, cholesterol-free egg product	¼ cup	25	1	5	0	80	½ lean meat
	Egg Beaters® with Cheez (99% real egg product)	¼ cup	65	2	7	3	220	1 lean meat

PANCAKES, WAFFLES, FRENCH TOAST
AUNT JEMIMA® (Quaker Oats Co.)

	PRODUCTS	SERVING SIZE	CALORIES	CARBO-HYDRATE	PROTEIN	FAT	SODIUM	EXCHANGES
	French Toast, frozen Regular	2 slices	170	26	6	5	560	2 starch, 1 fat

†For Occasional Use　**Not Recommended For Use　*Not Available　Ⓕ More Than 2 Fat Exchanges　Ⓢ Moderate To High Sugar Content

NUTRIENT VALUE

PRODUCTS	SERVING SIZE	CALORIES	CARBO-HYDRATE (g.)	PROTEIN (g.)	FAT (g.)	SODIUM (mg.)	EXCHANGES
Cinnamon Swirl	2 slices	210	31	6	7	470	2 starch, 1 fat
Raisin	2 slices	190	28	7	5	550	2 starch, 1 fat
Pancake Batter, frozen, all varieties (average)	three 4" cakes	210	43	7	3	905-1105	3 starch
Pancake and Waffle Mix (as prepared)							
Buckwheat	two 4" cakes	135	17	5	5	348	1 starch, 1 fat
Buttermilk	two 4" cakes	200	27	7	7	663	2 starch, 1 fat
Buttermilk Complete	two 4" cakes	175	38	5	2	643	2½ starch
Complete	two 4" cakes	188	35	5	3	308	2 starch, ½ fat
Original	two 4" cakes	145	17	5	5	369	1 starch, 1 fat
Whole Wheat	two 4" cakes	165	21	7	6	482	1½ starch, 1 fat
Pancakes, frozen, all varieties (average)	three 4" cakes	260	47	7	4	1010-1030	3 starch, ½ fat
Waffles, frozen, all varieties (average)	1 waffle	85	15	3	2	630-700	1 starch

BETTY CROCKER® (General Mills, Inc.)

PRODUCTS	SERVING SIZE	CALORIES	CARBO-HYDRATE (g.)	PROTEIN (g.)	FAT (g.)	SODIUM (mg.)	EXCHANGES
Buttermilk Pancake Mix (as prepared)	three 4" cakes	170	36	4	1	755	2 starch
Complete Buttermilk Pancake Mix (as prepared)	three 4" cakes	210	41	5	3	580	2½ starch

DIA-MEL® (Estee Corp.)

PRODUCTS	SERVING SIZE	CALORIES	CARBO-HYDRATE (g.)	PROTEIN (g.)	FAT (g.)	SODIUM (mg.)	EXCHANGES
Pancake Mix, Dietetic (as prepared)	three 3" cakes	100	21	3	0	175	1½ starch

EGGO® (Mrs. Smith's® Frozen Foods, A Kellogg Company)

PRODUCTS	SERVING SIZE	CALORIES	CARBO-HYDRATE (g.)	PROTEIN (g.)	FAT (g.)	SODIUM (mg.)	EXCHANGES
French Toast, frozen	1 slice	80	12	3	2	245	1 starch
Pancake Batter (as prepared)	3 cakes (4 oz.)	230	41	7	4	660	3 starch, ½ fat
Waffles, frozen, all varieties (average)	1	110-120	16	3	5	*	1 starch, 1 fat

†For Occasional Use   **Not Recommended For Use   *Not Available   F More Than 2 Fat Exchanges   S Moderate To High Sugar Content

NUTRIENT VALUE

PRODUCTS	SERVING SIZE	CALORIES	CARBO-HYDRATE (g.)	PROTEIN (g.)	FAT (g.)	SODIUM (mg.)	EXCHANGES
Nutri-Grain™ Waffles, frozen, all varieties (average)	1	130	18	3	5	300	1 starch, 1 fat
Waffle Batter (as prepared)	1 (4 oz.)	285	36	5	13	495	2½ starch, 2 fat
FEATHERWEIGHT® (Sandoz Nutrition)							
Pancake Mix, Low Sodium (as prepared)	three 4" cakes	130	24	6	1	70	1½ starch
HEALTH VALLEY® (Health Valley Foods)							
Pancake Mix, all varieties (average)	1 oz.	110	22	4	1	165-170	1½ starch
HUNGRY JACK® (The Pillsbury Co.) Pancake and Waffle Mix (as prepared)							
Blueberry	one 4" cake	105	13	2	5	270	1 starch, 1 fat
Buttermilk	two 4" cakes	160	20	5	7	382	1½ starch, 1 fat
Complete	two 4" cakes	120	25	3	1	475	1½ starch
Extra Lights®	two 4" cakes	140	20	4	4	328	1½ starch, ½ fat
Panshakes	one 4" cake	83	14	2	2	290	1 starch
PILLSBURY® (The Pillsbury Co.) Microwave Pancakes, frozen							
Buttermilk	2 cakes	175	34	4	3	395	2 starch
Original	2 cakes	160	31	4	3	370	2 starch

†For Occasional Use   **Not Recommended For Use   *Not Available   Ⓕ More Than 2 Fat Exchanges   Ⓢ Moderate To High Sugar Content

Candy, Frostings, Syrups

Authors' Note: We have included a variety of convenience items in this section. This is not meant to imply that all are readily approved for general use or for use by people with diabetes. Many of these products contain large amounts of fats and refined sugars. We recommend that these products be used in moderation, if at all. If you decide to use them, work the specific product into your meal plan, using the nutrition information supplied here. And if you have diabetes, remember that if you decide to eat a high sugar food, eat it with a meal, when it will be more slowly absorbed; or before exercise, so that it will be readily used for energy.

NUTRIENT VALUE

PRODUCTS	SERVING SIZE	CALORIES	CARBO-HYDRATE (g.)	PROTEIN (g.)	FAT (g.)	SODIUM (mg.)	EXCHANGES
CANDY							
ESTEE® (Estee Corp.)							
Candy, Dietetic							
⒮ Chocolate Bars	3 squares	90	7	2	7	15	½ starch, 1 fat†
⒮ Chocolate Coated Raisins	12 pieces	60	8	2	4	20	½ starch, ½ fat†
⒮ Crunch Chocolate Bar	4 squares	90	8	2	6	20	½ starch, 1 fat†
⒮ Fruit and Nut Mix	10 pieces	88	8	3	5	25	½ starch, 1 fat†
⒮ Peanut Butter Cups	2	90	6	2	6	20	½ starch, 1 fat†
Hard Candy, Dietetic							
⒮ Estee-ets	10 pieces	70	8	2	4	20	½ starch, ½ fat†
Gum Drops	4 pieces	12	3	0	0	5	Free
⒮ Hard Candy	5 pieces	63	15	0	0	13	1 fruit†
Lollipops	1	12	3	0	0	5	Free

†For Occasional Use   **Not Recommended For Use   *Not Available   Ⓕ More Than 2 Fat Exchanges   ⒮ Moderate To High Sugar Content

PRODUCTS	SERVING SIZE	CALORIES	CARBO-HYDRATE (g.)	PROTEIN (g.)	FAT (g.)	SODIUM (mg.)	EXCHANGES
		NUTRIENT VALUE					
FEATHERWEIGHT® (Sandoz Nutrition)							
Assorted Hard Candies	1 piece	12	3	0	0	*	Free
[S] Chocolate Crisp Bar (3 oz.)	2 pieces	100	9	2	6	*	½ starch, 1 fat†
[S] Milk Chocolate Bar (3 oz.)	2 pieces	90	8	2	6	*	½ starch, 1 fat†

FROSTING

PRODUCTS	SERVING SIZE	CALORIES	CARBO-HYDRATE (g.)	PROTEIN (g.)	FAT (g.)	SODIUM (mg.)	EXCHANGES
BETTY CROCKER® (General Mills, Inc.)							
[S] Creamy Deluxe® Ready to Spread Frostings, all varieties (average)	1/12 tub	170	26	0	7	50-100	**
[S] Creamy Frosting Mixes, all varieties (as prepared) (average)	1/12 mix	170	30	0	6	40-115	**
[S] Fluffy Frosting Mix	1/12 package	70	16	<1	0	40	1 fruit†
PILLSBURY® (The Pillsbury Co.)							
[S] Frosting Mix (as prepared)(average)	for 1/12 cake	160	18	0-1	7-10	85-105	**
[S] Ready to Spread Supreme Frosting (average)	for 1/12 cake	160	25	0	8	45-115	**

SYRUP

PRODUCTS	SERVING SIZE	CALORIES	CARBO-HYDRATE (g.)	PROTEIN (g.)	FAT (g.)	SODIUM (mg.)	EXCHANGES
AUNT JEMIMA® (Quaker Oats Corp.)							
Syrup							
[S] Butter Lite	2 Tbsp. (1 fl. oz.)	50	13	0	0	65	1 fruit†
[S] Lite	2 Tbsp. (1 fl. oz.)	60	15	0	0	65	1 fruit†

†For Occasional Use **Not Recommended For Use *Not Available [F] More Than 2 Fat Exchanges [S] Moderate To High Sugar Content

NUTRIENT VALUE

	PRODUCTS	SERVING SIZE	CALORIES	CARBO-HYDRATE (g.)	PROTEIN (g.)	FAT (g.)	SODIUM (mg.)	EXCHANGES
Ⓢ	Regular	2 Tbsp. (1 fl. oz.)	100	26	0	0	25	**
	DIA-MEL® (Estee Corp.) Syrup, Dietetic							
	Blueberry Syrup	1 Tbsp.	1	<1	0	0	15	Free
	Chocolate Syrup	1 Tbsp.	6	1	0	0	3	Free
	Pancake Syrup	1 Tbsp.	1	<1	0	0	10	Free
	FEATHERWEIGHT® (Sandoz Nutrition) Reduced Calorie Syrups, all flavors (average)	1 Tbsp.	12-14	3	0	0	25	Free
	GOLDEN GRIDDLE® AND KARO® (Best Foods, CPC International, Inc.)							
Ⓢ	Dark	1 Tbsp.	60	15	0	0	40	1 fruit†
Ⓢ	Regular	1 Tbsp.	60	15	0	0	35	1 fruit†
Ⓢ	White	1 Tbsp.	60	15	0	0	30	1 fruit†
	NUTRADIET® (S and W Fine Foods) Flavored Pancake Syrups	1 Tbsp.	12	3	0	0	*	Free

†For Occasional Use   **Not Recommended For Use   *Not Available   Ⓕ More Than 2 Fat Exchanges   Ⓢ Moderate To High Sugar Content

Crackers, Snack Crackers

NUTRIENT VALUE

PRODUCTS	SERVING SIZE	CALORIES	CARBO-HYDRATE (g.)	PROTEIN (g.)	FAT (g.)	SODIUM (mg.)	EXCHANGES
ESTEE® (Estee Corp.)							
6 Calorie Wheat Wafers	12 wafers	72	12	*	*	<60	1 starch
Unsalted Crackers	6	90	15	1-2	3	<15	1 starch, ½ fat
FEATHERWEIGHT® (Sandoz Nutrition)							
Crackers, Low Sodium	6	90	15	0	3	3	1 starch, ½ fat
FRITO-LAY® (Frito-Lay, Inc.)							
Cheese Filled Crackers	1.5 oz.	200	26	4	9	475	1½ starch, 2 fat
Cheese Peanut Butter Crackers	1.5 oz.	210	21	7	11	415	1½ starch, 2 fat
Toast Peanut Butter Crackers	1.5 oz.	220	22	7	11	385	1½ starch, 2 fat
HEALTH VALLEY® (Health Valley Foods)							
Amaranth Graham	1 oz.	100	18	2	2	50	1 starch
Cheese Wheels	1 oz.	140	14	4	7	170	1 starch, 1 fat
French Onion	1 oz.	130	16	3	6	160	1 starch, 1 fat
Herb	1 oz.	130	16	3	6	250	1 starch, 1 fat
Honey Graham	1 oz.	130	16	3	6	160	1 starch, 1 fat
Rye	1 oz.	130	16	3	6	160	1 starch, 1 fat
Sesame	1 oz.	130	16	3	6	190	1 starch, 1 fat
Seven Grain	1 oz.	130	16	3	6	125	1 starch, 1 fat
Stoned Wheat	1 oz.	130	16	3	6	190	1 starch, 1 fat

†For Occasional Use   **Not Recommended For Use   *Not Available   F More Than 2 Fat Exchanges   S Moderate To High Sugar Content

NUTRIENT VALUE

PRODUCTS	SERVING SIZE	CALORIES	CARBO-HYDRATE (g.)	PROTEIN (g.)	FAT (g.)	SODIUM (mg.)	EXCHANGES
KEEBLER® (Keebler Co.)							
Club® Crackers	8	120	16	2	6	310	1 starch, 1 fat
Harvest Wheat Crackers	6	140	16	2	8	230	1 starch, 1½ fat
Toasted Rye Crackers	8	128	16	2	6	232	1 starch, 1 fat
Toasted Sesame Crackers	8	128	16	2	6	224	1 starch, 1 fat
Toasted Wheat Crackers	8	128	16	2	6	240	1 starch, 1 fat
Townhouse® Crackers	8	128	15	2	8	232	1 starch, 1½ fat
Tuc® Snack Crackers	6	140	16	2	8	170	1 starch, 1½ fat
Zesta® Saltine Crackers	8	100	16	2	3	330	1 starch, ½ fat
MANISCHEWITZ (B. Manischewitz Co.)							
Matzo Crackers	8	65	14	2	0	*	1 starch
Matzos (average)	1 oz.	105	22	3	0	*	1½ starch
Passover Matzos (average)	1 oz.	120	23	4	2	*	1½ starch
Tarns (average)	6	85	13	1	2	*	1 starch
NABISCO® (Nabisco, Inc.)							
Cheese Nips®	20 (¾ oz.)	108	14	2	5	200	1 starch, 1 fat
Chicken in a Biskit®	14 (1 oz.)	140	16	2	8	230	1 starch, 1½ fat
Crown Pilot® Crackers	1 (½ oz.)	60	11	1	1	65	1 starch
Dandy® Soup and Oyster Crackers	30 (¾ oz.)	90	15	2	2	330	1 starch
Dip in a Chip®	16 (1 oz.)	140	16	2	8	260	1 starch, 1½ fat
Escort®	6 (1 oz.)	160	18	2	8	220	1 starch, 1½ fat
Holland Rusks®	2	120	20	4	2	70	1 starch
Meal Mates® Sesame Seed Wafers	6 (1 oz.)	140	18	2	6	280	1 starch, 1 fat
Oysterettes® Oyster Crackers	27 (¾ oz.)	90	15	2	2	195	1 starch

†For Occasional Use   **Not Recommended For Use   *Not Available   F More Than 2 Fat Exchanges   S Moderate To High Sugar Content

NUTRIENT VALUE

PRODUCTS	SERVING SIZE	CALORIES	CARBO-HYDRATE (g.)	PROTEIN (g.)	FAT (g.)	SODIUM (mg.)	EXCHANGES
Ritz® Crackers							
Original	8 (1 oz.)	140	18	2	8	240	1 starch, 1½ fat
Cheese	10 (1 oz.)	140	16	2	6	240	1 starch, 1 fat
Low Salt	8 (1 oz.)	140	18	2	8	120	1 starch, 1½ fat
Royal Lunch® Milk Crackers	2 (1 oz.)	120	20	2	4	160	1 starch, 1 fat
Sea Rounds® Crackers	2 (1 oz.)	120	20	2	4	280	1 starch, 1 fat
Sociables®	12 (1 oz.)	140	18	2	6	260	1 starch, 1 fat
Triscuit® Wafers							
Original	6 (1 oz.)	120	20	2	4	180	1 starch, 1 fat
Low Salt	6 (1 oz.)	120	20	2	4	70	1 starch, 1 fat
Uneeda® Biscuits, unsalted tops	6 (1 oz.)	120	20	2	4	200	1 starch, 1 fat
Waverly® Crackers	8 (1 oz.)	140	20	2	6	320	1 starch, 1 fat
Wheat Thins®							
Original	16 (1 oz.)	140	18	2	6	240	1 starch, 1 fat
Cheese	18 (1 oz.)	140	18	4	6	440	1 starch, 1 fat
Low Salt	16 (1 oz.)	140	18	2	6	70	1 starch, 1 fat
Nutty	14 (1 oz.)	160	16	2	10	500	1 starch, 2 fat
Wheatsworth®	10 (1 oz.)	140	18	2	6	270	1 starch, 1 fat
Zweiback Toast	3 (¾ oz.)	90	15	3	2	*	1 starch

PEPPERIDGE FARM® (Campbell Soup Co.)

PRODUCTS	SERVING SIZE	CALORIES	CARBO-HYDRATE (g.)	PROTEIN (g.)	FAT (g.)	SODIUM (mg.)	EXCHANGES
Distinctive Crackers							
Cracked Wheat and Hearty Wheat (average)	4	110	13	2	4	180-200	1 starch, ½ fat
English Water Biscuits	4	70	13	1	1	90	1 starch
Sesame	5	100	14	3	4	131	1 starch, ½ fat
Toasted Wheat with Onion	5	100	15	4	4	138	1 starch, ½ fat
Goldfish Crackers, all varieties (average)	45	140	18	3	6	160-250	1 starch, 1 fat
Snack Sticks, all varieties (average)	8	130	18	2	6	320-390	1 starch, 1 fat

†For Occasional Use   **Not Recommended For Use   *Not Available   Ⓕ More Than 2 Fat Exchanges   Ⓢ Moderate To High Sugar Content

NUTRIENT VALUE

PRODUCTS	SERVING SIZE	CALORIES	CARBO-HYDRATE (g.)	PROTEIN (g.)	FAT (g.)	SODIUM (mg.)	EXCHANGES
Thin Crackers, all varieties (average)	4	70	9	1	3	100-105	½ starch, ½ fat

RALSTON™ (Ralston Purina Co.)

PRODUCTS	SERVING SIZE	CALORIES	CARBO-HYDRATE (g.)	PROTEIN (g.)	FAT (g.)	SODIUM (mg.)	EXCHANGES
Animal Crackers	10 (⅔ oz.)	87	15	1	2	76	1 starch
Cheese Snacks	25 (1 oz.)	140	18	3	7	259	1 starch, 1 fat
Crackers, unsalted tops	8 (0.8 oz.)	96	17	2	3	170	1 starch, ½ fat
Oyster Crackers	50 (¾ oz.)	90	15	2	2	260	1 starch
Rich & Crisp	7 (¾ oz.)	105	14	1	5	140	1 starch, 1 fat
RyKrisp®, all varieties (average)	3 triple crackers (¾ oz.)	75	17	3	2	167-258	1 starch
Snackers	6 (¾ oz.)	105	14	2	5	141	1 starch, 1 fat
Wheat Snacks	11 (¾ oz.)	98	14	2	4	138	1 starch, ½ fat

†For Occasional Use   **Not Recommended For Use   *Not Available   F More Than 2 Fat Exchanges   S Moderate To High Sugar Content

Dairy Products

NUTRIENT VALUE

PRODUCTS	SERVING SIZE	CALORIES	CARBO-HYDRATE (g.)	PROTEIN (g.)	FAT (g.)	SODIUM (mg.)	EXCHANGES
BEVERAGES							
(MILK, MILK-BASED AND MILK SUBSTITUTES)							
ALBA® (H. J. Heinz Company)							
Fit 'N Frosty, all flavors (average)	1 package	70	12	6	1	150-250	1 skim milk
Hot Cocoa	1 package	62	10	5	0	134	1 skim milk
CARNATION® (Calreco®, Inc.)							
Hot Cocoa Mixes							
70 Calorie, packets, dry powder	1 envelope	70	15	3	0	125	1 starch **or** ½ fruit, ½ skim milk
Ⓢ Regular, packets, dry powder, all varieties (average)	1 envelope (1 oz.)	110	23	2	1	120	1 fruit, ½ skim milk **or** 1 fruit, ½ starch†
Sugar Free, packets, dry powder	1 envelope	50	8	4	<1	160	½ skim milk **or** ½ starch
Ⓢ Malted Milk Powder, all varieties (average)	3 heaping tsp.	80-90	17	2	1	53-98	½ starch, ½ fruit†
Milk, Evaporated Lowfat Milk	½ cup (4 oz.)	110	12	9	3	138	1 skim milk, ½ fat

†For Occasional Use   **Not Recommended For Use   *Not Available   Ⓕ More Than 2 Fat Exchanges   Ⓢ Moderate To High Sugar Content

NUTRIENT VALUE

PRODUCTS	SERVING SIZE	CALORIES	CARBO-HYDRATE (g.)	PROTEIN (g.)	FAT (g.)	SODIUM (mg.)	EXCHANGES
Milk	½ cup (4 oz.)	170	12	8	10	133	1 skim milk, 2 fat
Skimmed Milk	½ cup (4 oz.)	100	14	9	<1	140	1 skim milk
Ⓢ Sweetened Condensed Milk	⅓ cup	318	54	8	9	325	**
ESTEE® (Estee Corp.)							
Cocoa, Dietetic	6 oz.	50	9	4	<1	75	½ skim milk
FEATHERWEIGHT® (Sandoz Nutrition)							
Hot Cocoa Mix, Low Calorie (as prepared)	6 oz.	40	7	3	0	71	½ milk **or** ½ starch
HEALTH VALLEY® (Health Valley Foods)							
Soy Moo (Soybean Milk)	8 oz.	140	11	9	6	210	1 skim milk, 1 fat
KRAFT® (Kraft, Inc.)							
Ⓢ Instant Malted Milk, all flavors, (as prepared) (average)	3 tsp. powder and 8 oz. skim milk	180	28	10	1	160-210	1 fruit, 1 skim milk†
LAND O'LAKES® (Land O' Lakes, Inc.)							
Ⓢ Chocolate Milk	8 oz.	210	26	8	8	150	1 fruit, 1 skim milk, 1½ fat†
Ⓢ Chocolate 1% Milk	8 oz.	160	26	8	3	150	1 fruit, 1 skim milk, ½ fat†
Ⓢ Chocolate Skim Milk	8 oz.	140	26	8	<1	155	1 fruit, 1 skim milk†
Ⓕ Ⓢ Egg Nog	8 oz.	300	32	9	15	142	**
NESTLÉ® (Nestlé Foods Corp.)							
Ⓢ Hot Cocoa Mix	1.25 oz.	150	26	3	4	110	1 starch, ½ fruit, 1 fat **or** 1 fruit, ½ skim milk, 1 fat†
Quik, Chocolate or Strawberry flavor (average)	2 tsp.	90	20	1	0	0-35	**
Quik, Sugar Free	5.8 grams	18	3	1	0	40	Free

†For Occasional Use   **Not Recommended For Use   *Not Available   Ⓕ More Than 2 Fat Exchanges   Ⓢ Moderate To High Sugar Content

NUTRIENT VALUE

PRODUCTS	SERVING SIZE	CALORIES	CARBO-HYDRATE (g.)	PROTEIN (g.)	FAT (g.)	SODIUM (mg.)	EXCHANGES
OVALTINE® (Sandoz Nutrition)							
Cocoa Mix							
50 Calorie Cocoa Mix	.45 oz.	50	8	1	2	135	½ skim milk **or** ½ starch
ⓢ Hot 'n Rich Cocoa Mix	1 oz. 5 tsp.	120	22	1	3	140	½ starch, 1 fruit, ½ fat **or** 1 fruit, ½ skim milk, ½ fat†
Sugar Free Cocoa Mix	.41 oz.	40	7	2	1	195	½ milk **or** ½ starch
ⓢ Ovaltine, Chocolate or Malt Flavor Dry Mix (average)	¾ oz.	80	18	1	0	65-145	1 starch **or** 1 fruit†
ⓢ Ovaltine, reconstituted with 8 oz. skim milk (average)	¾ oz. mix, 8 oz. skim	160	30	10	1	*	1 starch, 1 milk **or** 1 fruit, 1 milk†

CHEESE
DORMAN'S® (N. Dorman and Company, Inc.)

PRODUCTS	SERVING SIZE	CALORIES	CARBO-HYDRATE (g.)	PROTEIN (g.)	FAT (g.)	SODIUM (mg.)	EXCHANGES
Chedda-DeLite™	1 oz.	90	1	7	7	100	1 high fat meat
Chedda-Jack™	1 oz.	90	1	7	7	100	1 high fat meat
Dorelle® Wedges	1 oz.	60	1	3	5	690	½ high fat meat
Dorelle® Wedges, Reduced Calorie	1 oz.	35	1	3	1	227	½ lean meat
Lo-Chol® Imitation Cheese	1 oz.	70	0	6	5	130	1 meat
Mozzarella, Low Sodium	1 oz.	80	1	8	5	95	1 meat
Mozzarella, Part Skim	1 oz.	80	1	7	5	132	1 meat
Muenster, Low Sodium	1 oz.	110	0	7	9	95	1 high fat meat
Slim Jack™	1 oz.	90	1	6	7	90	1 high fat meat
Swiss, No Salt Added	1 oz.	100	0	8	8	8	1 high fat meat

†For Occasional Use   **Not Recommended For Use   *Not Available   Ⓕ More Than 2 Fat Exchanges   ⓢ Moderate To High Sugar Content

NUTRIENT VALUE

PRODUCTS	SERVING SIZE	CALORIES	CARBO-HYDRATE (g.)	PROTEIN (g.)	FAT (g.)	SODIUM (mg.)	EXCHANGES
EASY CHEESE® (Nabisco Brands, Inc.)							
Pasteurized Process Cheese Spread, all varieties (average)	1 oz.	80	2	4	6	320-370	½ meat, 1 fat
KRAFT® (Kraft, Inc.)							
Grated Cheese							
American Cheese Food	1 oz.	70	5	5	4	430	1 meat
Italian Blend, Parmesan, Romano (average)	1 oz.	130	1	12	9	350-430	2 meat
Natural Cheeses							
Blue	1 oz.	100	1	6	9	330	1 high fat meat
Brick	1 oz.	110	0	7	9	170	1 high fat meat
Caraway	1 oz.	100	1	7	8	180	1 high fat meat
Cheddar	1 oz.	110	1	7	9	180	1 high fat meat
Colby	1 oz.	110	1	7	9	180	1 high fat meat
Edam	1 oz.	90	0	8	7	310	1 high fat meat
Gouda	1 oz.	110	0	7	9	200	1 high fat meat
Monterey Jack, all varieties, (average)	1 oz.	110	0	7	9	180-190	1 high fat meat
Mozzarella, Low Moisture, Part-Skim, all varieties (average)	1 oz.	80	1	8	5	190-230	1 meat
Muenster	1 oz.	110	0	7	9	180	1 high fat meat
Neufchâtel	1 oz.	80	1	3	7	115	½ meat, 1 fat
Parmesan Cheese, Natural	1 oz.	110	1	10	7	350	1½ meat
Provolone	1 oz.	100	1	7	7	260	1 high fat meat
Scamorze, Low Moisture, Part-Skim	1 oz.	80	0	8	5	190	1 meat
Swiss, all varieties (average)	1 oz.	110	1	8	8	40-50	1 high fat meat
Taco, Shredded	1 oz.	110	1	7	9	180	1 high fat meat

†For Occasional Use   **Not Recommended For Use   *Not Available   Ⓕ More Than 2 Fat Exchanges   Ⓢ Moderate To High Sugar Content

NUTRIENT VALUE

PRODUCTS	SERVING SIZE	CALORIES	CARBO-HYDRATE (g.)	PROTEIN (g.)	FAT (g.)	SODIUM (mg.)	EXCHANGES
Process Cheese Food, Singles, all varieties (average)	1 oz.	90	2	6	7	380-450	1 high fat meat
Process Cheese Spread, all varieties (average)	1 oz.	80	2	5	6	340-450	1 meat
Spreads: Pimento, Pineapple, Relish, etc. (average)	1 oz.	70	3	2	5	75-160	½ meat, ½ fat
KRAFT® CASINO® (Kraft, Inc.)							
Havarti	1 oz.	120	0	6	11	140	1 meat, 1 fat
Mozzarella, Low Moisture	1 oz.	90	1	6	7	180	1 high fat meat
Romano, Natural	1 oz.	100	1	9	7	350	1½ meat
KRAFT® CHEEZ 'N BACON® (Kraft, Inc.)							
Process Cheese Food Singles	1 oz.	90	2	6	7	390	1 high fat meat
KRAFT® CHEEZ WHIZ® (Kraft, Inc.)							
Process Cheese Spread, all varieties (average)	1 oz.	80	2	4	6	370-470	½ meat, 1 fat
KRAFT® CRACKER BARREL® (Kraft, Inc.)							
Cheese Ball or Log, all varieties (average)	1 oz.	90	4	5	6	410	1 high fat meat
Cold Pack Cheese Food, all varieties (average)	1 oz.	90	4	5	7	260-280	1 high fat meat
KRAFT® DELUXE® (Kraft, Inc.)							
Process Cheese, all varieties (average)	1 oz.	100	1	6	8	420-460	1 high fat meat
KRAFT® GOLDEN IMAGE® (Kraft, Inc.)							
Imitation Cheese Natural Cheddar Cheese	1 oz.	110	0	7	9	150	1 high fat meat
Colby Cheese	1 oz.	110	1	7	9	170	1 high fat meat
Process Cheese Food, American Flavored	1 oz.	90	2	7	6	360	1 meat

†For Occasional Use   **Not Recommended For Use   *Not Available   Ⓕ More Than 2 Fat Exchanges   Ⓢ Moderate To High Sugar Content

48

NUTRIENT VALUE

PRODUCTS	SERVING SIZE	CALORIES	CARBO-HYDRATE (g.)	PROTEIN (g.)	FAT (g.)	SODIUM (mg.)	EXCHANGES
KRAFT® HARVEST MOON® (Kraft, Inc.)							
Process Cheese Product, all varieties (average)	1 oz.	60	3	5	3	420-460	1 lean meat
KRAFT® LIGHT N'LIVELY® (Kraft, Inc.)							
Singles, all varieties (average)	1 oz.	70	2	6	4	350-410	1 meat
KRAFT® MOHAWK VALLEY® (Kraft, Inc.)							
Limburger, Little Gem Size Natural	1 oz.	90	0	6	8	250	1 high fat meat
Limburger, Process Cheese Spread	1 oz.	70	0	4	6	400	½ meat, 1 fat
KRAFT® OLD ENGLISH® (Kraft, Inc.)							
Process Cheese, all varieties (average)	1 oz.	110	1	6	9	390-440	1 high fat meat
Process Cheese Spread	1 oz.	90	1	5	7	330	1 high fat meat
KRAFT® ROKA® (Kraft, Inc.)							
Blue Process Cheese Spread	1 oz.	70	2	3	6	270	½ meat, 1 fat
KRAFT® SQUEEZ-A-SNAK® (Kraft, Inc.)							
Process Cheese Spread, all varieties (average)	1 oz.	90	1	5	7	280-320	1 high fat meat
KRAFT® VELVEETA® (Kraft, Inc.)							
Process Cheese Spread, all varieties (average)	1 oz.	80	2	5	6	400-520	1 high fat meat
LAND O' LAKES® (Land O' Lakes Inc.)							
Cheese, Natural, except part skim (average)	1 oz.	110	1	7	8	75-275	1 high fat meat
Cheese, Part Skim Mozzarella	1 oz.	80	1	8	5	150	1 meat
Cheese, Processed (average)	1 oz.	90	2	6	7	330-445	1 high fat meat
SARGENTO® (Sargento Cheese Co., Inc.)							
Blue Cheese	1 oz.	100	1	6	8	400	1 high fat meat
Brick	1 oz.	110	1	7	8	160	1 high fat meat

†For Occasional Use   **Not Recommended For Use   *Not Available   Ⓕ More Than 2 Fat Exchanges   Ⓢ Moderate To High Sugar Content

NUTRIENT VALUE

PRODUCTS	SERVING SIZE	CALORIES	CARBO-HYDRATE (g.)	PROTEIN (g.)	FAT (g.)	SODIUM (mg.)	EXCHANGES
Brie	1 oz.	100	<1	6	8	180	1 high fat meat
Burger Cheese	1 oz.	110	<1	6	9	410	1 high fat meat
Camembert	1 oz.	90	<1	6	7	240	1 high fat meat
Colby	1 oz.	110	1	7	9	170	1 high fat meat
Colby-Jack	1 oz.	110	<1	7	9	160	1 high fat meat
Cracker Snacks, processed cheese spreads (average)	1 oz.	105	1	6	9	390-430	1 high fat meat
Edam	1 oz.	100	<1	7	8	270	1 high fat meat
Farmers Cheese	1 oz.	100	1	7	8	130	1 high fat meat
Feta	1 oz.	80	1	4	6	320	½ high fat meat, ½ fat
Finland Swiss	1 oz.	110	<1	8	8	75	1 high fat meat
Fontina	1 oz.	110	<1	7	9	*	1 high fat meat
Gjetost	1 oz.	130	12	3	8	130	1 starch, 1½ fat
Gorgonzola	1 oz.	100	1	6	8	400	1 high fat meat
Gouda	1 oz.	100	1	7	8	230	1 high fat meat
Gruyere	1 oz.	120	<1	8	9	95	1 high fat meat
Havarti	1 oz.	120	<1	5	11	200	1 high fat meat, ½ fat
Imitation Cheeses Cheddar	1 oz.	90	<1	7	6	350	1 meat
Mozzarella	1 oz.	80	<1	7	6	310	1 meat
Parmesan	1 oz.	120	10	5	7	450	½ starch, ½ meat, 1 fat
Monterey Jack	1 oz.	110	<1	7	9	150	1 high fat meat
Mozzarella Low Moisture Part Skim	1 oz.	80	1	8	5	150	1 meat
Low Moisture Whole Milk	1 oz.	90	1	6	7	120	1 high fat meat
Muenster, Red Rind	1 oz.	100	<1	7	9	180	1 high fat meat
Nacho Cheese	1 oz.	110	<1	6	9	410	1 high fat meat
Norwegian Jarlsberg	1 oz.	100	1	7	7	130	1 high fat meat

†For Occasional Use   **Not Recommended For Use   *Not Available   F More Than 2 Fat Exchanges   S Moderate To High Sugar Content

NUTRIENT VALUE

PRODUCTS	SERVING SIZE	CALORIES	CARBO-HYDRATE (g.)	PROTEIN (g.)	FAT (g.)	SODIUM (mg.)	EXCHANGES
Nut Logs							
Port Wine	1 oz.	100	3	6	7	250	1 high fat meat
Sharp Cheddar	1 oz.	100	3	6	7	250	1 high fat meat
Swiss Almond	1 oz.	90	2	6	7	350	1 high fat meat
Pot Cheese	1 oz.	25	1	5	<1	1	½ lean meat
Provolone	1 oz.	100	1	7	8	250	1 high fat meat
Queso Blanco	1 oz.	100	<1	7	9	180	1 high fat meat
Queso de Papa	1 oz.	110	<1	7	9	180	1 high fat meat
Ricotta							
Part skim	1 oz.	30	1	3	2	30	½ meat
Whole milk	1 oz.	50	1	3	4	35	½ high fat meat
Smokestick	1 oz.	100	1	7	7	390	1 high fat meat
String Cheese	1 oz.	80	1	8	5	150	1 meat
Swiss	1 oz.	110	1	8	8	75	1 high fat meat
Taco	1 oz.	110	1	7	9	160	1 high fat meat
Tilsiter	1 oz.	100	1	7	7	210	1 high fat meat
Tybo-Red Wax	1 oz.	100	<1	7	7	200	1 high fat meat

WEIGHT WATCHERS® (Nutrition Industries Corp.)

PRODUCTS	SERVING SIZE	CALORIES	CARBO-HYDRATE (g.)	PROTEIN (g.)	FAT (g.)	SODIUM (mg.)	EXCHANGES
Natural, Part-Skim Cheese	1 oz.	80	1	8	5	150	1 meat
Process Cheese Product, singles all varieties (average)	1 oz.	50	1	7	2	360-400	1 lean meat
Process Cheese Product, Low Sodium, singles	1 oz.	50	1	7	2	140	1 lean meat

WHIPPED TOPPINGS
BIRD'S EYE® (General Foods Corp.)

PRODUCTS	SERVING SIZE	CALORIES	CARBO-HYDRATE (g.)	PROTEIN (g.)	FAT (g.)	SODIUM (mg.)	EXCHANGES
Cool Whip® Extra Creamy Dairy Recipe Whipped Topping	1 Tbsp.	16	1	0	1	0	Free
	3 Tbsp.	48	3	0	3	0	1 fat
Cool Whip® Non-Dairy Whipped Topping	1 Tbsp.	12	1	0	1	0	Free
	¼ cup	48	4	0	4	0	1 fat

†For Occasional Use   **Not Recommended For Use   *Not Available   F More Than 2 Fat Exchanges   S Moderate To High Sugar Content

NUTRIENT VALUE

PRODUCTS	SERVING SIZE	CALORIES	CARBO-HYDRATE (g.)	PROTEIN (g.)	FAT (g.)	SODIUM (mg.)	EXCHANGES
DREAM WHIP® (General Foods Corp.)							
Whipped Topping Mix (as prepared)	1 Tbsp.	10	1	0	0	0	Free
D-ZERTA® (General Foods Corp.)							
Reduced Calorie Whipped Topping Mix (as prepared)	1 Tbsp.	8	0	0	1	5	Free
	¼ cup	32	0	0	4	20	1 fat
ESTEE® (Estee Corp.)							
Whipped Topping (as prepared)	¼ cup	16	1	1	1	20	Free
FEATHERWEIGHT® (Sandoz Nutrition)							
Whipped Topping Mix (as prepared)	1 Tbsp.	2	0	0	0	4	Free
KRAFT® (Kraft, Inc.)							
Real Cream Topping	¼ cup	25	2	0	2	10	½ fat
Whipped Topping	¼ cup	35	2	0	3	10	1 fat
LA CREME® (Kraft, Inc.)							
Whipped Topping	1 Tbsp.	12	1	0	1	5	Free
	¼ cup	48	4	0	4	20	1 fat

YOGURT

PRODUCTS	SERVING SIZE	CALORIES	CARBO-HYDRATE (g.)	PROTEIN (g.)	FAT (g.)	SODIUM (mg.)	EXCHANGES
DANNON® (The Dannon Co., Inc.)							
Plain Yogurt	8 oz.	140	16	10	4	160	1¼ skim milk, ½ fat **or** 1 starch, 1 lean meat
[S] Extra Smooth Yogurt	6 oz.	190	33	7	4	60	1 skim milk, 1½ fruit, ½ fat **or** 1 starch, ½ meat, 1 fruit†
[S] Extra Smooth Yogurt Mini-Pack	4.4 oz.	130	24	5	2	80	1 fruit, ½ skim milk, ½ fat **or** 1 starch, ½ fruit†
[S] Flavored Yogurt, coffee, lemon, vanilla (average)	8 oz.	200	32	10	4	140	1¼ skim milk, 1 fruit, ½ fat **or** 1 starch, 1 lean meat, 1 fruit†

†For Occasional Use **Not Recommended For Use *Not Available [F] More Than 2 Fat Exchanges [S] Moderate To High Sugar Content

		NUTRIENT VALUE					
PRODUCTS	SERVING SIZE	CALORIES	CARBO-HYDRATE (g.)	PROTEIN (g.)	FAT (g.)	SODIUM (mg.)	EXCHANGES
[S] Fruit-on-the-Bottom Yogurt	8 oz.	240	43	9	3	120	1 milk, 2 fruit, ½ fat **or** 1 starch, 1 lean meat, 2 fruit†
[S] Hearty Nuts and Raisins Yogurt	8 oz.	260	48	11	3	120	1 starch, 1½ fruit, 1 skim milk **or** 1 starch, 1 lean meat, 2 fruit†
[S] Original Mini-Pack Yogurt	4.4 oz.	130	23	5	2	65	1 fruit, ½ skim milk, ½ fat **or** 1 starch, 1 fruit†
[S] Supreme Yogurt	6 oz.	190	33	6	4	50	1 fruit, 1 skim milk, 1 fat **or** 1 starch, 1 fruit, 1 fat†
DANNY® (The Dannon Co., Inc.)							
Frozen Yogurt Treats							
[S] Danny® in a Cup, chocolate, vanilla (average)	1 cup (8 fl. oz.)	180-190	32-33	8-9	2-3	105-115	1 skim milk, 1 fruit, ½ fat†
[S] Danny® in a Cup, fruit flavored (average)	1 cup (8 fl. oz.)	210-230	42-44	6-7	2-4	105-115	1 skim milk, 2 fruit, ½ fat†
[S] Danny® on a Stick (coated) (average)	1 bar (2½ fl. oz.)	130-140	12-15	2-3	7-8	30-35	1 starch, 1½ fat†
[S] Danny® on a Stick (uncoated) (average)	1 bar (2½ fl. oz.)	60-70	10-14	2-3	1	30	1 starch†
[S] Danny Yo®, all flavors (average)	3½ oz.	110-120	21-23	4-5	1	*	1½ starch†
GAYMONT™ (Old Home® Foods, Inc.)							
Yogurt, Low Fat							
French Vanilla	8 oz.	130	15	10	3	150	1 skim milk, ½ fat
[S] Other Flavors (average)	8 oz.	240	42	10	3	130	2 fruit, 1 skim milk, ½ fat†
OLD HOME® (Old Home® Foods Inc.)							
Yogurt							
Plain	8 oz.	150	13	9	7	120	1 skim milk, 1 fat

†For Occasional Use **Not Recommended For Use *Not Available [F] More Than 2 Fat Exchanges [S] Moderate To High Sugar Content

NUTRIENT VALUE

	PRODUCTS	SERVING SIZE	CALORIES	CARBO-HYDRATE (g.)	PROTEIN (g.)	FAT (g.)	SODIUM (mg.)	EXCHANGES
Ⓢ	Vanilla	8 oz.	180	22	8	7	120	1 fruit, 1 skim milk, 1 fat†
Ⓢ	Fruit on the Bottom® Lowfat Yogurt, all flavors (average)	6 oz.	190	38	7	1	170	1½ fruit, 1 skim milk†
Ⓢ	No Refined Sugar	8 oz.	230	38	10	5	150	2 fruit, 1 skim milk, 1 fat†
Ⓢ	Soft Whip® Lowfat Yogurt, all flavors (average)	4 oz.	130	25	5	2	60	1½ fruit, ½ skim milk†

WEIGHT WATCHERS® (Pro-Mark Companies, Inc.)

	PRODUCTS	SERVING SIZE	CALORIES	CARBO-HYDRATE (g.)	PROTEIN (g.)	FAT (g.)	SODIUM (mg.)	EXCHANGES
	Plain Nonfat Yogurt	8 oz.	90	12	9	<1	140	1 skim milk
Ⓢ	Fruit Flavored Yogurt	8 oz.	150	27	9	<1	120	1 fruit, 1 skim milk†

WHITNEY'S™ (Kellogg Company)

	PRODUCTS	SERVING SIZE	CALORIES	CARBO-HYDRATE (g.)	PROTEIN (g.)	FAT (g.)	SODIUM (mg.)	EXCHANGES
	Plain Yogurt	6 oz.	150	13	9	7	*	1 skim milk, 1½ fat
Ⓢ	Flavored Yogurt, all flavors (average)	6 oz.	200	31	7	5	*	1 fruit, 1 skim milk, 1 fat **or** 1 meat, 2 fruit†

YOPLAIT® (General Mills, Inc.)

	PRODUCTS	SERVING SIZE	CALORIES	CARBO-HYDRATE (g.)	PROTEIN (g.)	FAT (g.)	SODIUM (mg.)	EXCHANGES
	Extra Mild Plain	8 oz.	160	18	12	4	140	1½ skim milk, ½ fat
	Original® Plain	6 oz.	130	13	9	5	120	1 skim milk, 1 fat **or** 1 starch, 1 meat
Ⓢ	Fruit Flavors (average)	6 oz.	190	32	7	4	105	1 fruit, 1 skim milk, 1 fat†
Ⓢ	Breakfast Yogurt™ All varieties except Cherry and Strawberry with Almonds (average)	6 oz.	230	41	8	4	90-95	2 fruit, 1 skim milk, ½ fat **or** 1 starch, 1 meat, 1½ fruit†
Ⓢ	Cherry with Almonds and Strawberry with Almonds (average)	6 oz.	210	37	8	3	90	1½ fruit, 1 skim milk, ½ fat†

†For Occasional Use   **Not Recommended For Use   *Not Available   Ⓕ More Than 2 Fat Exchanges   Ⓢ Moderate To High Sugar Content

NUTRIENT VALUE

	PRODUCTS	SERVING SIZE	CALORIES	CARBO-HYDRATE (g.)	PROTEIN (g.)	FAT (g.)	SODIUM (mg.)	EXCHANGES
	Custard Style™							
Ⓢ	Fruit Flavors (average)	6 oz.	190	32	7	4	95	1 fruit, 1 skim milk, ½ fat†
Ⓢ	Vanilla	6 oz.	180	30	7	4	110	1 fruit, 1 skim milk, ½ fat†
	Yo Creme®							
Ⓢ	Amaretto Almond	5 oz.	240	31	7	10	80	1 fruit, 1 skim milk, 2 fat **or** 1 starch, ½ meat, 1 fruit, 1½ fat†
Ⓢ	Bavarian Chocolate	5 oz.	270	36	7	11	95	1½ fruit, 1 skim milk, 2 fat **or** 1 starch, ½ meat, 1½ fruit, 1½ fat†
Ⓢ	Cherries Jubilee, Raspberries and Cream, Strawberries Romanoff	5 oz.	220	30	6	8	80	1 fruit, 1 skim milk, 1½ fat **or** 1 starch, ½ meat, 1 fruit, 1 fat†

†For Occasional Use   **Not Recommended For Use   *Not Available   Ⓕ More Than 2 Fat Exchanges   Ⓢ Moderate To High Sugar Content

Desserts

Authors' Note: We have included a variety of convenience items with this section. This is not meant to imply that all are readily approved for general use or for use by people with diabetes. Many of these products contain large amounts of fats and refined sugars. We recommend that these products be used in moderation, if at all. If you decide to use them, work the specific product into your meal plan, using the nutrition information supplied here. And if you have diabetes, remember that if you decide to eat a high sugar food, eat it with a meal, when it will be more slowly absorbed; or before exercise, so that it will be readily used for energy.

PRODUCTS	SERVING SIZE	NUTRIENT VALUE CALORIES	CARBO-HYDRATE (g.)	PROTEIN (g.)	FAT (g.)	SODIUM (mg.)	EXCHANGES
BARS, BROWNIES, COOKIES							
BETTY CROCKER® (General Mills, Inc.)							
[S] Big Batch® Cookie Mix (as prepared) (average)	2 cookies	120	17	1	6	95-100	1 starch, 1 fat†
[S] Brownie Mix, regular size, all varieties (as prepared) (average)	1/16 package	150	23	1	6	100	1½ starch, 1 fat†
[S] Brownie Mix, family size, all varieties (as prepared) (average)	1/24 package	130	21	1	5	80-95	1 starch, ½ fruit, 1 fat†
[S] Brownie Mix, Frosted Family Fudge (as prepared) (average)	1/24 package	160	27	1	5	105	1 starch, 1 fruit, 1 fat†

†For Occasional Use **Not Recommended For Use *Not Available [F] More Than 2 Fat Exchanges [S] Moderate To High Sugar Content

PRODUCTS	SERVING SIZE	CALORIES	CARBO-HYDRATE (g.)	PROTEIN (g.)	FAT (g.)	SODIUM (mg.)	EXCHANGES
		NUTRIENT VALUE					
[S] Coconut Macaroon Mix (as prepared)	1/24 package	80	10	1	4	15	½ starch, 1 fat†
[S] Date Bar Mix (as prepared)	1/24 package	60	8	1	3	35	½ starch, ½ fat†
[S] Vienna Dream Bar Mix (as prepared)	1/24 package	90	10	1	5	65	½ starch, 1 fat†
ESTEE® (Estee Corp.)							
[S] Brownie Mix (as prepared)	2″ x 4″ piece	90	16	2	4	30	1 starch, ½ fat†
Cookies and Wafers, Dietetic							
[S] Assorted Creme Filled Wafers	4	120	16	1	8	20	1 starch, 1½ fat†
[S] Chocolate, Vanilla Creme Filled Wafers	5	100	15	1-2	5	<25	1 starch, 1 fat†
[S] Cookies	4	100	12	1-2	6	<20	1 starch, 1 fat†
[S] Duplex Sandwich Cookies	3	120	15	1-2	6	15	1 starch, 1 fat†
[S] Snack Wafers, Chocolate, Strawberry, Vanilla	1	80	11	<1	4	<5	½ starch, 1 fat†
[S] Snack Wafers, Chocolate Coated	1	120	14	2	7	10	1 starch, 1 fat†
FEATHERWEIGHT® (Sandoz Nutrition)							
[S] Chocolate Chip Cookies	2	80	8	2	4	12	½ starch, 1 fat†
[S] Chocolate Wafers	2	60	6	0	4	24	½ fruit, 1 fat†
[S] Lemon Cookies	2	80	8	2	4	6	½ starch, 1 fat†
[S] Peanut Butter Wafers	2	60	6	0	4	24	½ fruit, 1 fat†
[S] Vanilla Cookies	2	80	8	2	4	12	½ starch, 1 fat†
[S] Vanilla Wafers	2	60	6	0	4	24	½ fruit, 1 fat†
GRANDMA'S® (Frito-Lay, Inc.)							
[S] Chocolate Chip Cookie	3 oz.	400	55	5	18	260	**
[S] Duplex Creme Cookie	2½ oz.	340	51	4	13	420	**

†For Occasional Use **Not Recommended For Use *Not Available [F] More Than 2 Fat Exchanges [S] Moderate To High Sugar Content

		NUTRIENT VALUE					
PRODUCTS	**SERVING SIZE**	**CALORIES**	**CARBO-HYDRATE (g.)**	**PROTEIN (g.)**	**FAT (g.)**	**SODIUM (mg.)**	**EXCHANGES**
[S] Oatmeal Apple Spice Cookie	3 oz.	350	55	6	12	295	**
[S] Peanut Butter Big Cookie	3 oz.	410	49	9	19	*	**
[S] Raisin Cookie	3 oz.	350	59	4	11	260	**
HEALTH VALLEY® (Health Valley Foods)							
Cookies							
[S] Date Pecan	½ oz.	67	9	1	3	134	½ starch, ½ fat†
[S] Peanut Butter	½ oz.	70	10	1	4	40	½ starch, ½ fat†
[S] Raisin Bran	½ oz.	70	10	1	4	40	½ starch, ½ fat†
[S] Raisin Oatmeal	½ oz.	70	10	1	4	40	½ starch, ½ fat†
Jumbo Cookies							
[S] Amaranth	⅔ oz.	60	14	3	2	35	1 starch†
[S] Cinnamon	½ oz.	60	10	1	2	35	½ starch†
[S] Oatmeal	½ oz.	60	10	1	2	35	½ starch†
[S] Peanut Butter	½ oz.	70	11	2	2	35	1 starch†
[S] Jumbo Fruit Cookies, all varieties (average)	½ oz.	85	12	1	3	26	½ starch, ½ fruit, ½ fat†
KEEBLER® (Keebler Co.)							
[S] Chips Deluxe Cookies	2	180	20	<2	8	150	1 starch, 1½ fat†
[S] Deluxe Grahams	3	120	17	<2	6	75	1 starch, 1 fat†
[S] Fudge Cremes Sandwich Cookies	2	120	16	<2	6	60	1 starch, 1 fat†
[S] Fudge Stripes Cookies	2	100	14	<2	6	100	1 starch, 1 fat†
[S] Oatmeal Cremes Sandwich Cookies	1	80	11	<1	3	60	1 starch, ½ fat†
[S] Old Fashioned Oatmeal Cookies	1	80	12	1	3	115	1 starch, ½ fat†
[S] Pecan Sandies® Cookies	2	160	18	<2	10	150	1 starch, 2 fat†
[S] Pitter Patter® Sandwich Cookies	1	90	11	1	4	120	1 starch, ½ fat†

†For Occasional Use **Not Recommended For Use *Not Available [F] More Than 2 Fat Exchanges [S] Moderate To High Sugar Content

NUTRIENT VALUE

	PRODUCTS	SERVING SIZE	CALORIES	CARBO-HYDRATE (g.)	PROTEIN (g.)	FAT (g.)	SODIUM (mg.)	EXCHANGES
[S]	Rich 'n Chips Cookies	2	160	20	2	8	140	1 starch, 1½ fat†
[S]	Vanilla Wafers	6	120	16	<2	6	120	1 starch, 1 fat†
	NABISCO® (Nabisco, Inc.)							
[S]	Almost Home® Fruit Sticks, apple, blueberry, cherry, iced Dutch apple	1	70	14	0	2	30-100	1 fruit†
[S]	Animal Crackers	8	95	15	1	3	88	1 starch, ½ fat†
[S]	Arrowroot Biscuits	5	108	17	2	3	66	1 starch, ½ fat†
[S]	Brown Edge Wafers	4	112	16	1	5	64	1 starch, 1 fat†
[S]	Chocolate Grahams	2	100	13	1	5	47	1 starch, 1 fat†
[S]	Famous Chocolate Wafers	4	104	17	2	3	160	1 starch, ½ fat†
[S]	Giggles® Sandwich Cookies, Chocolate or Vanilla	2	140	17	1	6	50-70	1 starch, 1 fat†
[S]	Lorna Doone® Shortbread	3	105	14	2	5	98	1 starch, 1 fat†
[S]	Molasses Cookie	2	130	21	2	4	130	1½ starch, 1 fat†
	Newtons®							
[S]	Apple, Blueberry, or Cherry	2	147	27	1	1	60-107	1 starch, 1 fruit†
[S]	Fig	2	100	20	1	2	100	½ starch, 1 fruit†
[S]	Nilla® Wafers	5	93	15	1	3	*	1 starch, ½ fat†
[S]	Old Fashioned Ginger Snaps	3	90	17	2	2	160	1 starch†
[S]	Social Tea® Biscuit	5	108	17	2	3	87	1 starch, ½ fat†
	NANAK'S® (Nanak's Gourmet Cookie Co.)							
[S]	Bavarian Fudge Cookies	2	118	12	2	7	38	1 starch, 1 fat†
[S]	Carob Coconut Chip Cookies	2	116	12	2	7	32	1 starch, 1 fat†
[S]	Danish Butter Pecan Cookies	2	122	12	1	7	24	1 starch, 1 fat†

†For Occasional Use **Not Recommended For Use *Not Available [F] More Than 2 Fat Exchanges [S] Moderate To High Sugar Content

	PRODUCTS	SERVING SIZE	CALORIES	CARBO-HYDRATE (g.)	PROTEIN (g.)	FAT (g.)	SODIUM (mg.)	EXCHANGES
Ⓢ	Dutch Chocolate Chip Cookies	2	120	13	2	7	16	1 starch, 1 fat†
Ⓢ	Jamaican Ginger Cookies	2	126	14	2	7	24	1 starch, 1 fat†
Ⓢ	Pistachio Paradise Cookies	2	112	13	2	5	38	1 starch, 1 fat†
Ⓢ	Scottish Oatmeal Raisin Cookies	2	120	14	2	6	19	1 starch, 1 fat†

PEPPERIDGE FARM® (Campbell Soup, Co.)

	PRODUCTS	SERVING SIZE	CALORIES	CARBO-HYDRATE (g.)	PROTEIN (g.)	FAT (g.)	SODIUM (mg.)	EXCHANGES
Ⓢ	Fruit Cookies, all varieties (average)	3	150	23	1	6	70-80	½ starch, 1 fruit, 1 fat†
Ⓢ	Kitchen Hearth Cookies, all varieties (average)	3	160	20	1	8	60-95	1 starch, 1½ fat†
Ⓢ	Old Fashioned Cookies, all varieties (average)	3	150	19	1	8	65-170	1 starch, 1½ fat†

PILLSBURY® (The Pillsbury Co.)

	PRODUCTS	SERVING SIZE	CALORIES	CARBO-HYDRATE (g.)	PROTEIN (g.)	FAT (g.)	SODIUM (mg.)	EXCHANGES
Ⓢ	Brownies, all varieties (as prepared) (average)	one 2″ square	150	20	2	8	90-100	1 starch, 1½ fat†
Ⓢ	Cookies, all varieties (as prepared) (average)	1	100	15	2	4	75-95	1 starch, ½ fat†
Ⓢ	Fudge Jumbles™ (as prepared) (average)	1 bar	100	14	1	4	55-60	1 starch, ½ fat†

CAKE, CAKE MIXES

Authors' Note: Some of these products contain large amounts of sugars and fats. If you decide to use them occasionally, make them part of your meal plan and eat them with a meal or before exercise.

BETTY CROCKER® (General Mills, Inc.)

	PRODUCTS	SERVING SIZE	CALORIES	CARBO-HYDRATE (g.)	PROTEIN (g.)	FAT (g.)	SODIUM (mg.)	EXCHANGES
Ⓢ	Angel Food Cake Mix, all varieties, (as prepared) (average)	1/12 cake	150	34	3	0	165-310	2 starch†

†For Occasional Use   **Not Recommended For Use   *Not Available   Ⓕ More Than 2 Fat Exchanges   Ⓢ Moderate To High Sugar Content

NUTRIENT VALUE

	PRODUCTS	SERVING SIZE	CALORIES	CARBO-HYDRATE (g.)	PROTEIN (g.)	FAT (g.)	SODIUM (mg.)	EXCHANGES
[S]	Boston Cream Pie (as prepared)	⅛ cake	270	50	4	6	390	2 starch, 1 fruit, 1 fat†
[S]	Gingerbread Mix (as prepared)	1/9 cake	210	35	3	6	330	2 starch, 1 fat†
[S]	Golden Pound Cake (as prepared)	1/12 cake	200	28	2	9	170	2 starch, 1 fat†
[S]	Lemon Chiffon Cake Mix (as prepared)	1/12 cake	190	35	4	4	190	2 starch, ½ fat **or** 1 starch, 1 fruit, 1 fat†
[S]	Pineapple Upside Down Cake Mix, cake and topping (as prepared)	1/9 cake	250	39	2	9	210	1 starch, 1½ fruit, 1½ fat†
[S]	Pudding Cake Mix, all varieties (as prepared) (average)	1/6 cake	230	45	2	5	250-270	1 starch, 2 fruit, 1 fat†
[S]	Snackin' Cake® Mix, all varieties (as prepared) (average)	1/9 cake	190	33	2	6	210-270	2 starch, 1 fat **or** 1 starch, 1 fruit, 1 fat†
[S]	Stir 'N Frost Cake Mix with Frosting®, all varieties (as prepared) (average)	1/6 cake	230	42	2	6	200-310	1 starch, 2 fruit, 1 fat†
[S]	Supermoist® Cake Mix, all varieties except those listed below (as prepared) (average)	1/12 cake	260	36	3	12	250-430	2 starch, 2 fat **or** 1 starch, 1½ fruit, 2 fat†
[S]	Cherry Chip	1/12 cake	190	37	3	3	270	2½ starch **or** 1 starch, 1½ fruit, ½ fat†
[S]	Chocolate Chip	1/12 cake	280	36	3	14	300	2 starch, 2½ fat **or** 1 starch, 1½ fruit, ½ fat†
[S]	Sour Cream White	1/12 cake	180	36	3	3	300	2 starch, ½ fat **or** 1 starch, 1½ fruit, ½ fat†
	DROMEDARY® (Nabisco, Inc.)							
[S]	Gingerbread Mix (as prepared)	2″ square	100	19	1	2	190	1 starch†

†For Occasional Use   **Not Recommended For Use   *Not Available   [F] More Than 2 Fat Exchanges   [S] Moderate To High Sugar Content

NUTRIENT VALUE

PRODUCTS	SERVING SIZE	CALORIES	CARBO-HYDRATE (g.)	PROTEIN (g.)	FAT (g.)	SODIUM (mg.)	EXCHANGES
Ⓢ Pound Cake Mix (as prepared)	½" slice	150	21	2	6	340	1½ starch, 1 fat†
ESTEE® (Estee Corp.)							
Ⓢ Cake Mixes, Dietetic with Sorbitol, all varieties (as prepared) (average)	⅒ cake	100	18	2	2	60-110	1 starch, ½ fat†
PEPPERIDGE FARM® (Campbell Soup Co.)							
Ⓢ Butter Pound Cake	1 oz.	130	16	1	7	150	1 starch, 1 fat†
Ⓢ Layer Cakes, all varieties (average)	1⅝ oz.	180	23	1	9	110-170	½ starch, 1 fruit, 2 fat†
PILLSBURY® (The Pillsbury Co.)							
Ⓢ Bundt® Brand Cake Mix, all varieties (as prepared) (average)	¹⁄₂₄ cake	165	25	2	7	175-205	1 starch, ½ fruit, 1 fat†
Ⓢ Gingerbread Mix (as prepared)	1½" x 3" piece	95	18	1	2	155	1 starch†
Ⓢ Pillsbury Plus® Cake Mix, all varieties (as prepared) (average)	¹⁄₂₄ cake	125	17	2	6	130-190	1 starch, 1 fat†
Ⓢ Streusel Swirl® Cake Mix, all varieties (as prepared) (average)	¹⁄₂₄ cake	175	25	2	7	135-225	1 starch, ½ fruit, 1 fat†
SARA LEE® (Kitchens of Sara Lee)							
Ⓢ Pound Cake, all varieties (average)	⅒ cake	130	17	2	6	85-170	1 starch, 1 fat†
Single Layer Cakes							
Ⓢ Banana	⅛ cake	170	28	1	6	160	1 starch, 1 fruit, 1 fat†
Ⓕ Ⓢ Carrot	⅛ cake	260	31	3	13	240	1 starch, 1 fruit, 2½ fat†

†For Occasional Use   **Not Recommended For Use   *Not Available   Ⓕ More Than 2 Fat Exchanges   Ⓢ Moderate To High Sugar Content

PRODUCTS	SERVING SIZE	CALORIES	CARBO-HYDRATE (g.)	PROTEIN (g.)	FAT (g.)	SODIUM (mg.)	EXCHANGES
		NUTRIENT VALUE					
[S] Two Layer Cakes, all varieties (average)	⅛ cake	190	28	2	8	90-100	1 starch, 1 fruit, 1½ fat†
WEIGHT WATCHERS® (Foodways National, Inc.)							
[S] Carrot Cake (contains fructose)	3 oz.	180	27	4	6	340	1 starch, 1 fruit, 1 fat†
[S] Chocolate Cake	2½ oz.	190	30	4	6	290	1 starch, 1 fruit, 1 fat†
[S] German Chocolate Cake	2½ oz.	200	31	4	8	350	1 starch, 1 fruit, 1½ fat†
[S] Spice Cake	3 oz.	170	24	4	6	350	1 starch, ½ fruit, 1 fat†
[S] Strawberry Shortcake	3 oz.	160	29	2	4	165	1 starch, 1 fruit, ½ fat†
DESSERTS							
DIA-MEL® (Estee Corp.)							
Gelatins, Dietetic, all flavors (as prepared) (average)	½ cup	8	<1	1	0	10	Free
DROMEDARY® (Nabisco, Inc.)							
[S] Date Nut Roll	½" slice (1 oz.)	80	13	1	2	160	1 starch†
D-ZERTA® (General Foods Corp.)							
Low Calorie Gelatin, all flavors (as prepared) (average)	½ cup	8	0	2	0	0	Free
ESTEE® (Estee Corp.)							
Gelatin Desserts, Dietetic, all flavors (average)	½ cup	8	<1	1	0	10	Free
FEATHERWEIGHT® (Sandoz Nutrition)							
Gelatin, Dietetic, all flavors (average)	½ cup	10	1	2	0	3-5	Free
JELL-O® (General Foods Corp.)							
[S] Cheesecake (as prepared)	⅛ of 8" cake	280	36	5	13	350	2 starch, ½ fruit, 2 fat†

†For Occasional Use **Not Recommended For Use *Not Available [F] More Than 2 Fat Exchanges [S] Moderate To High Sugar Content

NUTRIENT VALUE

	PRODUCTS	SERVING SIZE	CALORIES	CARBO-HYDRATE (g.)	PROTEIN (g.)	FAT (g.)	SODIUM (mg.)	EXCHANGES
S	Gelatin, all flavors (average)	½ cup	80	19	2	0	35-75	1 starch†
	Sugar Free Gelatin, all flavors (average)	½ cup	8	0	1	0	50-80	Free
	KNOX® (Thomas J. Lipton, Inc.) Gelatine, Orange Flavor, drinking	1 envelope	50	7	6	0	20	½ starch
	Gelatine, unflavored	1 envelope	25	0	6	0	10	Free
S	**MRS. SMITH'S® (Mrs. Smith's Frozen Foods, A Kellogg Company)** Apple Crepes	1 crepe (3 oz.)	195	34	3	5	210	1 starch, 1 fruit, 1 fat†
S	Strawberry Crepes	1 crepe (3 oz.)	150	23	3	5	210	1 starch, ½ fruit, 1 fat†
F S	**PEPPERIDGE FARM® (Campbell Soup Co.)** Apple Dumplings	3 oz.	260	33	2	14	240	1 starch, 1 fruit, 2½ fat†
S	Apple Strudel	3 oz.	240	35	1	11	220	1 starch, 1 fruit, 2 fat†
S	Fruit Squares, all varieties (average)	1	230	29	1	12	180-190	1 starch, 1 fruit, 2 fat†
F S	Fruit Turnovers, all varieties (average)	1	310	34	3	18	220-290	1 starch, 1 fruit, 3½ fat†
	SARA LEE® (Kitchens of Sara Lee) Elegant Endings™							
F S	Chocolate Chip	⅙	420	38	7	27	390	**
F S	Classic	⅙	350	29	10	22	250	**
F S	Pecan Praline	⅙	430	32	7	30	410	**
	Light Classics							
F S	French Cheesecake	1/10	200	19	3	13	100	1 starch, 2½ fat†
S	Strawberry French Cheesecake	1/10	200	22	3	11	100	1 starch, ½ fruit, 2 fat†
S	**STOUFFER'S® (Stouffer Foods Corp.)** Escalloped Apples	⅓ of 12 oz. package	140	28	0	3	20	2 fruit, ½ fat†

†For Occasional Use   **Not Recommended For Use   *Not Available   F More Than 2 Fat Exchanges   S Moderate To High Sugar Content

PRODUCTS	SERVING SIZE	CALORIES	CARBO-HYDRATE (g.)	PROTEIN (g.)	FAT (g.)	SODIUM (mg.)	EXCHANGES
		NUTRIENT VALUE					
WEIGHT WATCHERS® (Foodways National, Inc.)							
[S] Cheesecake, Black Cherry (contains fructose)	3.9 oz.	190	26	5	7	190	1 starch, 1 fruit, 1 fat†
[S] Cheesecake, Plain	3.9 oz.	200	24	8	8	220	1 starch, ½ skim milk, 1½ fat†
[S] Cheesecake, Strawberry (contains fructose)	3.9 oz.	180	25	5	6	220	1 starch, 1 fruit, 1 fat†

ICE CREAM, FROZEN DESSERT PRODUCTS

BLUE BUNNY® (Wells' Dairy, Inc.)

PRODUCTS	SERVING SIZE	CALORIES	CARBO-HYDRATE (g.)	PROTEIN (g.)	FAT (g.)	SODIUM (mg.)	EXCHANGES
[S] Ice Cream, all plain varieties (average)	½ cup	130	16	2	7	70	1 starch, 1 fat†
[S] Ice Milk, Vanilla Flavor	½ cup	110	18	3	3	65	1 starch, ½ fat†
[S] Sherbet, all flavors	½ cup	120	28	0	1	35	2 starch†
Ice Cream Novelties							
[S] Citrus Sticks	1¾ fl. oz.	50	13	0	0	5	1 fruit†
[S] Cookies 'n Cream Ice Cream Sandwiches	3 fl. oz.	180	30	3	6	140	1 starch, 1 fruit, 1 fat†
[S] Drumstick	3 fl. oz.	190	27	5	7	80	2 starch, 1 fat†
[S] English Toffee Stick	3 fl. oz.	190	18	2	12	60	1 starch, 2 fat†
[S] Fudge Stick	2½ fl. oz.	100	22	3	0	90	1 starch, ½ fruit†
[S] Ice Cream Sandwich	2½ fl. oz.	170	27	3	6	120	2 starch, 1 fruit, 1 fat†
[S] Krunch Sticks	2½ fl. oz.	140	15	2	9	80	1 starch, 1½ fat†
[F] [S] Peanut Stick	3 fl. oz.	190	15	3	13	80	1 starch, 2 ½ fat†
[S] Polar Pies	3 fl. oz.	190	17	2	12	70	1 starch, 2 fat†
[S] Pudding Bars, all flavors (average)	1.7 fl. oz.	90	15	2	3	40	1 starch, ½ fat†

†For Occasional Use **Not Recommended For Use *Not Available [F] More Than 2 Fat Exchanges [S] Moderate To High Sugar Content

NUTRIENT VALUE

	PRODUCTS	SERVING SIZE	CALORIES	CARBO-HYDRATE (g.)	PROTEIN (g.)	FAT (g.)	SODIUM (mg.)	EXCHANGES
S	Rainbow Stick	3 fl. oz.	80	16	1	1	45	1 starch†
S	Sherbet Push-up	2½ fl. oz.	120	28	0	1	35	2 fruit†
S	Slush Pops	2 fl. oz.	50	13	0	0	5	1 fruit†
S	Star Sticks	2½ fl. oz.	140	15	2	8	50	1 starch, 1½ fat†
S	Twin Pop Stick	3 fl. oz.	70	16	0	0	5	1 fruit†

CARNATION® (Calreco®, Inc.)

	PRODUCTS	SERVING SIZE	CALORIES	CARBO-HYDRATE (g.)	PROTEIN (g.)	FAT (g.)	SODIUM (mg.)	EXCHANGES
S	Bon Bon Ice Cream Nuggets, all varieties (average)	5 nuggets	170	14	2	12	28-50	1 starch, 2 fat†

CHIQUITA® (Chiquita Brands, Inc.)

	PRODUCTS	SERVING SIZE	CALORIES	CARBO-HYDRATE (g.)	PROTEIN (g.)	FAT (g.)	SODIUM (mg.)	EXCHANGES
S	Fruit and Cream Pops, all varieties (average)	1 bar (2 fl. oz.)	75	14	0	1	15-24	1 fruit†
S	Fruit and Juice Pops, all varieties (average)	1 bar (2 fl. oz.)	50	12	0	0	5-9	1 fruit†

COMET® (Nabisco, Inc.)

	PRODUCTS	SERVING SIZE	CALORIES	CARBO-HYDRATE (g.)	PROTEIN (g.)	FAT (g.)	SODIUM (mg.)	EXCHANGES
	Cones or Cups (wafer)	1	20	4	0	0	*	Free
	Sugar Cone	1	40	9	1	0	*	½ starch **or** ½ fruit

DAD'S® (Wells' Dairy, Inc.)

	PRODUCTS	SERVING SIZE	CALORIES	CARBO-HYDRATE (g.)	PROTEIN (g.)	FAT (g.)	SODIUM (mg.)	EXCHANGES
S	Root Beer Float Bar	1 bar (2½ fl. oz.)	90	15	1	2	40	1 starch†

GOOD HUMOR® (Thomas J. Lipton, Inc.)

Bars, original

	PRODUCTS	SERVING SIZE	CALORIES	CARBO-HYDRATE (g.)	PROTEIN (g.)	FAT (g.)	SODIUM (mg.)	EXCHANGES
F S	Chip Crunch	1 bar (3 fl. oz.)	200	16	2	14	35	1 starch, 2½ fat†
S	Chocolate Eclair	1 bar (3 fl. oz.)	180	24	2	9	70	1½ starch, 1½ fat†
F S	Chocolate Fudge Cake	1 bar (3 fl. oz.)	260	25	3	16	95	1½ starch, 3 fat†
F S	Chocolate Malt	1 bar (3 fl. oz.)	190	16	2	13	50	1 starch, 2½ fat†
S	Strawberries and Ice Cream	1 bar (3 fl. oz.)	100	18	1	2	40	1 starch†
S	Toasted Almond	1 bar (3 fl. oz.)	190	28	1	8	30	1 starch, 1 fruit, 1½ fat†

†For Occasional Use   **Not Recommended For Use   *Not Available   F More Than 2 Fat Exchanges   S Moderate To High Sugar Content

NUTRIENT VALUE

	PRODUCTS	SERVING SIZE	CALORIES	CARBO-HYDRATE (g.)	PROTEIN (g.)	FAT (g.)	SODIUM (mg.)	EXCHANGES
Ⓢ	Toasted Caramel	1 bar (3 fl. oz.)	170	21	2	9	55	1½ starch, 1½ fat†
Ⓢ	Vanilla Ice Cream Bar	1 bar (3 fl. oz.)	170	16	2	11	40	1 starch, 2 fat†
	Ice Cream Cookie Sandwiches							
Ⓢ	All Flavors	1 sandwich (2.7 fl. oz. ice cream)	290	42	4	11	195	**
Ⓢ	All Flavors	1 sandwich (4 fl. oz. ice cream)	400	59	5	16	270	**
	Shaped Novelties							
Ⓢ	Fat Frog	1 pop (3 fl. oz.)	140	17	2	7	45	1 starch, 1½ fat†
Ⓢ	Heart	1 pop (4 fl. oz.)	200	21	3	12	60	1½ starch, 2 fat†
Ⓢ	Shark	1 pop (3 fl. oz.)	70	17	0	0	0	1 fruit†
	Slices							
Ⓢ	Vanilla Ice Cream Slices	1 slice (3.2 fl. oz.)	110	13	2	6	45	1 starch, 1 fat†
Ⓢ	Cal-Control Vanilla Slices	1 slice (3.2 fl. oz.)	60	11	2	1	45	1 starch†
	Special Favorites							
Ⓢ	Assorted Whammys	1 bar (1.6 fl. oz.)	90	9	1	6	25	½ starch, 1 fat†
Ⓢ	Ice Stripes	1 pop (1.5 fl. oz.)	40	10	0	0	0	½ fruit†
Ⓢ	Pudding Stix	1 pop (1.75 fl. oz.)	90	15	4	2	65	1 starch†
Ⓢ	Vanilla Ice Cream Sandwich	1 sandwich (2.5 fl. oz.)	170	28	3	5	120	1 starch, 1 fruit, 1 fat†

HÄAGEN-DAZS® (The Pillsbury Co.)

	PRODUCTS	SERVING SIZE	CALORIES	CARBO-HYDRATE (g.)	PROTEIN (g.)	FAT (g.)	SODIUM (mg.)	EXCHANGES
Ⓢ	Fruit Ice, all flavors (average)	4 fl. oz. (½ cup)	120	29	0-1	0	10-20	2 fruit†
Ⓢ Ⓕ	Ice Cream, all flavors (average)	4 fl. oz. (½ cup)	270	25	5	17	45-220	1½ starch, 3 fat†

†For Occasional Use   **Not Recommended For Use   *Not Available   Ⓕ More Than 2 Fat Exchanges   Ⓢ Moderate To High Sugar Content

NUTRIENT VALUE

	PRODUCTS	SERVING SIZE	CALORIES	CARBO-HYDRATE (g.)	PROTEIN (g.)	FAT (g.)	SODIUM (mg.)	EXCHANGES
F S	Ice Cream Bars coated with chocolate, all flavors (average)	1	330	30	4	23	50-60	**
S	Sorbet and Cream, all flavors (average)	4 fl. oz. (½ cup)	200	27	3	9	40-45	1 starch, 1 fruit, 1½ fat†

JELLO® (General Foods Corp.)

	PRODUCTS	SERVING SIZE	CALORIES	CARBO-HYDRATE (g.)	PROTEIN (g.)	FAT (g.)	SODIUM (mg.)	EXCHANGES
S	Fruit Bars, all flavors (average)	1	45	11	1	0	10	1 fruit†
S	Gelatin Pops® Bars, all flavors (average)	1	35	8	1	0	5	½ fruit†
S	Pudding Pops® Bars All flavors, not chocolate-coated (average)	1	80	13	2	2	50-80	1 starch†
S	Chocolate-Coated Bars, all flavors (average)	1	130	14	2	7	50-75	1 starch, 1 fat†

KEMPS® (Marigold Foods, Inc.)

	PRODUCTS	SERVING SIZE	CALORIES	CARBO-HYDRATE (g.)	PROTEIN (g.)	FAT (g.)	SODIUM (mg.)	EXCHANGES
S	Ice Cream (average)	½ cup	130	17	2	6	*	1 starch, 1 fat†
S	Ice Milk (average)	½ cup	100	17	2	2	*	1 starch†
S	Sherbet (average)	½ cup	120	27	1	1	*	2 starch†
S	Sugar Lo	½ cup	135	14	3	7	*	1 starch, 1 fat†
S	Vegetable Fat Frozen Dessert	½ cup	120	15	1	6	*	1 starch, 1 fat†

LAND O' LAKES® (Land O' Lakes, Inc.)

	PRODUCTS	SERVING SIZE	CALORIES	CARBO-HYDRATE (g.)	PROTEIN (g.)	FAT (g.)	SODIUM (mg.)	EXCHANGES
S	Ice Cream, all varieties (average)	½ cup	140	16	2	7	60	1 starch, 1½ fat†
S	Ice Milk, all varieties (average)	½ cup	90	14	3	3	50	1 starch, ½ fat†
S	Sherbet, Fruit Flavors	½ cup	130	27	1	2	25	2 fruit†

MINUTE MAID® (Coca-Cola Foods)

	PRODUCTS	SERVING SIZE	CALORIES	CARBO-HYDRATE (g.)	PROTEIN (g.)	FAT (g.)	SODIUM (mg.)	EXCHANGES
S	Fruit Juicees, all flavors (average)	2¼ fl. oz.	60	14	0	0	7	1 fruit†

†For Occasional Use   **Not Recommended For Use   *Not Available   F More Than 2 Fat Exchanges   S Moderate To High Sugar Content

NUTRIENT VALUE

PRODUCTS	SERVING SIZE	CALORIES	CARBO-HYDRATE (g.)	PROTEIN (g.)	FAT (g.)	SODIUM (mg.)	EXCHANGES
NESTLÉ® (Nestlé Foods Corp.)							
Ⓕ Ⓢ Crunch Ice Cream Bars	1	180	15	2	13	*	1 starch, 2½ fat†
Ⓕ Ⓢ Quik Ice Cream Bars	1	210	19	3	14	40	1 starch, 3 fat†
SALADA® (Kellogg Co.)							
Ⓢ Ice Cream Mix, all flavors (as prepared) (average)	½ cup	155	16	2	10	30	1 starch, 2 fat†
SUGARLO® (Wells' Dairy, Inc.)							
Ⓢ Frozen Dietary Dessert, all flavors (average)	½ cup	120	14	2	6	45-50	1 starch, 1 fat†
SUNKIST® (Thomas J. Lipton, Inc.)							
Ⓢ Frozen Novelties, all flavors (average)	1	70	18	0	0	5	1 fruit†
TOFUTTI® (Tofutti Brands, Inc.) Novelties, single serving							
Ⓢ Chocolate Cuties	1	140	21	2	5	130	½ starch, 1 fruit, 1 fat†
Ⓢ Vanilla Cuties	1	130	21	2	5	110	½ starch, 1 fruit, 1 fat†
Pints							
Ⓢ Vanilla, Chocolate (average)	½ cup	200	21	2	12	90-130	½ starch, 1 fruit, 2 fat†
Ⓕ Ⓢ Other flavors (average)	½ cup	220	24	3	13	95-120	½ starch, 1 fruit, 2½ fat†
Soft Serve							
Ⓢ Regular	½ cup	158	20	1	8	65	1 starch, 1½ fat†
Ⓢ Hi-Lite, Chocolate or Vanilla (average)	½ cup	95	18	2	1	75	1 starch†
WEIGHT WATCHERS® (Foodways National, Inc.)							
Ⓢ Frozen Dietary Dessert, all varieties (average)	4.6 fl. oz.	100	18	4	1	75-105	1 starch†

†For Occasional Use   **Not Recommended For Use   *Not Available   Ⓕ More Than 2 Fat Exchanges   Ⓢ Moderate To High Sugar Content

NUTRIENT VALUE

	PRODUCTS	SERVING SIZE	CALORIES	CARBO-HYDRATE (g.)	PROTEIN (g.)	FAT (g.)	SODIUM (mg.)	EXCHANGES
	Frozen Novelties							
Ⓢ	Chocolate Dip Bar	1 bar (1.7 fl. oz.)	100	10	2	6	60	½ starch, 1 fat†
Ⓢ	Vanilla Sandwich Bar	1 bar (2.75 fl. oz.)	130	26	3	2	170	1 starch, 1 fruit†
Ⓢ	Quenchers, all flavors	1.7 fl. oz.	35	9	0	0	10	½ fruit†
Ⓢ	Treats, frozen, all varieties (average)	1 bar (1.75 fl. oz.)	60	12	3	1	45-50	½ fruit, ½ skim milk **or** 1 starch†

PIES, PUDDINGS, PIE CRUST

Authors' Note: Some of these products contain large amounts of sugars and fats. If you decide to use them occasionally, make them part of your meal plan and eat them with a meal or before exercise.

BANQUET® (ConAgra® Frozen Foods Co.)

	PRODUCTS	SERVING SIZE	CALORIES	CARBO-HYDRATE (g.)	PROTEIN (g.)	FAT (g.)	SODIUM (mg.)	EXCHANGES
Ⓢ	Cream Pies, all varieties (average)	⅛ of 14 oz. pie	135	15	2	8	80-110	1 starch, 1½ fat†
Ⓢ	Fruit Pies, all varieties (average)	⅛ of 20 oz. pie	190	28	2	8	193-273	1 starch, 1 fruit, 1½ fat†
Ⓢ	Pumpkin Pie	⅛ of 20 oz. pie	150	22	2	6	256	1 starch, ½ fruit, 1 fat†

BETTY CROCKER® (General Mills, Inc.)

	PRODUCTS	SERVING SIZE	CALORIES	CARBO-HYDRATE (g.)	PROTEIN (g.)	FAT (g.)	SODIUM (mg.)	EXCHANGES
	Pie Crust Mix	1/16 package	120	10	1	8	140	½ starch, 1½ fat
	Pie Crust Sticks	1/16 package	120	10	1	8	140	½ starch, 1½ fat

DIA-MEL® (Estee Corp.)

	PRODUCTS	SERVING SIZE	CALORIES	CARBO-HYDRATE (g.)	PROTEIN (g.)	FAT (g.)	SODIUM (mg.)	EXCHANGES
	Puddings, Dietetic, (as prepared) Butterscotch, Chocolate, Vanilla (average)	½ cup	50	9	4	0	80	½ skim milk
	Lemon	½ cup	14	4	0	0	20	Free

D-ZERTA® (General Foods Corp.)

	PRODUCTS	SERVING SIZE	CALORIES	CARBO-HYDRATE (g.)	PROTEIN (g.)	FAT (g.)	SODIUM (mg.)	EXCHANGES
Ⓢ	Reduced Calorie Pudding, all varieties (as prepared) (average)	½ cup	60-70	12	4	0	65-70	1 skim milk **or** 1 starch†

†For Occasional Use   **Not Recommended For Use   *Not Available   Ⓕ More Than 2 Fat Exchanges   Ⓢ Moderate To High Sugar Content

NUTRIENT VALUE

PRODUCTS	SERVING SIZE	CALORIES	CARBO-HYDRATE (g.)	PROTEIN (g.)	FAT (g.)	SODIUM (mg.)	EXCHANGES
ESTEE® (Estee Corp.)							
S Puddings, Dietetic, all varieties (as prepared) (average)	½ cup	70	13	4	<1	75-80	1 starch **or** 1 skim milk†
FEATHERWEIGHT® (Sandoz Nutrition)							
S Chocolate Mousse Mix, Reduced Calorie (as prepared)	½ cup	100	14	4	3	74	1 starch, ½ fat **or** ½ fruit, ½ skim milk, ½ fat†
S Pudding Mix, Low Calorie, all varieties (as prepared) (average)	½ cup	60	9	5	0	70-78	¾ skim milk†
FLAKO® (Quaker Oats Co.)							
F Pie Crust Mix	⅙ of 9″ crust	260	29	3	14	350	2 starch, 2½ fat
HORMEL® (George A. Hormel and Co.)							
S Dulcita, Apple or Cherry, frozen (average)	4 oz.	295	46	5	10	345-350	**
JELL-O® (General Foods Corp.) Americana®							
S Golden Egg Custard Mix (as prepared with skim milk)	½ cup	130	23	5	2	200	½ starch, 1 fruit, ½ skim milk **or** 1 starch, 1 fruit†
S Rice Pudding (as prepared with skim milk)	½ cup	140	30	5	1	160	½ starch, 1 fruit, ½ skim milk **or** 1 starch, 1 fruit†
S Tapioca Pudding, all flavors (as prepared with skim milk) (average)	½ cup	135	27	5	2	170	½ starch, 1 fruit, ½ skim milk **or** 1 starch, 1 fruit†
Mousse							
S Chocolate Mousse Pie, filling only (as prepared with skim milk)	⅛ pie	220	28	4	11	330	½ starch, 1 fruit, ½ skim milk, 2 fat†

†For Occasional Use **Not Recommended For Use *Not Available F More Than 2 Fat Exchanges S Moderate To High Sugar Content

NUTRIENT VALUE

	PRODUCTS	SERVING SIZE	CALORIES	CARBO-HYDRATE (g.)	PROTEIN (g.)	FAT (g.)	SODIUM (mg.)	EXCHANGES
S	Rich and Luscious® Mousse, all flavors (as prepared with skim milk) (average)	½ cup	120	21	5	4	85	1 starch, ½ fruit, ½ fat†
S	Pudding and Pie Filling Cooked or Instant, filling only, all flavors, (as prepared with skim milk) (average)	½ cup	140	28	4	1	170-520	½ starch, 1 fruit, ½ skim milk **or** 1 starch, 1 fruit†
S	Sugar Free Cooked or Instant, filling only, all flavors (as prepared with skim milk) (average)	½ cup	70	13	4	1	170-430	1 skim milk **or** 1 starch†
JUNKET® (Kellogg Co.)								
S	Rennet Custard Dessert Mix, all flavors (as prepared with skim milk) (average)	½ cup	90	16	4	0	65-70	½ fruit, ½ skim milk†
	Rennet Tablets	1 tablet	1	0	0	0	165	Free
KEEBLER® (Keebler Co.)								
	Tart Shells	1	160	19	2	9	45	1 starch, 2 fat
PEPPERIDGE FARM® (Campbell Soup Co.)								
F S	Fruit Pie Tarts, all varieties (average)	1	277	34	2	15	176-196	1½ fruit, 1 starch, 3 fat†
F	Patty Shells	1	210	17	2	15	180	1 starch, 3 fat
F	Puff Pastry Sheets	¼ sheet	260	22	4	17	290	1½ starch, 3 fat
PILLSBURY® (The Pillsbury Co.)								
F	All-Ready Pie Crust	⅛ of 2 crust pie	240	24	2	15	310	1½ starch, 3 fat
F	Pie Crust Mix or Sticks (as prepared)	⅙ of 2 crust pie	270	25	4	17	430	2 starch, 3 fat

†For Occasional Use   **Not Recommended For Use   *Not Available   F More Than 2 Fat Exchanges   S Moderate To High Sugar Content

NUTRIENT VALUE

PRODUCTS	SERVING SIZE	CALORIES	CARBO-HYDRATE (g.)	PROTEIN (g.)	FAT (g.)	SODIUM (mg.)	EXCHANGES
ROYAL® (Nabisco Brands, Inc.)							
[S] Cooked Puddings, all varieties (as prepared) (average)	½ cup	160	25	4	4	115-210	1 starch, ½ fruit, 1 fat†
[S] Instant Pudding, all varieties (as prepared) (average)	½ cup	180	29	4	5	350-390	1 starch, 1 fruit, 1 fat†
Sugar Free Instant Puddings, all varieties (as prepared) (average)	½ cup	105	16	4	3	470-480	1 starch, ½ fat
SALADA® (Kellogg Co.)							
[S] Danish Dessert™ Pie Glaze-Filling and Pudding (as prepared)	½ cup	130	32	0	0	5	**
SARA LEE® (Kitchens of Sara Lee)							
Light Classics							
[F] [S] Chocolate Mousse	1/10	200	18	2	14	80	1 starch, 2½ fat†
[S] Strawberry Mousse	1/10	180	18	1	11	60	1 starch, 2 fat†
WEIGHT WATCHERS® (Foodways National, Inc.)							
[S] Apple Pie	3.5 oz.	180	37	1	6	310	1 starch, 1½ fruit, 1 fat†
[S] Boston Cream Pie	3 oz.	180	37	4	4	320	1½ starch, 1 fruit, ½ fat†
[S] Cherry Pie	3.5 oz.	200	40	1	6	160	1 starch, 1½ fruit, 1 fat†
[S] Chocolate Mousse	2.5 oz.	170	25	6	6	190	1½ starch, 1 fat†

†For Occasional Use   **Not Recommended For Use   *Not Available   [F] More Than 2 Fat Exchanges   [S] Moderate To High Sugar Content

Dips

NUTRIENT VALUE

PRODUCTS	SERVING SIZE	CALORIES	CARBO-HYDRATE (g.)	PROTEIN (g.)	FAT (g.)	SODIUM (mg.)	EXCHANGES
DURKEE® (Durkee Famous Foods)							
Bacon Cheese Dip Mix (as prepared)	⅓ cup	127	10	6	6	552	½ starch, ½ meat, ½ fat
Cheese Dip Mix	⅓ cup	132	11	6	7	529	1 starch, ½ meat, ½ fat
Nacho Cheese Dip Mix	⅓ cup	122	9	6	6	427	½ starch, ½ meat, ½ fat
ESTEE® (Estee Corp.)							
Dip Mixes (as prepared)	2 Tbsp.	50	1	<1	5	20	1 fat
FRITOS® (Frito-Lay, Inc.)							
Enchilada Dip	1 oz.	35	4	2	1	*	1 veg.
KRAFT® (Kraft, Inc.)							
Premium Dips, all varieties (average)	1 oz. or 2 Tbsp.	45-60	2	1	4	125-250	1 fat
Other Dips, all varieties (average)	2 Tbsp.	60	3	1	4	160-260	1 fat
LAND O' LAKES® (Land O' Lakes)							
Dips, flavored (average)	2 oz.	70	4	2	5	315	1 veg., 1 fat

†For Occasional Use   **Not Recommended For Use   *Not Available   F More Than 2 Fat Exchanges   S Moderate To High Sugar Content

NUTRIENT VALUE

PRODUCTS	SERVING SIZE	CALORIES	CARBO-HYDRATE (g.)	PROTEIN (g.)	FAT (g.)	SODIUM (mg.)	EXCHANGES
Lean Cream™ Dip, all varieties (average)	1 Tbsp.	20	2	1	1	82-117	Free
TOSTITOS® (Frito-Lay, Inc.) Picante Sauce (average)	1 oz.	14	3	0	0	163	Free

†For Occasional Use   **Not Recommended For Use   *Not Available   F More Than 2 Fat Exchanges   S Moderate To High Sugar Content

Entrees

NUTRIENT VALUE

PRODUCTS	SERVING SIZE	CALORIES	CARBO-HYDRATE (g.)	PROTEIN (g.)	FAT (g.)	SODIUM (mg.)	EXCHANGES
BEANS, BEAN COMBINATIONS							
BANQUET® (ConAgra® Frozen Foods Co.)							
Beans and Franks Dinner	10¼ oz.	500	64	19	19	1377	4 starch, 1 high fat meat, 2 fat
CAMPBELL'S® (Campbell Soup Co.)							
Barbecue Beans	7⅞ oz.	250	43	10	4	1110	3 starch, ½ fat
Beans and Franks	7⅞ oz.	360	43	14	14	1140	3 starch, 1 high fat meat, 1 fat
Home Style Beans	8 oz.	270	48	11	4	1130	3 starch, ½ fat
Pork and Beans in Tomato Sauce	8 oz.	240	42	9	3	820	3 starch
DENNISON'S® (American Home Foods)							
Lima Beans with Ham	7½ oz.	250	33	14	7	935	2 starch, 1 meat
HEALTH VALLEY® (Health Valley Foods)							
Boston Baked Beans	4 oz.	130	23	6	1	390	1½ starch
Boston Baked Beans, No Salt	4 oz.	130	23	6	1	20	1½ starch
Vegetarian Beans with Miso	4 oz.	120	19	6	1	310	1 starch, ½ lean meat
HEINZ® (H.J. Heinz Co.)							
Pork 'n Beans	8 oz.	250	46	11	4	745	3 starch
Vegetarian Beans	8 oz.	230	43	11	1	910	3 starch

†For Occasional Use   **Not Recommended For Use   *Not Available   Ⓕ More Than 2 Fat Exchanges   Ⓢ Moderate To High Sugar Content

NUTRIENT VALUE

PRODUCTS	SERVING SIZE	CALORIES	CARBO-HYDRATE (g.)	PROTEIN (g.)	FAT (g.)	SODIUM (mg.)	EXCHANGES
HORMEL® (George A. Hormel and Co.)							
Beans and Bacon	7½ oz.	330	40	16	12	813	2½ starch, 1 meat, 1 fat
Beans and Ham	7½ oz.	360	32	16	18	1182	2 starch, 1½ meat, 2 fat
Beans and Wieners	7½ oz.	280	29	12	14	1342	2 starch, 1 high fat meat, 1 fat
VAN CAMP'S® (Quaker Oats Co.)							
Beanee Weenee®	1 cup	330	32	15	15	990	2 starch, 1 high fat meat, 1 fat
Pork and Beans	½ cup	110	20	6	1	505	1½ starch
Vegetarian Style Beans	½ cup	105	20	6	1	445	1½ starch

CHICKEN
BANQUET® (ConAgra® Frozen Foods Co.)

PRODUCTS	SERVING SIZE	CALORIES	CARBO-HYDRATE (g.)	PROTEIN (g.)	FAT (g.)	SODIUM (mg.)	EXCHANGES
Breaded Chicken Drum Snackers	3 oz.	202	14	14	10	532	1 starch, 1½ lean meat, 1 fat
Breaded Chicken Nuggets	3 oz.	233	14	14	14	573	1 starch, 1½ lean meat, 2 fat
Breaded Chicken Patties	3 oz.	225	13	13	14	513	1 starch, 1½ lean meat, 2 fat
Breaded Chicken Sticks	3 oz.	228	15	14	13	566	1 starch, 1½ lean meat, 1½ fat
Breaded Chicken Winglets	3 oz.	202	14	14	10	532	1 starch, 1½ lean meat, 1 fat
F Chicken and Cheddar Nuggets	3 oz.	275	11	14	19	*	1 starch, 1½ lean meat, 3 fat
F Fried Chicken	6½ oz.	325	20	18	19	1201	1 starch, 2 lean meat, 2½ fat
Fried Chicken Breast Portions	4½ oz.	238	14	17	12	772	1 starch, 2 lean meat, 1 fat

†For Occasional Use   **Not Recommended For Use   *Not Available   F More Than 2 Fat Exchanges   S Moderate To High Sugar Content

NUTRIENT VALUE

PRODUCTS	SERVING SIZE	CALORIES	CARBO-HYDRATE (g.)	PROTEIN (g.)	FAT (g.)	SODIUM (mg.)	EXCHANGES
Fried Chicken Thighs and Drumsticks	5 oz.	277	16	16	16	892	1 starch, 2 lean meat, 2 fat
Hot and Spicy Chicken Nuggets	3 oz.	235	13	13	14	*	1 starch, 1½ lean meat, 2 fat
F Hot 'n Spicy Fried Chicken	6½ oz.	325	20	18	19	1201	1 starch, 2 lean meat, 2½ fat

CHICKEN HELPER® (General Mills, Inc.)

PRODUCTS	SERVING SIZE	CALORIES	CARBO-HYDRATE (g.)	PROTEIN (g.)	FAT (g.)	SODIUM (mg.)	EXCHANGES
Chicken and Dumpling (as prepared)	1 serving	530	41	34	26	1320	3 starch, 3½ meat, 1 fat
Chicken and Mushroom (as prepared)	1 serving	470	29	31	25	900	2 starch, 3½ meat, 1 fat
F Potato and Gravy (as prepared)	1 serving	600	45	34	32	1000	3 starch, 3½ meat, 2½ fat
F Stuffing (as prepared)	1 serving	570	34	33	33	1600	2 starch, 4 meat, 2½ fat
Teriyaki Chicken (as prepared)	1 serving	480	35	31	23	1010	2 starch, 3½ meat, 1 fat

TYSON® (Tyson Foods, Inc.)
Chick'n Quick® Products

PRODUCTS	SERVING SIZE	CALORIES	CARBO-HYDRATE (g.)	PROTEIN (g.)	FAT (g.)	SODIUM (mg.)	EXCHANGES
Breast Patties	3 oz.	240	10	13	17	*	½ starch, 2 lean meat, 2 fat
Breast Fillets	3 oz.	190	14	15	8	*	1 starch, 2 lean meat
Chick'n Cheddar®	3 oz.	260	13	13	17	*	1 starch, 1½ lean meat, 2 fat
Chick'n Chunks™	6 pieces (3 oz.)	250	13	13	16	*	1 starch, 1½ lean meat, 2 fat
Chick'n Dippers™	4 dippers (3 oz.)	250	13	13	16	*	1 starch, 1½ lean meat, 2 fat
Chick'n Sticks™	3 sticks (3 oz.)	240	14	13	15	*	1 starch, 1½ lean meat, 2 fat

†For Occasional Use   **Not Recommended For Use   *Not Available   F More Than 2 Fat Exchanges   S Moderate To High Sugar Content

NUTRIENT VALUE

PRODUCTS	SERVING SIZE	CALORIES	CARBO-HYDRATE (g.)	PROTEIN (g.)	FAT (g.)	SODIUM (mg.)	EXCHANGES
Chicken Bologna	1 slice	90	1	4	7	*	½ high fat meat, ½ fat
Chicken Corn Dogs	1 frank (2 oz.)	280	28	9	14	*	2 starch, ½ meat, 2 fat
Chicken Franks	3½ oz.	150	1	8	13	*	1 high fat meat, 1 fat
Chicken Patties, Thick'n Crispy™	3 oz.	220	11	13	14	*	1 starch, 1½ lean meat, 1½ fat
Southern Fried Chick'n Chunks™	3 oz.	250	13	13	16	*	1 starch, 1½ lean meat, 2 fat
F Swiss'n Bacon™	3 oz.	280	14	12	20	*	1 starch, 1½ lean meat, 3 fat
Thick'n Zesty™ Chicken Patties, Italian Recipe	3 oz.	240	14	12	15	*	1 starch, 1½ lean meat, 2 fat
Turkey Patties	3 oz.	220	12	13	14	*	1 starch, 1½ lean meat, 1½ fat

CHILI
ARMOUR® (Armour-Dial, Inc.)

PRODUCTS	SERVING SIZE	CALORIES	CARBO-HYDRATE (g.)	PROTEIN (g.)	FAT (g.)	SODIUM (mg.)	EXCHANGES
F Chili with Beans or Texas Chili with Beans (average)	7½ oz.	380	28	12	25	1080-1240	2 starch, 1 meat, 3½ fat
F Chili without Beans or Texas Chili without Beans (average)	7½ oz.	390	14	14	31	1140-1550	1 starch, 1½ meat, 4½ fat
Chili Mac	7½ oz.	220	20	7	12	1190	1 starch, ½ meat, 2 fat

CHEF BOY-AR-DEE® (American Home Foods)

PRODUCTS	SERVING SIZE	CALORIES	CARBO-HYDRATE (g.)	PROTEIN (g.)	FAT (g.)	SODIUM (mg.)	EXCHANGES
Beef Chili with Beans	7½ oz.	330	30	15	17	1005	2 starch, 1 meat, 2 fat
F Beef Chili without Beans	7½ oz.	370	14	14	29	875	1 starch, 1½ meat, 4 fat
Chili Mac	7½ oz.	230	24	8	11	1410	1½ starch, ½ meat, 1½ fat

†For Occasional Use   **Not Recommended For Use   *Not Available   F More Than 2 Fat Exchanges   S Moderate To High Sugar Content

NUTRIENT VALUE

PRODUCTS	SERVING SIZE	CALORIES	CARBO-HYDRATE (g.)	PROTEIN (g.)	FAT (g.)	SODIUM (mg.)	EXCHANGES
DENNISON'S® (American Home Foods)							
Chili Beans in Chili Gravy	7½ oz.	180	30	12	1	770	2 starch, 1 lean meat
Chili Con Carne with Beans	7½ oz.	320	27	16	17	840	2 starch, 1½ meat, 1½ fat
Chili Con Carne with Beans, Hot	7½ oz.	310	26	16	16	910	2 starch, 1½ meat, 1½ fat
Chili Con Carne without Beans	7½ oz.	300	15	17	19	1380	1 starch, 2 meat, 1½ fat
Chili Mac	7½ oz.	210	22	8	10	1360	1½ starch, ½ meat, 1 fat
FEATHERWEIGHT® (Sandoz Nutrition)							
Chili with Beans, Low Sodium	7½ oz.	270	25	15	13	85	1½ starch, 1½ high fat meat
HAMBURGER HELPER® (General Mills, Inc.)							
Chili Tomato (as prepared)	1 serving	330	31	20	14	1360	2 starch, 2 meat, 1 fat
HEALTH VALLEY® (Health Valley Foods)							
Chili Con Carne	4 oz.	170	12	9	8	482	1 starch, 1 meat, ½ fat
Chili, Lentil	4 oz.	130	6	16	6	200	½ starch, 2 lean meat
Chili, Vegetarian, all varieties (average)	4 oz.	170	18	9	7	780	1 starch, 1 lean meat, ½ fat
Chili, Vegetarian, No Salt, all varieties (average)	4 oz.	170	18	9	7	25	1 starch, 1 lean meat, ½ fat
HEINZ® (H.J. Heinz Co.)							
F Chili Con Carne	7¾ oz.	350	27	15	21	1000	2 starch, 1½ meat, 2½ fat
Chili Mac	7½ oz.	250	26	10	12	860	2 starch, ½ meat, ½ fat
Hot Chili with Beans	7¾ oz.	330	30	15	16	1140	2 starch, 1½ meat, 1½ fat

†For Occasional Use   **Not Recommended For Use   *Not Available   F More Than 2 Fat Exchanges   S Moderate To High Sugar Content

PRODUCTS	SERVING SIZE	CALORIES	CARBO-HYDRATE (g.)	PROTEIN (g.)	FAT (g.)	SODIUM (mg.)	EXCHANGES
HORMEL® (George A. Hormel and Co.)							
Chili with Beans or Hot Chili with Beans (average)	7½ oz.	290	23	17	15	1086-1134	1½ starch, 2 meat, 1 fat
Ⓕ Chili, No Beans	7½ oz.	360	11	18	27	961	1 starch, 2 meat, 3 fat
Chili Mac	7½ oz.	200	16	11	10	1418	1 starch, 1 meat, 1 fat
STOUFFER'S® (Stouffer Foods Corp.)							
Chili Con Carne with Beans	8¾ oz.	280	23	21	11	1190	1½ starch, 2 meat
VAN CAMP'S® (Quaker Oats Co.)							
Chili Weenee®	1 cup	310	28	14	16	1060	2 starch, 1 high fat meat, 1 fat
Ⓕ Chili with Beans	1 cup	350	21	15	23	1220	1½ starch, 1½ high fat meat, 2½ fat
Ⓕ Chili without Beans	1 cup	410	12	15	34	1500	1 starch, 2 high fat meat, 3½ fat

COMBINATION DISHES, DINNERS

PRODUCTS	SERVING SIZE	CALORIES	CARBO-HYDRATE (g.)	PROTEIN (g.)	FAT (g.)	SODIUM (mg.)	EXCHANGES
ARMOUR® (Armour-Dial, Inc.)							
Beef Stew	8 oz.	210	16	12	11	1190	1 starch, 1½ meat, ½ fat
Ⓕ Corned Beef Hash	7½ oz.	410	18	18	28	1420	1 starch, 2 meat, 3½ fat
Roast Beef Hash	7½ oz.	350	21	19	22	1110	1½ starch, 2 meat, 2 fat
Sloppy Joe Beef	7.6 oz.	360	28	14	20	1700	2 starch, 1½ meat, 2 fat
ARMOUR® (ConAgra® Frozen Foods Co.)							
Classic Lites							
Baby Bay Shrimp in Sherried Cream Sauce	10½ oz.	280	34	17	8	1220	2 starch, 1½ lean meat, ½ fat
Beef Pepper Steak	10 oz.	240	28	16	7	1020	2 starch, 1½ lean meat

†For Occasional Use   **Not Recommended For Use   *Not Available   Ⓕ More Than 2 Fat Exchanges   Ⓢ Moderate To High Sugar Content

NUTRIENT VALUE

PRODUCTS	SERVING SIZE	CALORIES	CARBO-HYDRATE (g.)	PROTEIN (g.)	FAT (g.)	SODIUM (mg.)	EXCHANGES
Chicken Burgundy	11¼ oz.	230	26	21	5	1220	2 starch, 2 lean meat
Chicken Chow Mein	10½ oz.	220	25	20	4	1180	1½ starch, 2 lean meat
Chicken Oriental	10 oz.	250	26	24	6	880	1½ starch, 3½ lean meat
Medallions of Chicken Breast Marsala	11 oz.	270	28	22	7	970	2 starch, 2 lean meat
Roast Breast of Chicken	11 oz.	270	26	22	9	1220	2 starch, 2 lean meat
Salisbury Steak	10 oz.	290	25	20	13	870	1½ starch, 2 meat
Seafood Natural Herbs	11½ oz.	250	38	12	6	1240	2½ starch, 1 lean meat
Steak Diane Mignonettes	10 oz.	290	23	29	9	770	1½ starch, 3½ lean meat
Stuffed Cabbage	12 oz.	290	43	13	8	600	3 starch, ½ meat, 1 fat
Sweet and Sour Chicken	11 oz.	250	33	23	3	640	1 starch, 1 fruit, 3 lean meat
Szechuan Beef	10 oz.	280	26	23	9	1010	2 starch, 2½ lean meat
Turf and Surf	10 oz.	250	14	31	7	890	1 starch, 4 lean meat
Turkey Parmesan	11 oz.	240	25	19	8	480	1½ starch, 2 lean meat
Dinner Classics Beef Burgundy	10½ oz.	330	23	28	15	990	1 starch, 1 veg., 3 lean meat, 1 fat
Beef Stroganoff	11¼ oz.	370	25	30	17	1330	1 starch, 1 veg., 3½ meat
F Boneless Beef Short Ribs with BBQ Sauce	10½ oz.	460	33	25	26	1180	2 starch, 1 veg., 2½ meat, 2½ fat
Boneless Beef Short Ribs with Horseradish Sauce	10½ oz.	370	21	25	21	1160	1 starch, 1 veg., 2½ meat, 1½ fat
Chicken Fricassee	11¾ oz.	340	35	23	12	1210	2 starch, 1 veg., 2 lean meat, 1 fat

†For Occasional Use   **Not Recommended For Use   *Not Available   F More Than 2 Fat Exchanges   S Moderate To High Sugar Content

NUTRIENT VALUE

	PRODUCTS	SERVING SIZE	CALORIES	CARBO-HYDRATE (g.)	PROTEIN (g.)	FAT (g.)	SODIUM (mg.)	EXCHANGES
	Chicken Hawaiian	11½ oz.	360	47	21	10	700	2 starch, 1 fruit, 2 lean meat, ½ fat
	Chicken Milan	11½ oz.	350	38	24	12	1360	2 starch, 1 veg., 2 lean meat, 1 fat
	Chicken Tetrazzini	11½ oz.	320	26	23	14	850	1½ starch, 1 veg., 2½ lean meat, 1 fat
	Cod Almondine	12 oz.	360	33	23	15	1440	2 starch, 1 veg., 2 lean meat, 1½ fat
	Lasagna	10 oz.	380	42	17	16	1120	3 starch, 1 meat, 2 fat
Ⓕ	Salisbury Steak	11 oz.	480	39	20	27	1400	2½ starch, 2 meat, 3 fat
	Seafood Newburg	10½ oz.	280	36	11	10	1500	2 starch, 1 veg., ½ lean meat, 1½ fat
	Sherried Chicken Breast	10 oz.	300	19	29	12	830	1 starch, 1 veg., 3½ lean meat
	Shrimp Americana	11½ oz.	280	31	18	10	1210	1½ starch, 1 veg., 1½ lean meat, 1 fat
	Sirloin Roast	11 oz.	280	24	25	9	780	1 starch, 1 veg., 3 lean meat
	Sirloin Tips	11 oz.	370	27	29	16	1180	1½ starch, 1 veg., 3 lean meat, 1 fat
Ⓕ	Spaghetti with Meatballs	11 oz.	350	27	14	21	1130	2 starch, 1 meat, 3 fat
	Stuffed Green Peppers	12 oz.	390	41	16	18	1750	2 starch, 2 veg., 1 meat, 2 fat
Ⓕ	Swedish Meatballs	11½ oz.	470	32	23	28	1560	2 starch, 1 veg., 2 meat, 3 fat
Ⓕ Ⓢ	Sweet and Sour Chicken	11 oz.	450	51	16	20	1240	1 starch, 1 veg., 1½ meat, 2 fruit, 2½ fat†
	Teriyaki Chicken	10½ oz.	250	28	22	5	1120	1½ starch, 1 veg., 2 lean meat

†For Occasional Use   **Not Recommended For Use   *Not Available   Ⓕ More Than 2 Fat Exchanges   Ⓢ Moderate To High Sugar Content

NUTRIENT VALUE

	PRODUCTS	SERVING SIZE	CALORIES	CARBO-HYDRATE (g.)	PROTEIN (g.)	FAT (g.)	SODIUM (mg.)	EXCHANGES
	Teriyaki Steak	10 oz.	360	32	24	16	1440	2 starch, 1 veg., 2 meat, 1 fat
F	Veal Parmigiana	10¾ oz.	400	34	17	22	1430	2 starch, 1 veg., 1 lean meat, 3½ fat
	Yankee Pot Roast	11 oz.	380	32	30	15	820	1½ starch, 1 veg., 3 meat

BANQUET® (ConAgra® Frozen Foods Co.)
American Favorites
Dinners

	PRODUCTS	SERVING SIZE	CALORIES	CARBO-HYDRATE (g.)	PROTEIN (g.)	FAT (g.)	SODIUM (mg.)	EXCHANGES
	Beans and Franks	10¼ oz.	500	64	19	19	1377	4 starch, 1 high fat meat, 2 fat
	Beef with Gravy	10 oz.	345	19	23	19	1009	1 starch, 1 veg., 2½ meat, 1 fat
F	Chopped Beef	11 oz.	434	23	19	30	1199	1 starch, 1 veg., 2 meat, 4 fat
F	Fish	8¾ oz.	553	45	18	33	927	3 starch, 1½ lean meat, 5 fat
	Fried Chicken	11 oz.	359	46	18	11	1831	2½ starch, 1 veg., 1 lean meat, 1½ fat
F	Ham	10 oz.	532	61	21	22	1148	3½ starch, 1 veg., 1 lean meat, 3½ fat
F	Meat Loaf	11 oz.	437	30	20	27	1525	1½ starch, 1 veg., 2 meat, 3 fat
F	Salisbury Steak	11 oz.	395	24	17	26	1333	1 starch, 1 veg., 2 meat, 3 fat
	Turkey	11 oz.	320	41	19	9	1416	2 starch, 1 veg., 1½ lean meat, 1 fat
F	Western	11 oz.	513	43	22	29	1548	2½ starch, 1 veg., 2 meat, 3½ fat

Casseroles

	PRODUCTS	SERVING SIZE	CALORIES	CARBO-HYDRATE (g.)	PROTEIN (g.)	FAT (g.)	SODIUM (mg.)	EXCHANGES
	Macaroni and Cheese	8 oz.	344	36	11	17	930	2½ starch, ½ high fat meat, 2 fat
	Spaghetti with Meat Sauce	8 oz.	270	35	14	8	1242	2 starch, 1 veg., 1 meat, ½ fat

†For Occasional Use   **Not Recommended For Use   *Not Available   F More Than 2 Fat Exchanges   S Moderate To High Sugar Content

NUTRIENT VALUE

PRODUCTS	SERVING SIZE	CALORIES	CARBO-HYDRATE (g.)	PROTEIN (g.)	FAT (g.)	SODIUM (mg.)	EXCHANGES
Entrees for One							
Barbecue Sauce and Sliced Beef	4 oz.	90	10	9	2	789	½ starch, 1 lean meat
Breaded Veal Parmigiana	5 oz.	230	20	10	11	842	1 starch, 1 meat, 1 fat
Chicken Ala King	4 oz.	110	9	8	5	551	½ starch, 1 meat
Creamed Chipped Beef	4 oz.	90	10	9	2	818	½ starch, 1 lean meat
Gravy with Sliced Beef	4 oz.	90	4	12	3	426	2 lean meat
Gravy and Sliced Turkey	5 oz.	110	7	8	5	586	½ starch, 1 meat
Meat Loaf	5 oz.	240	12	12	15	827	1 starch, 1 meat, 2 fat
F Salisbury Steak	5 oz.	230	7	10	18	766	½ starch, 1 meat, 2½ fat
Extra Helping Dinners							
F Beef	16 oz.	864	72	40	46	1731	4½ starch, 1 veg., 3½ meat, 5 fat
F Mexican Style	21¼ oz.	777	105	31	27	4778	6½ starch, 1 veg., 1 meat, 4 fat
F Salisbury Steak	19 oz.	1024	72	39	65	2175	4½ starch, 1 veg., 3 meat, 9½ fat
F Turkey	19 oz.	723	98	31	23	2165	6 starch, 1 veg., 1½ lean meat, 3 fat
Family Entrees							
Beef Enchilada	8 oz.	264	37	11	8	1477	2½ starch, ½ meat, ½ fat
Beef Stew	8 oz.	254	21	12	13	977	1½ starch, 1 meat, 1½ fat
F Chicken and Dumplings	8 oz.	430	31	18	25	928	2 starch, 2 lean meat, 3½ fat
Gravy and Salisbury Steak	5⅓ oz.	210	8	10	15	850	½ starch, 1 meat, 2 fat
Gravy and Sliced Beef	8 oz.	160	9	19	6	900	½ starch, 2½ lean meat

†For Occasional Use   **Not Recommended For Use   *Not Available   F More Than 2 Fat Exchanges   S Moderate To High Sugar Content

NUTRIENT VALUE

PRODUCTS	SERVING SIZE	CALORIES	CARBO-HYDRATE (g.)	PROTEIN (g.)	FAT (g.)	SODIUM (mg.)	EXCHANGES
Gravy and Sliced Turkey	8 oz.	160	8	14	8	1010	½ starch, 2 lean meat
Lasagna with Meat Sauce	8 oz.	330	39	19	11	1000	2½ starch, 2 meat
Macaroni and Cheese	8 oz.	230	31	9	8	790	2 starch, ½ high fat meat, ½ fat
Mostaccioli and Meat Sauce	8 oz.	240	38	12	4	1180	2½ starch, ½ high fat meat
Mushroom Gravy and Charbroil Beef Patties	5⅓ oz.	210	8	10	15	850	½ starch, 1 meat, 2 fat
F Noodles and Beef	8 oz.	283	21	10	18	877	1½ starch, 1 meat, 2½ fat
F Veal Parmigiana	6½ oz.	282	21	15	18	961	1½ starch, 1½ meat, 2½ fat
Family Favorite Dinners Chicken and Dumplings	9 oz.	286	28	13	13	944	1½ starch, 1 veg., 1 lean meat, 1½ fat
Macaroni and Cheese	9 oz.	334	37	11	16	940	2 starch, 1 veg., ½ high fat meat, 2 fat
Noodles and Chicken	9½ oz.	361	50	13	11	964	3 starch, 1 veg., ½ lean meat, 1½ fat
Spaghetti and Meatballs	9½ oz.	418	57	15	14	1317	3½ starch, 1 veg., 1 meat, 1½ fat
Gourmet Entrees Chicken Cacciatore	10 oz.	260	35	17	5	510	2 starch, 1 veg., 1½ lean meat
French Chicken	10 oz.	190	25	12	4	850	1 starch, 1 veg., 1 lean meat
Green Pepper Steak	10 oz.	310	44	21	5	1125	2½ starch, 1 veg., 2 lean meat
Pasta Shells and Sauce	10 oz.	310	41	17	8	950	2½ starch, 1 veg., 1 meat
Rigatoni with Ham and Peas	10 oz.	280	36	16	8	1215	2½ starch, 1 meat

†For Occasional Use   **Not Recommended For Use   *Not Available   F More Than 2 Fat Exchanges   S Moderate To High Sugar Content

NUTRIENT VALUE

PRODUCTS	SERVING SIZE	CALORIES	CARBO-HYDRATE (g.)	PROTEIN (g.)	FAT (g.)	SODIUM (mg.)	EXCHANGES
Sirloin Tips Supreme	10 oz.	160	24	13	1	1030	1 starch, 1 veg., 1 lean meat
Sliced Beef and Vegetables	10 oz.	300	17	38	9	770	1 starch, 1 veg., 4½ lean meat
Turkey Tetrazzini	10 oz.	270	38	19	4	1025	2 starch, 1 veg., 1½ lean meat
International Favorites Dinners Beef Enchilada	12 oz.	497	72	19	15	1801	4½ starch, 1 veg., ½ meat, 2 fat
F Cheese Enchilada	12 oz.	543	71	22	19	2166	4½ starch, 1 veg., 1 lean meat, 2½ fat
F Italian Style	12 oz.	597	71	21	26	1783	4½ starch, 1 veg., 1 meat, 3½ fat
Mexican Style	12 oz.	483	62	18	18	1995	3½ starch, 1 veg., 1 meat, 2 fat
F Mexican Style Combination	12 oz.	518	72	20	17	1978	4½ starch, 1 veg., ½ meat, 2½ fat
F Veal Parmigiana	11 oz.	413	43	14	21	1310	2½ starch, 1 veg., ½ meat, 3½ fat
Meat Pies F Beef	8 oz.	449	44	14	24	1292	3 starch, 1 meat, 3 fat
F Chicken	8 oz.	450	44	15	24	966	3 starch, 1 meat, 3 fat
Tuna	8 oz.	395	43	16	18	565	3 starch, 1 meat, 2 fat
F Turkey	8 oz.	437	46	13	23	1263	3 starch, 1 meat, 3 fat

BENIHANA® (Benihana Frozen Foods, Corp.)

PRODUCTS	SERVING SIZE	CALORIES	CARBO-HYDRATE (g.)	PROTEIN (g.)	FAT (g.)	SODIUM (mg.)	EXCHANGES
Oriental Lites Beef and Mushrooms in Sauce with Rice and Vegetables	9 oz.	280	35	20	7	*	2 starch, 1 veg., 2 lean meat
Chicken in Spicy Garlic Sauce	9 oz.	280	39	20	5	870	2 starch, 1 veg., 2 lean meat

†For Occasional Use   **Not Recommended For Use   *Not Available   F More Than 2 Fat Exchanges   S Moderate To High Sugar Content

NUTRIENT VALUE

PRODUCTS	SERVING SIZE	CALORIES	CARBO-HYDRATE (g.)	PROTEIN (g.)	FAT (g.)	SODIUM (mg.)	EXCHANGES
Glazed Chicken	8½ oz.	230	37	18	1	920	2 starch, 1 veg., 1½ lean meat
Shrimp and Cashews with Rice	9 oz.	250	37	14	6	1070	2 starch, 1 veg., 1 lean meat, ½ fat

CHEF BOY-AR-DEE® (American Home Foods)

PRODUCTS	SERVING SIZE	CALORIES	CARBO-HYDRATE (g.)	PROTEIN (g.)	FAT (g.)	SODIUM (mg.)	EXCHANGES
Canned Meats							
Beef Stew	7 oz.	220	16	9	13	1360	1 starch, 1 meat, 1½ fat
Chicken Stew	7 oz.	140	17	6	5	1150	1 starch, ½ meat, ½ fat
[F] Corned Beef Hash	7 oz.	370	20	16	25	1165	1 starch, 2 meat, 3 fat
[F] Meatball Stew	8 oz.	330	24	10	21	1315	1½ starch, 1 meat, 3 fat
Dinners							
Lasagna Dinner	¼ of 23⅞ oz. dinner	280	42	15	8	900	3 starch, 1 meat
Pac Man and Cheese Dinner (as prepared)	⅔ cup	290	40	8	11	780	2½ starch, ½ meat, 1 fat
Spaghetti and Meatball Dinner	¼ of 21¼ oz. dinner	310	43	12	10	900	3 starch, ½ meat, 1 fat
Spaghetti Dinner with Condensed Meat Sauce	⅛ of 26 oz. dinner	250	37	12	6	595	2½ starch, 1 meat
Mama Leone's Products							
Pasta Suprema Cheese Ravioli in Sauce	7½ oz.	180	33	9	2	955	2 starch, ½ lean meat
Pasta Suprema Elbow Macaroni in Sauce with Green Peppers	7½ oz.	180	31	11	4	1135	2 starch, ½ meat
Pasta Suprema Mini Lasagna	7½ oz.	170	37	5	1	720	2½ starch
Pasta Suprema Shells in Meat Flavored Sauce	7½ oz.	160	32	4	5	875	2 starch, 1 fat

†For Occasional Use   **Not Recommended For Use   *Not Available   [F] More Than 2 Fat Exchanges   [S] Moderate To High Sugar Content

NUTRIENT VALUE

PRODUCTS	SERVING SIZE	CALORIES	CARBO-HYDRATE (g.)	PROTEIN (g.)	FAT (g.)	SODIUM (mg.)	EXCHANGES
Pasta Suprema Spaghetti in Tomato Sauce	7½ oz.	140	29	6	1	745	2 starch
Pasta Suprema Ziti in Meat Flavored Sauce	7½ oz.	150	30	6	4	910	2 starch, ½ fat
Pasta Products ABC's and 1,2,3's in Sauce	7½ oz.	160	31	5	1	840	2 starch
ABC's and 1,2,3's with Mini Meatballs	7½ oz.	240	31	8	9	1200	2 starch, ½ meat, 1 fat
Beefaroni	8 oz.	250	36	9	8	1090	2 starch, ½ meat, 1 fat
Beef-O-Ghetti	7½ oz.	220	25	7	9	1240	1½ starch, ½ meat, 1 fat
Cosmic Kids in Tomato Sauce	7½ oz.	150	31	5	1	895	2 starch
Cosmic Kids in Chicken Sauce	7½ oz.	160	21	6	6	910	1½ starch, ½ meat, ½ fat
Cosmic Kids with Meatballs	7½ oz.	220	29	7	8	1115	2 starch, ½ meat, 1 fat
Lasagna, canned	7½ oz.	230	30	9	8	920	2 starch, ½ meat, 1 fat
Macaroni and Cheese	7 oz.	180	23	8	6	890	1½ starch, ½ meat, ½ fat
Macaroni Shells in Tomato Sauce	7½ oz.	150	31	6	1	930	2 starch
Mini Bites	7½ oz.	260	30	8	12	925	2 starch, ½ meat, 1½ fat
Mini Cannelloni	7½ oz.	230	33	9	7	980	2 starch, ½ meat, 1 fat
Pac Man in Chicken Sauce	7½ oz.	170	22	6	7	905	1½ starch, ½ meat, ½ fat
Pac Man in Tomato Sauce	7½ oz.	150	30	6	1	830	2 starch
Pac Man with Meatballs	7½ oz.	230	31	8	9	1140	2 starch, ½ meat, 1 fat
Roller Coasters	7½ oz.	230	29	8	9	980	2 starch, ½ meat, 1 fat

†For Occasional Use   **Not Recommended For Use   *Not Available   Ⓕ More Than 2 Fat Exchanges   Ⓢ Moderate To High Sugar Content

NUTRIENT VALUE

PRODUCTS	SERVING SIZE	CALORIES	CARBO-HYDRATE (g.)	PROTEIN (g.)	FAT (g.)	SODIUM (mg.)	EXCHANGES
Smurf Beef Ravioli and Pasta in Meat Sauce	7½ oz.	220	34	9	5	990	2 starch, ½ meat, ½ fat
Smurf Beef Ravioli and Pasta in Papa's Sauce	7½ oz.	220	39	7	4	980	2½ starch, ½ fat
Smurf Beef in Spaghetti Sauce with Cheese Flavor	7½ oz.	150	29	6	1	830	2 starch
Smurf Pasta with Meatballs	7½ oz.	230	30	8	9	900	2 starch, ½ meat, 1 fat
Zooroni with Meatballs in Sauce	7½ oz.	240	32	8	8	920	2 starch, ½ meat, 1 fat
Zooroni with Tomato Sauce	7½ oz.	160	32	5	1	810	2 starch
Ravioli Products Beef Ravioli in Sauce	8 oz.	220	35	8	5	1095	2 starch, ½ meat, ½ fat
Beef Ravioli in Tomato and Meat Sauce	7½ oz.	210	35	8	5	1055	2 starch, ½ meat, ½ fat
Cheese Ravioli in Tomato Sauce	7½ oz.	200	33	7	5	990	2 starch, ½ meat
Cheese Ravioli in Beef and Tomato Sauce	7½ oz.	200	33	7	5	990	2 starch, ½ meat
Chicken Ravioli	7½ oz.	180	29	7	4	1100	2 starch, ½ lean meat
Mini Ravioli, Beef	8 oz.	220	36	8	5	1213	2 starch, ½ meat, ½ fat
Mini Ravioli, Chicken	7½ oz.	220	29	7	8	1050	2 starch, ½ meat, ½ fat
Sausage Ravioli in Tomato and Meat Sauce	7½ oz.	210	31	9	5	835	2 starch, ½ meat, ½ fat
Spaghetti Products Spaghetti 'n Beef in Tomato Sauce	7½ oz.	240	30	8	9	995	2 starch, ½ meat, 1 fat
Spaghetti and Meatballs	8½ oz.	260	30	9	11	1210	2 starch, ½ meat, 1½ fat

†For Occasional Use   **Not Recommended For Use   *Not Available   F More Than 2 Fat Exchanges   S Moderate To High Sugar Content

NUTRIENT VALUE

PRODUCTS	SERVING SIZE	CALORIES	CARBO-HYDRATE (g.)	PROTEIN (g.)	FAT (g.)	SODIUM (mg.)	EXCHANGES
Spaghetti and Meatballs with Tomato Sauce	7½ oz.	230	30	8	8	935	2 starch, ½ meat, 1 fat
Spaghetti with Tomato Sauce and Cheese	8 oz.	150	30	5	1	1040	2 starch

CHUN KING® (ConAgra® Frozen Foods Co.)
Boil-in-Bag Entrees

PRODUCTS	SERVING SIZE	CALORIES	CARBO-HYDRATE (g.)	PROTEIN (g.)	FAT (g.)	SODIUM (mg.)	EXCHANGES
Beef Pepper Oriental	10 oz.	244	39	14	9	1257	2 starch, 1 veg., 1 meat, ½ fat
Chicken Chow Mein	10 oz.	227	33	13	5	1209	2 starch, 1 veg., 1 lean meat
Chunky Walnut Chicken	10 oz.	315	42	16	10	1115	2½ starch, 1 veg., 1 lean meat, 1 fat
Fried Rice with Pork	10 oz.	306	47	13	7	1382	3 starch, 1 meat
Oriental Chicken	10 oz.	267	45	14	4	1441	2½ starch, 1 veg., 1 lean meat
Ⓢ Sweet and Sour Chicken	10 oz.	335	63	16	3	1240	2 starch, 1 veg., 1 lean meat, 2 fruit†
Ⓢ Sweet and Sour Pork	10 oz.	338	57	13	7	1104	2 starch, 1 veg., 1 meat, 1½ fruit†

CON AGRA® (ConAgra® Frozen Foods Co.)
Light and Elegant Entrees

PRODUCTS	SERVING SIZE	CALORIES	CARBO-HYDRATE (g.)	PROTEIN (g.)	FAT (g.)	SODIUM (mg.)	EXCHANGES
Beef Burgundy	9 oz.	230	25	23	4	1240	1 starch, 1 veg., 2½ lean meat
Beef Julienne	8½ oz.	260	27	21	7	990	1½ starch, 1 veg., 2 lean meat
Beef Stroganoff	9 oz.	260	27	24	6	790	2 starch, 2½ lean meat
Beef Teriyaki	8 oz.	240	37	18	3	625	2 starch, 1 veg., 1½ lean meat
Chicken/Cheese	8¾ oz.	293	30	19	11	800	2 starch, 2 lean meat, ½ fat
Chicken Parmigiana	8 oz.	260	23	28	6	680	1 starch, 1 veg., 3 lean meat

†For Occasional Use   **Not Recommended For Use   *Not Available   Ⓕ More Than 2 Fat Exchanges   Ⓢ Moderate To High Sugar Content

NUTRIENT VALUE

PRODUCTS	SERVING SIZE	CALORIES	CARBO-HYDRATE (g.)	PROTEIN (g.)	FAT (g.)	SODIUM (mg.)	EXCHANGES
Glazed Chicken	8 oz.	240	23	29	4	660	1 starch, 1 veg., 3½ lean meat
Lasagna Florentine	11¼ oz.	280	35	24	5	980	2 starch, 1 veg., 2 lean meat
Macaroni and Cheese	9 oz.	300	38	16	9	1010	2½ starch, 1 high fat meat
Shrimp Creole	10 oz.	218	36	14	2	1050	2 starch, 1 veg., 1 lean meat
Sliced Turkey	8 oz.	230	25	20	5	1020	1 starch, 1 veg., 2 lean meat
Spaghetti and Meat Sauce	10¼ oz.	290	40	16	8	700	2½ starch, 1 meat, ½ fat

DEL MONTE® (ConAgra® Frozen Foods Co.)
Dinners

PRODUCTS	SERVING SIZE	CALORIES	CARBO-HYDRATE (g.)	PROTEIN (g.)	FAT (g.)	SODIUM (mg.)	EXCHANGES
F Fried Chicken - Dark	11 oz.	560	50	20	30	1100	3 starch, 1 veg., 1½ meat, 4 fat
F Fried Chicken - White	11 oz.	590	60	20	25	1300	3½ starch, 1 veg., 1½ meat, 3 fat
F Meat Loaf	11 oz.	555	35	20	35	1000	2 starch, 1 veg., 2 meat, 5 fat
Salisbury Steak	12 oz.	460	50	20	20	900	3 starch, 1 veg., 1½ meat, 2 fat
Turkey	11⅝ oz.	360	40	20	10	900	2 starch, 1 veg., 2 lean meat, ½ fat

Entrees

PRODUCTS	SERVING SIZE	CALORIES	CARBO-HYDRATE (g.)	PROTEIN (g.)	FAT (g.)	SODIUM (mg.)	EXCHANGES
Chicken Ala King	9½ oz.	370	35	15	15	400	2 starch, 1 veg., 1 meat, 1½ fat
Lasagna	10½ oz.	435	35	30	15	500	2 starch, 1 veg., 3 meat
F Macaroni and Cheese	12 oz.	490	45	20	25	1500	3 starch, 2 meat, 2½ fat

Frozen Dinners

PRODUCTS	SERVING SIZE	CALORIES	CARBO-HYDRATE (g.)	PROTEIN (g.)	FAT (g.)	SODIUM (mg.)	EXCHANGES
F Chicken Breast Parmigiana	12½ oz.	410	42	21	18	1120	2½ starch, 1 veg., 1½ lean meat, 2½ fat
Chicken Chow Mein	12¼ oz.	320	48	18	6	960	3 starch, 1 veg., 1 lean meat
F Chopped Beef Sirloin	12½ oz.	500	36	23	29	930	2 starch, 1 veg., 2 meat, 3½ fat

†For Occasional Use   **Not Recommended For Use   *Not Available   F More Than 2 Fat Exchanges   S Moderate To High Sugar Content

NUTRIENT VALUE

	PRODUCTS	SERVING SIZE	CALORIES	CARBO-HYDRATE (g.)	PROTEIN (g.)	FAT (g.)	SODIUM (mg.)	EXCHANGES
F	Fried Chicken - Dark Meat	12½ oz.	690	56	29	39	990	3½ starch, 1 veg., 2½ meat, 5 fat
F	Fried Chicken - White Meat	12⅞ oz.	700	57	31	38	1300	3½ starch, 1 veg., 2½ meat, 5 fat
	Meat Loaf	12⅞ oz.	450	42	24	21	940	2½ starch, 1 veg., 2 meat, 2 fat
F	Salisbury Steak	12⅝ oz.	490	46	22	24	1050	2½ starch, 1 veg., 2 meat, 2½ fat
F	Sweet and Sour Chicken	12 oz.	400	66	20	5	920	2 starch, 1 veg., 2 lean meat, 2 fruit†
	Turkey	13 oz.	430	51	20	16	1270	3 starch, 1 veg., 2 lean meat, 1½ fat
	Yankee Pot Roast	11 oz.	370	35	29	12	830	2 starch, 1 veg., 3 lean meat
	Meat Pies							
F	Beef and Vegetable	8 oz.	540	50	20	30	700	3 starch, 1 veg., 1½ meat, 4 fat
F	Chicken and Vegetable	8 oz.	515	50	15	25	700	3 starch, 1 veg., 1 lean meat, 4 fat
F	Turkey and Vegetable	8 oz.	505	50	15	25	700	3 starch, 1 veg., 1 lean meat, 4 fat

DENNISON'S® (American Home Foods)

	PRODUCTS	SERVING SIZE	CALORIES	CARBO-HYDRATE (g.)	PROTEIN (g.)	FAT (g.)	SODIUM (mg.)	EXCHANGES
F	Tamalitos in Chili Gravy	7½ oz.	310	37	6	16	1395	2 starch, 1 veg., 3 fat

DIA-MEL® (Estee Corp.)
Dinners, Dietetic

	PRODUCTS	SERVING SIZE	CALORIES	CARBO-HYDRATE (g.)	PROTEIN (g.)	FAT (g.)	SODIUM (mg.)	EXCHANGES
	Beef Ravioli	8 oz.	260	35	8	10	75	2 starch, 1 veg., 1½ fat
	Beef Stew	8 oz.	200	19	13	8	70	1 starch, 1 veg., 1 meat, ½ fat
	Chicken Stew	8 oz.	150	19	11	3	65	1 starch, 1 veg., 1 lean meat
F	Chili with Beans	8 oz.	360	31	14	19	50	2 starch, 1 meat, 2½ fat

†For Occasional Use   **Not Recommended For Use   *Not Available   F More Than 2 Fat Exchanges   S Moderate To High Sugar Content

NUTRIENT VALUE

PRODUCTS	SERVING SIZE	CALORIES	CARBO-HYDRATE (g.)	PROTEIN (g.)	FAT (g.)	SODIUM (mg.)	EXCHANGES
Spaghetti and Meatballs	8 oz.	220	24	8	10	55	1½ starch, ½ meat, 1 fat
Stuffed Dumplings	8 oz.	160	15	10	6	70	1 starch, 1 meat

DINING LITE® (Blue Star Foods, Inc.)

PRODUCTS	SERVING SIZE	CALORIES	CARBO-HYDRATE (g.)	PROTEIN (g.)	FAT (g.)	SODIUM (mg.)	EXCHANGES
Beef Teriyaki with Vegetables and Rice	8⅝ oz.	250	35	20	4	980	2 starch, 1 veg., 2 lean meat
Carne Picado with Rice and Bacon	9 oz.	250	26	22	7	900	2 starch, 2 lean meat
Cheese Cannelloni with Tomato Sauce	9 oz.	260	34	16	7	990	2 starch, 1 veg., 1 meat
Cheese Vegetable Lasagna	11 oz.	290	38	20	8	720	2 starch, 1 veg., 2 lean meat
Chicken Ala King with Rice	9½ oz.	290	35	18	9	910	2 starch, 1 veg., 1½ lean meat, ½ fat
Chicken Aloha- Chicken and Sauce with Rice	8½ oz.	240	33	20	4	1010	1½ starch, 1 fruit, 2 lean meat
Chicken Cacciatore with Vermicelli	11 oz.	290	36	26	5	680	2 starch, 1 veg., 2½ lean meat
Chicken Chow Mein with Rice	11¼ oz.	240	38	19	2	1440	2 starch, 1 veg., 1½ lean meat
Glazed Chicken with Rice	8½ oz.	250	28	20	6	960	1½ starch, 1 veg., 2 lean meat
Chicken Vegetable Medley with Vermicelli	12¾ oz.	290	35	24	7	930	2 starch, 1 veg., 2 lean meat
Cod Fillets and Vegetables with Sauce	10 oz.	200	13	24	7	570	½ starch, 1 veg., 3 lean meat
Oriental Pepper Steak with Rice	9¼ oz.	270	33	22	7	1400	2 starch, 1 veg., 2 lean meat
Salisbury Steak with Creole Sauce and Vegetables	9½ oz.	220	14	22	8	1380	½ starch, 1 veg., 2½ lean meat
Seafood Vegetable Medley with Rice	11 oz.	250	48	10	3	1080	3 starch, 1 veg., ½ lean meat
Shrimp Creole with Rice	10 oz.	210	38	11	2	850	2 starch, 1 veg., ½ lean meat

†For Occasional Use   **Not Recommended For Use   *Not Available   Ⓕ More Than 2 Fat Exchanges   Ⓢ Moderate To High Sugar Content

PRODUCTS	SERVING SIZE	CALORIES	CARBO-HYDRATE (g.)	PROTEIN (g.)	FAT (g.)	SODIUM (mg.)	EXCHANGES
Spaghetti with Beef and Mushroom Sauce	11½ oz.	280	37	19	7	1530	2 starch, 1 veg., 1½ meat
Veal and Vegetable Cannelloni	9 oz.	280	37	19	7	890	2 starch, 1 veg., 1½ meat
Zucchini Lasagna	11 oz.	280	33	23	8	780	2 starch, 1 veg., 2 meat

DINTY MOORE® (George A. Hormel and Co.)

PRODUCTS	SERVING SIZE	CALORIES	CARBO-HYDRATE (g.)	PROTEIN (g.)	FAT (g.)	SODIUM (mg.)	EXCHANGES
Beef Stew	7½ oz.	180	14	12	9	939	1 starch, 1 meat, ½ fat
Brunswick Stew	7½ oz.	220	15	11	13	*	1 starch, 1 meat, 1½ fat
Chicken Stew	7½ oz.	240	14	11	16	1010	1 starch, 1 meat, 2 fat
Meatball Stew	8 oz.	240	15	13	15	*	1 starch, 1½ meat, 1 fat
Noodles and Chicken	7½ oz.	210	15	9	12	1144	1 starch, 1 meat, 1 fat
Sliced Potatoes and Beef	7½ oz.	250	25	11	12	*	1½ starch, 1 meat, 1 fat
Vegetable Stew	8 oz.	170	20	5	8	1047	1 starch, 1 veg., 1½ fat

FEATHERWEIGHT® (Sandoz Nutrition)

PRODUCTS	SERVING SIZE	CALORIES	CARBO-HYDRATE (g.)	PROTEIN (g.)	FAT (g.)	SODIUM (mg.)	EXCHANGES
Beef Ravioli, Low Sodium	8 oz.	260	35	8	10	75	2 starch, ½ meat, 1½ fat
Beef Stew, Low Sodium	7½ oz.	210	24	13	8	95	1½ starch, 1 meat
Chicken Stew, Low Sodium	7½ oz.	170	21	10	6	55	1 starch, 1 veg., 1 lean meat, ½ fat
Dumplings and Chicken, Low Sodium	7½ oz.	160	18	12	5	115	1 starch, 1 meat
Spaghetti with Meatballs, Low Sodium	7½ oz.	200	28	8	5	95	1½ starch, 1 veg., ½ meat, ½ fat

FRANCO-AMERICAN® (Campbell Soup Co.)

PRODUCTS	SERVING SIZE	CALORIES	CARBO-HYDRATE (g.)	PROTEIN (g.)	FAT (g.)	SODIUM (mg.)	EXCHANGES
Beef Ravioli in Meat Sauce	7½ oz.	230	36	9	5	1090	2 starch, 1 veg., 1 fat

†For Occasional Use   **Not Recommended For Use   *Not Available   Ⓕ More Than 2 Fat Exchanges   Ⓢ Moderate To High Sugar Content

NUTRIENT VALUE

PRODUCTS	SERVING SIZE	CALORIES	CARBO-HYDRATE (g.)	PROTEIN (g.)	FAT (g.)	SODIUM (mg.)	EXCHANGES
Beef RavioliOs in Meat Sauce	7½ oz.	250	35	10	7	890	2 starch, 1 veg., 1 fat
Elbow Macaroni and Cheese	7⅜ oz.	170	23	6	6	910	1½ starch, 1 fat
Macaroni and Cheese	7⅜ oz.	170	24	6	6	960	1½ starch, 1 fat
Spaghetti in Meat Sauce	7½ oz.	210	26	8	8	1110	2 starch, 1½ fat
Spaghetti in Tomato Sauce with Cheese	7⅜ oz.	190	36	5	2	810	2 starch, 1 veg.
Spaghetti with Meatballs in Tomato Sauce	7⅜ oz.	220	28	9	8	820	2 starch, ½ meat, 1 fat
"SpaghettiOs" in Tomato and Cheese Sauce	7⅜ oz.	170	34	4	2	910	2 starch
"SpaghettiOs" with Meatballs in Tomato Sauce	7⅜ oz.	210	25	9	8	910	1½ starch, ½ meat, 1 fat
"SpaghettiOs" with Sliced Franks in Tomato Sauce	7⅜ oz.	210	28	7	7	990	2 starch, 1 fat
UFO's	7½ oz.	180	35	5	3	780	2 starch, ½ fat
UFO's with Meteors (Meatballs)	7½ oz.	240	30	9	9	790	2 starch, ½ high fat meat, 1 fat

GOLDEN GRAIN® (Golden Grain Macaroni Co.)

PRODUCTS	SERVING SIZE	CALORIES	CARBO-HYDRATE (g.)	PROTEIN (g.)	FAT (g.)	SODIUM (mg.)	EXCHANGES
Macaroni and Cheddar (as prepared)	¾ cup	190	35	7	2	430	2 starch, ½ fat

GREEN GIANT® (Van de Kamp's® Frozen Foods)

PRODUCTS	SERVING SIZE	CALORIES	CARBO-HYDRATE (g.)	PROTEIN (g.)	FAT (g.)	SODIUM (mg.)	EXCHANGES
Chicken A La King with Biscuits	9 oz.	370	40	20	15	1500	2½ starch, 2 lean meat, 1½ fat
Chicken and Broccoli with Rice in Cheese Sauce	9½ oz.	340	30	25	15	890	1½ starch, 1 veg., 2½ lean meat, 1 fat
Chicken and Noodles	9 oz.	370	35	20	15	1045	2 starch, 2 lean meat, 1½ fat

†For Occasional Use   **Not Recommended For Use   *Not Available   Ⓕ More Than 2 Fat Exchanges   Ⓢ Moderate To High Sugar Content

NUTRIENT VALUE

PRODUCTS	SERVING SIZE	CALORIES	CARBO-HYDRATE (g.)	PROTEIN (g.)	FAT (g.)	SODIUM (mg.)	EXCHANGES
Chicken and Pea Pods in Sauce with Rice and Vegetables	10 oz.	320	35	15	15	1005	2 starch, 1 veg., 1 lean meat, 2 fat
Chicken Chow Mein with Rice and Vegetables	9 oz.	240	30	20	5	1070	1½ starch, 1 veg., 2 lean meat
Lasagna with Meat and Sauce	10½ oz.	430	45	25	15	1515	3 starch, 2 meat, 1 fat
Lasagna with Meat and Sauce	12 oz.	490	45	35	20	1660	3 starch, 3½ meat
Macaroni and Cheese	9 oz.	290	35	15	10	1115	2 starch, 1½ meat, ½ fat
Shrimp Creole with Rice	9 oz.	230	35	10	5	370	2 starch, 1 veg., ½ lean meat, ½ fat
Shrimp Fried Rice	10 oz.	300	50	15	5	1130	3 starch, 1 lean meat
Shrimp with Linguini	9½ oz.	330	35	15	15	780	2 starch, 1½ lean meat, 2 fat
Stuffed Cabbage Rolls with Beef in Tomato Sauce	7 oz.	220	20	10	10	800	1 starch, 1 veg., 1 meat, 1 fat

HAMBURGER HELPER® (General Mills, Inc.)

PRODUCTS	SERVING SIZE	CALORIES	CARBO-HYDRATE (g.)	PROTEIN (g.)	FAT (g.)	SODIUM (mg.)	EXCHANGES
Beef Noodle (as prepared)	1 serving	320	26	20	15	1050	2 starch, 2 meat, 1 fat
Beef Romanoff (as prepared)	1 serving	350	30	22	16	1080	2 starch, 2 meat, 1 fat
Cheeseburger Macaroni (as prepared)	1 serving	360	28	21	18	1030	2 starch, 2 meat, 1 fat
Hamburger Hash (as prepared)	1 serving	320	27	18	15	1020	2 starch, 2 meat, 1 fat
Hamburger Pizza Dish (as prepared)	1 serving	360	37	21	14	1010	2½ starch, 2 meat, ½ fat
Hamburger Stew (as prepared)	1 serving	300	25	18	14	1010	1½ starch, 2 meat, ½ fat
Lasagna (as prepared)	1 serving	340	33	20	14	1070	2 starch, 2 meat, ½ fat

†For Occasional Use   **Not Recommended For Use   *Not Available   Ⓕ More Than 2 Fat Exchanges   Ⓢ Moderate To High Sugar Content

NUTRIENT VALUE

PRODUCTS	SERVING SIZE	CALORIES	CARBO-HYDRATE (g.)	PROTEIN (g.)	FAT (g.)	SODIUM (mg.)	EXCHANGES
Pizzabake (as prepared)	1 serving	320	29	19	14	840	2 starch, 2 meat, ½ fat
Potatoes Au Gratin (as prepared)	1 serving	320	28	19	15	910	2 starch, 2 meat, 1 fat
Potato Stroganoff (as prepared)	1 serving	320	28	18	15	900	2 starch, 2 meat, 1 fat
Rice Oriental (as prepared)	1 serving	340	38	19	14	1120	2 starch, 1 veg., 1½ meat, 1 fat
Spaghetti (as prepared)	1 serving	340	32	20	15	1110	2 starch, 2 meat, 1 fat
Tacobake (as prepared)	1 serving	320	31	17	14	960	2 starch, 1½ meat, 1 fat
Tamale Pie (as prepared)	1 serving	380	39	19	16	940	2½ starch, 1½ meat, 1½ fat

HEINZ® (H.J. Heinz Co.)

PRODUCTS	SERVING SIZE	CALORIES	CARBO-HYDRATE (g.)	PROTEIN (g.)	FAT (g.)	SODIUM (mg.)	EXCHANGES
Beans 'N' Franks	7¾ oz.	330	34	14	15	905	2 starch, 1 meat, 2 fat
Beef Goulash	7½ oz.	240	22	13	11	920	1½ starch, 1½ meat, ½ fat
Beef Stew	7½ oz.	210	19	12	9	1245	1 starch, 1 veg., 1 meat, 1 fat
Chicken Stew with Dumplings	7½ oz.	210	22	9	9	850	1 starch, 1 veg., 1 meat, 1 fat
Mac 'N' Beef in Tomato Sauce	7¼ oz.	200	23	8	8	850	1 starch, 1 veg., 1 meat, ½ fat
Macaroni and Cheese	7½ oz.	190	26	5	8	1105	2 starch, 1 fat
Noodles and Tuna	7½ oz.	170	20	11	5	950	1 starch, 1 veg., 1 meat
Noodles and Chicken	7½ oz.	160	19	6	7	930	1 starch, ½ meat, 1 fat
Noodles and Beef in Sauce	7½ oz.	170	17	8	8	825	1 starch, 1 meat, ½ fat
Spaghetti in Tomato Sauce with Cheese	7¾ oz.	160	30	4	2	1105	2 starch
Spaghetti in Tomato Sauce with Meat	7½ oz.	170	21	8	6	965	1½ starch, ½ meat, ½ fat

†For Occasional Use   **Not Recommended For Use   *Not Available   F More Than 2 Fat Exchanges   S Moderate To High Sugar Content

NUTRIENT VALUE

PRODUCTS	SERVING SIZE	CALORIES	CARBO-HYDRATE (g.)	PROTEIN (g.)	FAT (g.)	SODIUM (mg.)	EXCHANGES
HORMEL® (George A. Hormel and Co.)							
Beef Goulash	7½ oz.	230	17	14	12	*	1 starch, 1½ meat, ½ fat
F Beef Tamales, canned	2	140	8	4	10	550	½ starch, 2 fat
Beef Tamales, frozen	1	140	13	6	7	555	1 starch, ½ meat, ½ fat
Beef Tamales, canned	7½ oz.	270	17	9	19	1140	1 starch, 1 meat, 2½ fat
Burrito Grande, frozen	5½ oz.	380	45	14	16	877	3 starch, 1 meat, 2 fat
Burritos Beef, frozen	1	205	31	9	8	780	2 starch, ½ meat, 1 fat
Cheese, frozen	1	210	32	9	5	792	2 starch, ½ meat, ½ fat
Chicken and Rice	1	200	32	9	4	594	2 starch, ½ meat
Hot Chili, frozen	1	240	33	9	8	619	2 starch, ½ meat, 1 fat
Enchiladas Beef	1	140	17	6	5	573	1 starch, ½ meat, ½ fat
Cheese	1	151	18	6	6	676	1 starch, ½ meat, ½ fat
Lasagna, Beef, frozen	10 oz.	370	30	28	15	*	2 starch, 3 meat
Lasagna, canned	7½ oz.	260	25	8	14	1083	1½ starch, ½ meat, 2 fat
Macaroni and Cheese, canned	7½ oz.	170	22	8	6	*	1½ starch, 1 meat
Meatball Stew	7½ oz.	240	15	11	16	*	1 starch, 1 meat, 2 fat
Mexacali Dogs, frozen	5 oz.	400	41	14	21	952	3 starch, 1 high fat meat, 2 fat
Noodles 'N Beef	7½ oz.	230	16	10	14	974	1 starch, 1 meat, 1½ fat
Pork Chow Mein, canned	7½ oz.	140	13	7	7	*	½ starch, 1 veg., ½ meat, 1 fat

†For Occasional Use   **Not Recommended For Use   *Not Available   F More Than 2 Fat Exchanges   S Moderate To High Sugar Content

NUTRIENT VALUE

PRODUCTS	SERVING SIZE	CALORIES	CARBO-HYDRATE (g.)	PROTEIN (g.)	FAT (g.)	SODIUM (mg.)	EXCHANGES
Potato Dinners							
Au Gratin Potatoes and Bacon, canned	7½ oz.	240	20	9	14	942	1 starch, 1 high fat meat, 1 fat
Scalloped Potatoes and Ham, canned	7½ oz.	260	19	9	16	1189	1 starch, 1 meat, 2 fat
Scalloped Potatoes and Pepperoni	7½ oz.	246	21	8	15	*	1½ starch, ½ meat, 2 fat
Sloppy Joes, canned	7½ oz.	340	15	21	22	*	1 starch, 3 meat, 1½ fat
Spaghetti and Beef	7½ oz.	260	25	8	14	1091	1½ starch, ½ meat, 2 fat
Spaghetti and Italian Sausage	7½ oz.	187	19	9	9	1369	1 starch, 1 meat, ½ fat
Spaghetti and Meatballs	7½ oz.	210	26	10	8	*	2 starch, ½ meat, ½ fat

KRAFT® (Kraft, Inc.)

PRODUCTS	SERVING SIZE	CALORIES	CARBO-HYDRATE (g.)	PROTEIN (g.)	FAT (g.)	SODIUM (mg.)	EXCHANGES
Egg Noodle Dinners							
F Egg Noodles and Cheese (as prepared)	¾ cup	340	37	10	17	630-760	2½ starch, ½ meat, 2½ fat
Egg Noodles with Chicken (as prepared)	¾ cup	240	31	8	9	880-950	2 starch, ½ meat, 1 fat
Macaroni Dinners							
Deluxe Macaroni and Cheese (as prepared)	¾ cup	260	36	11	8	580-650	2½ starch, ½ meat, ½ fat
Macaroni and Cheese (as prepared)	¾ cup	290	34	9	13	530-630	2 starch, ½ meat, 2 fat
F Spiral Macaroni and Cheese (as prepared)	¾ cup	330	36	9	17	560-670	2½ starch, ½ meat, 2½ fat
Spaghetti Dinners							
American Style Spaghetti (as prepared)	1 cup	310	51	10	8	570-710	3½ starch, 1 fat
Spaghetti with Meat Sauce (as prepared)	1 cup	370	47	12	14	720-860	3 starch, ½ meat, 2 fat

†For Occasional Use   **Not Recommended For Use   *Not Available   F More Than 2 Fat Exchanges   S Moderate To High Sugar Content

NUTRIENT VALUE

PRODUCTS	SERVING SIZE	CALORIES	CARBO-HYDRATE (g.)	PROTEIN (g.)	FAT (g.)	SODIUM (mg.)	EXCHANGES
Tangy Italian Style Spaghetti (as prepared)	1 cup	310	49	11	8	730-830	3 starch, ½ meat, ½ fat

LA CHOY® (Beatrice Companies, Inc.)
Bi-Pack Products
Beef Pepper Oriental, (as prepared)	¾ cup	100	11	9	3	590	½ starch, 1 veg., ½ meat
Chow Mein							
Beef (as prepared)	¾ cup	90	11	8	2	740	½ starch, 1 veg., ½ lean meat
Chicken (as prepared)	¾ cup	130	9	7	7	870	2 veg., ½ lean meat, 1 fat
Pork (as prepared)	¾ cup	80	7	5	4	950	1 veg., ½ lean meat, ½ fat
Shrimp (as prepared)	¾ cup	70	10	6	1	860	2 veg., ½ lean meat
Vegetable (as prepared)	¾ cup	50	8	2	2	640	2 veg.
Sukiyaki (as prepared)	¾ cup	70	8	7	1	740	2 veg., ½ lean meat

Canned Products
Beef Pepper Oriental	¾ cup	90	10	8	2	1060	2 veg., ½ meat
Chow Mein							
Beef	¾ cup	60	5	6	1	890	1 veg., ½ lean meat
Chicken	¾ cup	70	5	7	2	800	1 veg., 1 lean meat
Meatless	¾ cup	35	6	2	1	780	1 veg.
Shrimp	¾ cup	45	4	5	1	820	1 veg., ½ lean meat
Ⓢ Sweet and Sour Oriental with Chicken	¾ cup	230	47	8	1	1300	1 starch, 1 veg., ½ lean meat, 1½ fruit†
Ⓢ Sweet and Sour Oriental with Pork	¾ cup	250	48	5	4	1500	1½ starch, 1 veg., 1½ fruit, ½ fat†

Frozen Entrees
Beef Pepper Oriental	⅔ cup	80	11	7	1	820	2 veg., ½ lean meat

†For Occasional Use   **Not Recommended For Use   *Not Available   Ⓕ More Than 2 Fat Exchanges   Ⓢ Moderate To High Sugar Content

		NUTRIENT VALUE					
PRODUCTS	SERVING SIZE	CALORIES	CARBO-HYDRATE (g.)	PROTEIN (g.)	FAT (g.)	SODIUM (mg.)	EXCHANGES
Chicken Chow Mein	2/3 cup	90	11	8	2	720	2 veg., ½ meat
Shrimp Chow Mein	2/3 cup	70	11	4	1	820	2 veg., ½ lean meat
[S] Sweet and Sour Chicken	2/3 cup	190	33	11	<1	1005	1 starch, 1 veg., 1 lean meat, 1 fruit†
[S] Sweet and Sour Pork	2/3 cup	180	32	7	3	1100	1 starch, 1 veg., ½ meat, 1 fruit†
Packaged Dinners							
Egg Foo Young Dinner (as prepared)	1 patty, ¼ cup sauce	125	10	6	7	760	½ starch, ½ meat, 1 fat
Pepper Steak Dinner (as prepared)	¾ cup	210	9	22	9	960	½ starch, 3 lean meat
Sukiyaki Dinner (as prepared)	¾ cup	210	9	23	9	990	½ starch, 3 lean meat
[S] Sweet and Sour Dinner (as prepared)	¾ cup	410	30	26	21	1210	½ starch, 1 veg., 3 meat, 1 fruit, 1 fat†
LE MENU® (Campbell Soup Co.)							
Beef Sirloin Tips	11½ oz.	390	26	30	18	840	2 starch, 3 meat
Beef Stroganoff	9¼ oz.	430	24	28	24	930	1½ starch, 3 meat, 1½ fat
Breast of Chicken Parmigiana	11½ oz.	380	28	27	18	890	2 starch, 3 lean meat, 1½ fat
Chicken A La King	10¼ oz.	320	29	22	13	1050	2 starch, 2 lean meat, 1 fat
[F] Chicken Cordon Bleu	11 oz.	460	47	26	19	870	3 starch, 2 lean meat, 2½ fat
[F] Chicken Florentine	12½ oz.	480	40	28	23	880	2½ starch, 3 lean meat, 2½ fat
Chopped Sirloin Beef	12¼ oz.	410	28	26	23	1080	2 starch, 3 meat, 1 fat
Flounder Fillet with Salmon Mousse	10½ oz.	340	26	20	18	1060	2 starch, 2 lean meat, 2 fat
Ham Steak	9¼ oz.	320	35	19	12	1510	2 starch, 2 lean meat, 1 fat

†For Occasional Use **Not Recommended For Use *Not Available [F] More Than 2 Fat Exchanges [S] Moderate To High Sugar Content

NUTRIENT VALUE

	PRODUCTS	SERVING SIZE	CALORIES	CARBO-HYDRATE (g.)	PROTEIN (g.)	FAT (g.)	SODIUM (mg.)	EXCHANGES
	Pepper Steak	11½ oz.	360	32	27	14	1110	2 starch, 3 meat
F	Sliced Breast of Turkey with Mushrooms	11¼ oz.	460	34	28	24	1140	2 starch, 3 lean meat, 3 fat
S	Sweet and Sour Chicken	11¼ oz.	450	43	22	22	980	2 starch, 2½ lean meat, 1 fruit, 2½ fat
F	Vegetable Lasagna	11 oz.	360	32	14	20	1010	2 starch, 1 meat, 3 fat
	Yankee Pot Roast	11 oz.	360	28	28	15	810	2 starch, 3 meat

MARY KITCHEN® (George A. Hormel and Co.)

	PRODUCTS	SERVING SIZE	CALORIES	CARBO-HYDRATE (g.)	PROTEIN (g.)	FAT (g.)	SODIUM (mg.)	EXCHANGES
	Corned Beef Hash	7½ oz.	360	17	20	24	1368	1 starch, 2½ meat, 2 fat
	Roast Beef Hash	7½ oz.	360	18	20	23	1156	1 starch, 2½ meat, 2 fat

MORTON® (ConAgra® Frozen Foods Co.)
Light Dinners

PRODUCTS	SERVING SIZE	CALORIES	CARBO-HYDRATE (g.)	PROTEIN (g.)	FAT (g.)	SODIUM (mg.)	EXCHANGES
Boneless Chicken Dinner	11 oz.	250	30	16	7	1150	1½ starch, 1 veg., 1½ lean meat, ½ fat
Chicken Chow Mein Dinner	11 oz.	260	43	11	5	700	2 starch, 2 veg., ½ lean meat, ½ fat
Italian Style Ziti Dinner	11 oz.	280	43	12	6	790	2½ starch, 1 veg., ½ lean meat, ½ fat
Sliced Beef Dinner	11 oz.	260	20	28	7	850	1 starch, 1 veg., 3 lean meat
Turkey Tetrazzini Dinner	11 oz.	280	47	13	4	900	3 starch, 1 veg., ½ lean meat
Veal Parmigiana Dinner	11 oz.	290	39	17	7	1300	2 starch, 1 veg., 1½ meat
Western Style Dinner	11 oz.	290	31	13	12	1010	1½ starch, 1 veg., 1 meat, 1 fat

Light Entrees

PRODUCTS	SERVING SIZE	CALORIES	CARBO-HYDRATE (g.)	PROTEIN (g.)	FAT (g.)	SODIUM (mg.)	EXCHANGES
Chicken a la King	8 oz.	280	33	13	10	600	2 starch, 1 veg., 1 lean meat, 1 fat
Chicken Chow Mein	8 oz.	210	35	10	3	500	2 starch, 1 veg., ½ lean meat

†For Occasional Use   **Not Recommended For Use   *Not Available   F More Than 2 Fat Exchanges   S Moderate To High Sugar Content

NUTRIENT VALUE

PRODUCTS	SERVING SIZE	CALORIES	CARBO-HYDRATE (g.)	PROTEIN (g.)	FAT (g.)	SODIUM (mg.)	EXCHANGES
Gravy and Salisbury Steak	8 oz.	290	34	13	12	670	2 starch, 1 meat, 1 fat
Gravy and Sliced Beef	8 oz.	280	30	20	9	490	2 starch, 2 lean meat
Gravy and Sliced Chicken	8 oz.	240	32	7	9	600	2 starch, ½ lean meat, 1 fat
Gravy and Sliced Turkey	8 oz.	270	45	14	4	1310	3 starch, ½ lean meat
Meat Sauce and Spaghetti	8 oz.	220	36	9	4	750	2½ starch, ½ meat

MRS. SMITH'S® (Mrs. Smith's Frozen Foods, A Kellogg Company)

Cannelloni

PRODUCTS	SERVING SIZE	CALORIES	CARBO-HYDRATE (g.)	PROTEIN (g.)	FAT (g.)	SODIUM (mg.)	EXCHANGES
F Beef with Tomato Sauce	8¼ oz.	430	39	19	22	1660	2 starch, 2 veg., 1½ meat, 2½ fat
F Chicken with Cheese Sauce	8¼ oz.	540	37	23	33	1440	2 starch, 1 veg., 2 meat, 4½ fat
F Shrimp with Cheese Sauce	8¼ oz.	500	35	19	31	1370	2 starch, 1 veg., 1½ meat, 4½ fat

Crepes

PRODUCTS	SERVING SIZE	CALORIES	CARBO-HYDRATE (g.)	PROTEIN (g.)	FAT (g.)	SODIUM (mg.)	EXCHANGES
Chicken Continental Crepes	2 crepes (6½ oz.)	320	23	22	15	1235	1½ starch, 2½ lean meat, 1½ fat
F Chicken Maison Crepes	2 crepes (6½ oz.)	350	24	19	20	1087	1½ starch, 2 lean meat, 3 fat
F Ham and Vegetable Crepes	2 crepes (6½ oz.)	305	29	11	16	1000	2 starch, 1 lean meat, 2½ fat
F Shrimp Crepes	2 crepes (6½ oz.)	305	26	13	16	1335	2 starch, 1 lean meat, 2½ fat

Manicotti

PRODUCTS	SERVING SIZE	CALORIES	CARBO-HYDRATE (g.)	PROTEIN (g.)	FAT (g.)	SODIUM (mg.)	EXCHANGES
F Cheese with Meat Sauce	8¼ oz.	500	33	24	30	1270	2 starch, 1 veg., 2 meat, 3½ fat
F Cheese and Spinach with Cheese Sauce	8¼ oz.	505	34	22	31	1325	2 starch, 1 veg., 2 meat, 4 fat

PATIO® (ConAgra® Frozen Foods Co.)

Boil-in-Bag Items

PRODUCTS	SERVING SIZE	CALORIES	CARBO-HYDRATE (g.)	PROTEIN (g.)	FAT (g.)	SODIUM (mg.)	EXCHANGES
Beef Enchiladas and Beef Chili Gravy	½ package	250	29	7	12	*	2 starch, ½ meat, 1½ fat

†For Occasional Use   **Not Recommended For Use   *Not Available   F More Than 2 Fat Exchanges   S Moderate To High Sugar Content

NUTRIENT VALUE

	PRODUCTS	SERVING SIZE	CALORIES	CARBO-HYDRATE (g.)	PROTEIN (g.)	FAT (g.)	SODIUM (mg.)	EXCHANGES
	Cheese Enchiladas and Chili Gravy	½ package	200	31	7	5	*	2 starch, ½ meat
	Refried Beans	⅓ package	190	23	8	7	*	1½ starch, ½ lean meat, ½ fat
	Tamales and Beef Chili Gravy	½ package	280	27	7	16	*	2 starch, ½ meat, 2 fat
	Frozen Burritos Beef and Bean	1	190	21	5	9	*	1½ starch, 1½ fat
	Beef and Bean with Green or Red Chilis (average)	1	190	23	6	8	*	1½ starch, 1½ fat
F	Large Beef and Bean	2	450	49	13	22	*	3 starch, ½ meat, 3½ fat
F	Large Beef and Bean with Green or Red Chilis (average)	2	445	54	14	20	*	3½ starch, ½ meat, 3 fat
	Frozen Dinner Items							
F	Beef Enchilada Dinner	13 oz.	550	70	17	23	*	4 starch, 1 veg., 1 meat, 3 fat
F	4 Beef Enchiladas, Chili and Beans	16 oz.	850	76	24	50	*	5 starch, 1 meat, 8½ fat
F	2 Beef and 2 Cheese Enchiladas, Chili and Beans	16 oz.	820	83	31	40	*	5½ starch, 2 meat, 5 fat
F	3 Beef Tacos, Chili and Beans	11 oz.	640	64	26	32	*	4 starch, 2 meat, 4 fat
	Cheese Enchilada Dinner	12¾ oz.	470	68	17	14	*	4 starch, 1 veg., 1 meat, 1 fat
F	Combination Dinner	11¼ oz.	590	66	19	28	*	4 starch, 1 veg., 1 meat, 4 fat
	Fiesta Dinner	12¾ oz.	510	68	17	19	*	4 starch, 1 veg., 1 meat, 2 fat
F	Mexican Dinner	12¼ oz.	510	60	16	23	*	3½ starch, 1 veg., 1 meat, 3 fat

†For Occasional Use   **Not Recommended For Use   *Not Available   F More Than 2 Fat Exchanges   S Moderate To High Sugar Content

NUTRIENT VALUE

PRODUCTS	SERVING SIZE	CALORIES	CARBO-HYDRATE (g.)	PROTEIN (g.)	FAT (g.)	SODIUM (mg.)	EXCHANGES
Frozen Products							
Enchiladas							
Beef	2	260	30	8	12	*	2 starch, ½ meat, 1½ fat
Cheese	2	170	26	7	5	*	2 starch, ½ meat
Tacos							
Beef	2	240	29	10	9	*	2 starch, ½ meat, 1 fat
Snack Beef	4	130	17	5	5	*	1 starch, ½ meat, ½ fat
Tortillas	2	100	21	2	1	*	1½ starch

PILLSBURY® (The Pillsbury Co.)
Microwave Classic™

PRODUCTS	SERVING SIZE	CALORIES	CARBO-HYDRATE (g.)	PROTEIN (g.)	FAT (g.)	SODIUM (mg.)	EXCHANGES
Casseroles							
Ⓕ Beef	1 package	400	32	15	23	1030	2 starch, 1½ meat, 3 fat
Chicken	1 package	380	30	20	20	980	2 starch, 2 meat, 2 fat
Turkey	1 package	410	32	20	22	840	2 starch, 2 meat, 2 fat

RAGÚ® (Chesebrough-Ponds, Inc.)
Pasta Meals

PRODUCTS	SERVING SIZE	CALORIES	CARBO-HYDRATE (g.)	PROTEIN (g.)	FAT (g.)	SODIUM (mg.)	EXCHANGES
Elbows in Sauce with Ground Beef, Mushrooms and Green Peppers	7½ oz.	170	22	9	5	760	1½ starch, ½ meat, ½ fat
Mini Lasagna in Sauce, Spaghetti in Sauce, Twists in Sauce (average)	7½ oz.	170	26	6	3	630	2 starch
Shells in Sauce with Ground Beef	7½ oz.	180	23	10	6	510	1½ starch, 1 meat
Spaghetti in Sauce with Ground Beef	7½ oz.	190	24	10	5	550	1½ starch, 1 meat

SARA LEE® (Kitchens of Sara Lee)
Le San★wich™

PRODUCTS	SERVING SIZE	CALORIES	CARBO-HYDRATE (g.)	PROTEIN (g.)	FAT (g.)	SODIUM (mg.)	EXCHANGES
Croissants							
Ⓕ Broccoli and Cheese	1	320	31	10	18	560	2 starch, ½ high fat meat, 2½ fat

†For Occasional Use   **Not Recommended For Use   *Not Available   Ⓕ More Than 2 Fat Exchanges   Ⓢ Moderate To High Sugar Content

NUTRIENT VALUE

	PRODUCTS	SERVING SIZE	CALORIES	CARBO-HYDRATE (g.)	PROTEIN (g.)	FAT (g.)	SODIUM (mg.)	EXCHANGES
F	Cheddar Cheese	1	380	29	13	23	910	2 starch, 1 high fat meat, 3 fat
	Chicken and Broccoli	1	340	32	16	17	600	2 starch, 1½ lean meat, 2 fat
F	Ham and Swiss Cheese	1	340	30	14	18	860	2 starch, 1 meat, 2½ fat
	Roast Beef in Wine Sauce	1	300	26	14	15	570	2 starch, 1 meat, 2 fat
	Turkey, Bacon and Cheese	1	360	28	17	20	895	2 starch, 1½ meat, 2 fat

STOUFFER'S® (Stouffer Foods Corp.)

	PRODUCTS	SERVING SIZE	CALORIES	CARBO-HYDRATE (g.)	PROTEIN (g.)	FAT (g.)	SODIUM (mg.)	EXCHANGES
	Beef Chop Suey with Rice	12 oz.	340	38	19	12	1590	2 starch, 2 veg., 1½ meat, 1 fat
	Beef and Spinach Stuffed Pasta Shells with Tomato Sauce	9 oz.	300	27	21	12	1100	1½ starch, 1 veg., 2 meat
	Beef Stew	10 oz.	310	19	22	16	1460	1 starch, 2½ meat, 1 fat
	Beef Stroganoff with Parsley Noodles	9¾ oz.	410	29	25	21	1180	2 starch, 2½ meat, 1½ fat
	Beef Teriyaki with Rice and Vegetables	9¾ oz.	330	35	22	9	1260	2 starch, 1 veg., 2 meat
	Cashew Chicken in Sauce with Rice	9½ oz.	410	33	31	17	1240	2 starch, 3½ meat
F	Cheese Soufflé	½ of 12 oz. package	380	12	18	29	950	1 starch, 2 meat, 3½ fat
	Cheese Stuffed Pasta Shells with Meat Sauce	9 oz.	340	25	23	16	1200	2 starch, 2 meat, 1 fat
	Chicken à la King with Rice	9½ oz.	320	37	19	11	840	2½ starch, 2 meat
	Chicken Chow Mein without Noodles	8 oz.	140	11	12	5	1170	2 veg., 1 lean meat, ½ fat
	Chicken Crepe with Mushroom Sauce	8¼ oz.	370	18	27	21	930	1 starch, 3½ meat, ½ fat

†For Occasional Use   **Not Recommended For Use   *Not Available   F More Than 2 Fat Exchanges   S Moderate To High Sugar Content

NUTRIENT VALUE

PRODUCTS	SERVING SIZE	CALORIES	CARBO-HYDRATE (g.)	PROTEIN (g.)	FAT (g.)	SODIUM (mg.)	EXCHANGES
F Chicken Divan	8½ oz.	350	14	23	22	850	1 starch, 3 lean meat, 2½ fat
Chicken Paprikash with Egg Noodles	10½ oz.	390	31	32	15	1250	2 starch, 4 lean meat
F Chicken Stuffed Pasta Shells with Cheese Sauce	9 oz.	420	21	29	24	810	1½ starch, 3 lean meat, 3 fat
F Creamed Chicken	6½ oz.	320	7	19	24	700	½ starch, 2½ lean meat, 3 fat
Creamed Chipped Beef	½ of 11 oz. package	240	8	13	17	890	½ starch, 1½ meat, 2 fat
F Escalloped Chicken and Noodles	½ of 11½ oz. package	260	16	12	16	720	1 starch, 1 lean meat, 2½ fat
Green Pepper Steak with Rice	10½ oz.	340	38	22	11	1470	2 starch, 1 veg., 2 meat
F Ham and Asparagus Crepes	6¼ oz.	310	24	14	18	750	1 starch, 1 veg., 1 meat, 2½ fat
F Ham and Swiss Cheese Crepes with Cheese Sauce	7½ oz.	410	21	23	26	980	1½ starch, 2½ meat, 2½ fat
Lasagna	10½ oz.	370	34	28	13	1030	2 starch, 1 veg., 3 meat
F Lobster Newburg	6½ oz.	360	8	15	30	840	½ starch, 2 lean meat, 5 fat
Macaroni and Beef with Tomatoes	11½ oz.	360	32	21	16	1600	2 starch, 2 meat, 1 fat
Macaroni and Cheese	½ of 12 oz. package	250	24	11	12	750	1½ starch, 1 meat, 1 fat
Meat Pies							
F Beef Pie	1-10 oz. pie	560	36	21	37	1300	2 starch, 1 veg., 2 meat, 5 fat
F Chicken Pie	1-10 oz. pie	530	34	21	34	1210	2 starch, 1 veg., 2 lean meat, 5 fat
F Turkey Pie	1-10 oz. pie	540	36	20	35	1260	2 starch, 1 veg., 2 meat, 5 fat
Roast Beef Hash	½ of 11½ oz. package	250	11	18	15	710	1 starch, 2 high fat meat

†For Occasional Use   **Not Recommended For Use   *Not Available   F More Than 2 Fat Exchanges   S Moderate To High Sugar Content

NUTRIENT VALUE

PRODUCTS	SERVING SIZE	CALORIES	CARBO-HYDRATE (g.)	PROTEIN (g.)	FAT (g.)	SODIUM (mg.)	EXCHANGES
Salisbury Steak with Onion Gravy	½ of 12 oz. package	230	6	20	14	1120	½ starch, 2½ meat
Scallops and Shrimp Mariner with Rice	10¼ oz.	390	35	21	18	850	2½ starch, 2 lean meat, 2 fat
Short Ribs of Beef with Vegetable Gravy	½ of 11½ oz. package	280	2	24	20	510	3½ meat, ½ fat
Spaghetti with Meatballs	12⅝ oz.	370	43	21	13	1560	3 starch, 2 meat
Spaghetti with Meat Sauce	14 oz.	440	53	22	15	1730	3½ starch, 2 meat, ½ fat
F Spinach Crepes with Cheddar Cheese Sauce	9½ oz.	420	27	17	27	1100	2 starch, 1½ meat, 4 fat
Stuffed Green Peppers with Beef in Tomato Sauce	½ of 15½ oz. package	220	18	11	11	870	1 starch, 1 veg., 1 meat, 1 fat
Swedish Meatballs with Parsley Noodles	11 oz.	470	36	25	25	1460	2½ starch, 2½ meat, 2 fat
Tuna Noodle Casserole	½ of 11½ oz. package	190	18	11	8	680	1 starch, 1 meat, ½ fat
Turkey Casserole with Gravy and Dressing	9¾ oz.	380	28	24	19	1250	2 starch, 2½ meat, 1 fat
Turkey Tetrazzini	½ of of 12 oz. package	230	14	13	14	650	1 starch, 1½ lean meat, 1½ fat
Vegetable Lasagna	10½ oz.	450	29	26	25	910	2 starch, 3 meat, 2 fat
F Welsh Rarebit	½ of 10 oz. package	360	9	13	30	700	½ starch, 1½ meat, 4½ fat

STOUFFER'S® LEAN CUISINE® (Stouffer Foods Corp.)

PRODUCTS	SERVING SIZE	CALORIES	CARBO-HYDRATE (g.)	PROTEIN (g.)	FAT (g.)	SODIUM (mg.)	EXCHANGES
Beef and Pork Cannelloni with Mornay Sauce	9⅝ oz.	270	25	19	10	940	1½ starch, 1 veg., 1½ lean meat, 1 fat
Cheese Cannelloni with Tomato Sauce	9⅛ oz.	270	24	22	10	900	1½ starch, 1 veg., 2 meat

†For Occasional Use   **Not Recommended For Use   *Not Available   F More Than 2 Fat Exchanges   S Moderate To High Sugar Content

NUTRIENT VALUE

PRODUCTS	SERVING SIZE	CALORIES	CARBO-HYDRATE (g.)	PROTEIN (g.)	FAT (g.)	SODIUM (mg.)	EXCHANGES
Chicken à l'Orange with Almond Rice	8 oz.	270	31	26	5	460	2 starch, 3 lean meat
Chicken and Vegetables with Vermicelli	12¾ oz.	270	29	23	7	1120	1½ starch, 1 veg., 2 lean meat
Chicken Cacciatore with Vermicelli	10⅞ oz.	280	25	23	10	950	1½ starch, 1 veg., 2 meat
Chicken Chow Mein with Rice	11¼ oz.	250	36	16	5	1160	2 starch, 1 veg., 1 lean meat
Fillet of Fish Divan	12⅜ oz.	270	17	31	9	700	½ starch, 1 veg., 4 lean meat
Fillet of Fish Florentine	9 oz.	240	13	27	9	700	½ starch, 1 veg., 3 lean meat
Fillet of Fish Jardiniere with Souffléed Potatoes	11¼ oz.	280	18	30	10	840	1 starch, 4 lean meat
Glazed Chicken with Vegetable Rice	8½ oz.	270	23	26	8	750	1 starch, 1 veg., 3 lean meat
Linguini with Clam Sauce	9⅝ oz.	260	32	16	7	800	2 starch, 1½ lean meat
Meatball Stew	10 oz.	270	21	21	11	1120	1 starch, 1 veg., 2 meat
Oriental Beef with Vegetables and Rice	8⅝ oz.	270	30	20	8	1150	1½ starch, 1 veg., 2 lean meat
Oriental Scallops and Vegetables with Rice	11 oz.	220	32	15	3	1100	1½ starch, 1 veg., 1 lean meat
Salisbury Steak with Italian Style Sauce and Vegetables	9½ oz.	270	14	25	13	700	½ starch, 1 veg., 3 lean meat, 1 fat
Spaghetti with Beef and Mushroom Sauce	11½ oz.	280	38	15	7	1300	2 starch, 1 veg., 1 meat, ½ fat
Stuffed Cabbage with Meat in Tomato Sauce	10¾ oz.	220	20	15	9	830	1 starch, 1 veg., 1½ meat
Tuna Lasagna with Spinach Noodles and Vegetables	9¾ oz.	260	30	18	8	990	1½ starch, 1 veg., 1½ lean meat, ½ fat
Turkey Dijon	9½ oz.	280	20	25	11	1030	1 starch, 1 veg., 3 lean meat

†For Occasional Use **Not Recommended For Use *Not Available [F] More Than 2 Fat Exchanges [S] Moderate To High Sugar Content

NUTRIENT VALUE

PRODUCTS	SERVING SIZE	CALORIES	CARBO-HYDRATE (g.)	PROTEIN (g.)	FAT (g.)	SODIUM (mg.)	EXCHANGES
Veal Primavera	9⅛ oz.	250	19	23	9	790	1 starch, 1 veg., 2½ lean meat
Zucchini Lasagna	11 oz.	260	28	21	7	975	1½ starch, 1 veg., 2 lean meat

SWANSON® (Campbell Soup Co.)
Breakfast Entrees, Frozen

PRODUCTS	SERVING SIZE	CALORIES	CARBO-HYDRATE (g.)	PROTEIN (g.)	FAT (g.)	SODIUM (mg.)	EXCHANGES
F French Toast with Sausages	6½ oz.	450	36	17	26	770	2½ starch, 1½ high fat meat, 2½ fat
Pancakes and Sausage	6 oz.	460	52	14	22	940	3½ starch, 1 high fat meat, 2 fat
F Scrambled Eggs and Sausage with Hash Brown Potatoes	6¼ oz.	410	17	12	33	790	1 starch, 1 high fat meat, 5 fat
Spanish Style Omelet	7¾ oz.	250	14	9	17	840	1 starch, 1 high fat meat, 2 fat
Canned Products							
Chicken a la King	5¼ oz.	180	9	10	12	690	½ starch, 1 lean meat, 2 fat
Chicken and Dumplings	7½ oz.	220	19	11	12	960	1 starch, 1 veg., 1 lean meat, 2 fat
Chicken Stew	7⅝ oz.	170	16	9	7	960	1 starch, 1 lean meat, 1 fat
Chunky Pies, Frozen							
F Beef	10 oz.	530	53	19	28	900	3 starch, 1 veg., 1 meat, 4 fat
F Chicken	10 oz.	580	53	19	33	850	3 starch, 1 veg., 1 lean meat, 5½ fat
F Turkey	10 oz.	530	45	19	31	950	3 starch, 1½ lean meat, 5 fat
Dinners, Frozen							
F Barbecue Flavored Fried Chicken	9¼ oz.	560	49	24	30	960	3 starch, 1 veg., 2 lean meat, 4½ fat
F Beans and Beef Burrito	15¼ oz.	720	88	21	32	1630	6 starch, ½ high fat meat, 5 fat

†For Occasional Use   **Not Recommended For Use   *Not Available   F More Than 2 Fat Exchanges   S Moderate To High Sugar Content

NUTRIENT VALUE

	PRODUCTS	SERVING SIZE	CALORIES	CARBO-HYDRATE (g.)	PROTEIN (g.)	FAT (g.)	SODIUM (mg.)	EXCHANGES
	Beef	11½ oz.	320	35	27	8	870	2 starch, 1 veg., 3 lean meat
F	Beef Enchiladas	15 oz.	510	57	18	23	1400	4 starch, 1 meat, 3 fat
F	Fish 'n Chips	10½ oz.	570	58	21	28	970	4 starch, 1 lean meat, 4½ fat
	Ham	10¼ oz.	320	46	19	9	1250	3 starch, 2 meat
	Loin of Pork	11¼ oz.	290	26	22	11	710	2 starch, 2 meat
	Macaroni and Cheese	12¼ oz.	380	46	13	15	980	3 starch, ½ high fat meat, 2 fat
F	Meat Loaf	11 oz.	500	48	19	26	970	3 starch, 1½ meat, 3 fat
F	Mexican Style Combination	16 oz.	580	67	20	26	1780	4 starch, 1 veg., 1 meat, 4 fat
	Polynesian Style	12 oz.	360	52	21	8	1430	3 starch, 1 veg., 1½ lean meat
	Spaghetti and Meatballs	12½ oz.	360	44	12	15	1040	3 starch, ½ meat, 2 fat
	Swiss Steak	10 oz.	350	33	23	14	830	2 starch, 2½ meat
	Turkey	11½ oz.	330	39	21	10	1260	2 ½ starch, 2 lean meat, ½ fat
	Veal Parmigiana	12¾ oz.	470	49	22	21	1120	3 starch, 2 meat, 2 fat
	Entrees, Frozen							
F	Chicken Nibbles	5 oz.	390	28	13	25	880	2 starch, 1 lean meat, 4 fat
F	Fish 'n' Chips	5½ oz.	320	32	11	17	600	2 starch, 1 lean meat, 2½ fat
	Gravy and Sliced Beef	8 oz.	200	18	18	6	760	1 starch, 2 lean meat
	Meatballs with Brown Gravy	8½ oz.	290	19	14	18	900	1 starch, 1½ meat, 2 fat
	Spaghetti in Tomato Sauce with Breaded Veal	8¼ oz.	280	29	15	12	810	2 starch, 1 meat, 1 fat
	Turkey	8¾ oz.	250	24	17	10	1090	1½ starch, 2 lean meat, ½ fat

†For Occasional Use   **Not Recommended For Use   *Not Available   F More Than 2 Fat Exchanges   S Moderate To High Sugar Content

NUTRIENT VALUE

	PRODUCTS	SERVING SIZE	CALORIES	CARBO-HYDRATE (g.)	PROTEIN (g.)	FAT (g.)	SODIUM (mg.)	EXCHANGES
	Hungry Man Dinners, Frozen							
	Boneless Chicken	17½ oz.	670	60	47	27	1640	4 starch, 5 lean meat, 2 fat
	Chopped Beefsteak	17½ oz.	600	48	36	29	1640	3 starch, 3½ meat, 2 fat
[F]	Fish n' Chips	14¾ oz.	770	73	36	36	1350	5 starch, 3 lean meat, 4 fat
[F]	Lasagna with Meat	18¾ oz.	730	99	25	26	1510	6½ starch, 1 meat, 4 fat
	Western Style	17½ oz.	750	71	41	34	1930	5 starch, 4 meat, 2 fat
	Hungry Man Entrees, Frozen							
[F]	Fried Chicken, White Portions	11¾ oz.	670	50	34	37	1760	3 starch, 1 veg., 3 lean meat, 5 fat
	Sliced Beef	12¼ oz.	330	24	40	8	1040	1½ starch, 4 lean meat
	Turkey	13¼ oz.	390	36	30	14	1740	2 starch, 1 veg., 3 lean meat, 1 fat
	Hungry Man Meat Pies, Frozen							
[F]	Beef	16 oz.	670	68	23	34	1750	4 starch, 1 veg., 1 meat, 5½ fat
[F]	Chicken	16 oz.	700	64	26	37	1670	4 starch, 1 veg., 2 lean meat, 5½ fat
[F]	Steak Burger	16 oz.	750	61	27	44	1520	4 starch, 2 meat, 6 fat
[F]	Turkey	16 oz.	740	66	27	41	1590	4 starch, 1 veg., 2 lean meat, 6½ fat
	Main Course Entrees, Frozen							
	Salisbury Steak	10 oz.	380	26	26	21	1400	2 starch, 3 meat, 1 fat
	Turkey with Gravy	9¼ oz.	300	24	28	10	1120	1½ starch, 3 lean meat
	Meat Pies, Frozen							
[F]	Beef	8 oz.	400	42	11	21	900	3 starch, 4 fat
[F]	Chicken	8 oz.	420	39	13	24	840	2½ starch, 1 lean meat, 4 fat

†For Occasional Use **Not Recommended For Use *Not Available [F] More Than 2 Fat Exchanges [S] Moderate To High Sugar Content

NUTRIENT VALUE

	PRODUCTS	SERVING SIZE	CALORIES	CARBO-HYDRATE (g.)	PROTEIN (g.)	FAT (g.)	SODIUM (mg.)	EXCHANGES
	Macaroni and Cheese	7 oz.	210	26	8	9	880	2 starch, 1½ fat
F	Turkey	8 oz.	430	41	12	24	800	3 starch, ½ lean meat, 4 fat

TUNA HELPER® (General Mills, Inc.)

	PRODUCTS	SERVING SIZE	CALORIES	CARBO-HYDRATE (g.)	PROTEIN (g.)	FAT (g.)	SODIUM (mg.)	EXCHANGES
	Au Gratin (as prepared)	1 serving	300	29	16	13	1110	2 starch, 1½ meat, 1 fat
	Cheesy Noodles 'n Tuna (as prepared)	1 serving	250	30	15	8	910	2 starch, 1½ meat
F	Cold Salad (as prepared)	1 serving	440	29	14	30	1020	2 starch, 1 meat, 5 fat
	Creamy Mushroom (as prepared)	1 serving	250	28	13	9	800	2 starch, 1 meat, ½ fat
	Creamy Noodles 'n Tuna (as prepared)	1 serving	290	32	14	12	960	2 starch, 1 meat, 1 fat
	Tuna Tetrazzini (as prepared)	1 serving	270	26	17	11	850	2 starch, 1½ meat, ½ fat

TYSON® (Tyson Foods, Inc.)
Chicken Entrees

	PRODUCTS	SERVING SIZE	CALORIES	CARBO-HYDRATE (g.)	PROTEIN (g.)	FAT (g.)	SODIUM (mg.)	EXCHANGES
	Chicken à l'Orange	9½ oz.	300	31	26	8	440	1½ starch, 1 veg., 3 lean meat
	Chicken Cacciatore	10½ oz.	300	18	30	12	770	1 starch, 1 veg., 3½ lean meat
	Chicken Cannelloni	11½ oz.	400	36	23	18	850	2 starch, 1 veg., 2 lean meat, 2 fat
	Chicken Fiesta	10½ oz.	440	43	29	17	1510	3 starch, 3 lean meat, 1 fat
	Chicken Francais	8¾ oz.	320	16	28	16	940	½ starch, 1 veg., 3½ lean meat, 1 fat
	Chicken Jambalaya	12¼ oz.	400	38	22	18	1040	2½ starch, 2 lean meat, 2 fat
F	Chicken Kiev	9¼ oz.	520	40	15	33	1020	2 starch, 1 veg., 1 lean meat, 6 fat
	Chicken Marsala	10½ oz.	300	24	26	11	760	1 starch, 1 veg., 3 lean meat
	Chicken Oriental	10¼ oz.	270	35	24	4	1050	2 starch, 1 veg., 2 lean meat

†For Occasional Use   **Not Recommended For Use   *Not Available   F More Than 2 Fat Exchanges   S Moderate To High Sugar Content

NUTRIENT VALUE

PRODUCTS	SERVING SIZE	CALORIES	CARBO-HYDRATE (g.)	PROTEIN (g.)	FAT (g.)	SODIUM (mg.)	EXCHANGES
Chicken Parmigiana	11¾ oz.	450	38	34	18	1100	2½ starch, 3½ lean meat, 1 fat
Chicken Picatta	9 oz.	215	18	23	5	660	1 starch, 1 veg., 2½ lean meat
[S] Chicken Sweet and Sour	11 oz.	450	53	24	16	840	2 starch, 1 veg., 2 lean meat, 1 fruit, 2 fat†

VAN CAMP'S® (Quaker Oats Co.)

Noodlee Weenee	1 cup	240	33	9	8	1250	2 starch, ½ high fat meat, ½ fat
Skettee Weenee	1 cup	240	35	9	7	1130	2 starch, ½ high fat meat, ½ fat

VAN DE KAMP'S® (Van de Kamp's® Frozen Foods)

Burritos

Bean and Cheese Burrito	5 oz.	320	39	12	11	450	2½ starch, ½ meat, 1½ fat
Beef and Bean Burrito	5 oz.	320	46	11	9	400	3 starch, ½ meat, 1 fat
Beef and Cheese Burrito	5 oz.	320	41	12	11	370	2½ starch, ½ meat, 1½ fat
Green Chili Beef/ Bean Burrito	5 oz.	330	43	12	11	340	3 starch, ½ meat, 1½ fat
Red Chili Beef/ Bean Burrito	5 oz.	320	39	13	12	340	2½ starch, 1 meat, 1 fat

Dinners

Beef Enchilada	12 oz.	390	45	20	15	2175	3 starch, 1½ meat, 1 fat
Cheese Enchilada	12 oz.	450	45	20	20	1665	3 starch, 1½ meat, 2 fat
Fillet of Fish	12 oz.	300	25	25	10	1820	1½ starch, 3 lean meat
Mexican Style	11½ oz.	420	45	20	20	1040	3 starch, 1½ meat, 2 fat

Enchiladas

Beef Enchilada	7½ oz.	250	20	10	15	1200	1 starch, 1 meat, 2 fat
4 Beef Enchiladas	8½ oz.	340	30	15	15	1480	2 starch, 1½ meat, 1 fat
Cheese Enchilada	7½ oz.	270	25	10	15	965	1½ starch, 1 meat, 2 fat

†For Occasional Use   **Not Recommended For Use   *Not Available   [F] More Than 2 Fat Exchanges   [S] Moderate To High Sugar Content

NUTRIENT VALUE

PRODUCTS	SERVING SIZE	CALORIES	CARBO-HYDRATE (g.)	PROTEIN (g.)	FAT (g.)	SODIUM (mg.)	EXCHANGES
4 Cheese Enchiladas	8½ oz.	370	30	15	20	1175	2 starch, 1½ meat, 2 fat
Chicken Enchilada	7½ oz.	250	25	15	10	1105	1½ starch, 1½ lean meat, 1 fat
Italian Classics							
Beef and Mushroom Lasagna	11 oz.	430	30	25	25	970	2 starch, 2½ meat, 2 fat
Italian Sausage Lasagna	11 oz.	440	35	25	25	1190	2 starch, 1 veg., 2½ meat, 2 fat
Mexican Classic Combinations							
Beef/Cheese Enchilada with Rice and Beans	14¾ oz.	540	60	25	20	1380	4 starch, 2 meat, 1½ fat
F Cheese Enchilada with Rice and Beans	14¾ oz.	620	60	25	30	1460	4 starch, 2 meat, 3½ fat
Chicken Suiza with Rice and Beans	14¾ oz.	550	65	25	20	1210	4 starch, 2 meat, 1½ fat
F Grande Burrito with Rice and Corn	14¾ oz.	530	70	20	20	1210	4½ starch, 1 meat, 2½ fat
Shredded Beef Enchilada with Rice and Corn	14¾ oz.	490	60	25	15	1170	4 starch, 2 meat, ½ fat
Mexican Classic Entrees							
F Beef Tostada Supreme	8½ oz.	530	40	25	30	900	2½ starch, 2½ meat, 3 fat
Cheese Enchilada Ranchero	5½ oz.	250	20	10	15	540	1½ starch, 1 meat, 2 fat
Chicken Enchilada Suiza	5½ oz.	220	20	10	10	590	1½ starch, 1 meat, 1 fat
Crispy Fried Burrito	6 oz.	365	40	10	15	825	½ starch, ½ meat, 2 fat
with Guacamole Packet	1¼ oz.	45	0	0	5	85	1 fat
Shredded Beef Enchilada	5½ oz.	180	15	10	10	930	1 starch, 1 meat, 1 fat

†For Occasional Use   **Not Recommended For Use   *Not Available   F More Than 2 Fat Exchanges   S Moderate To High Sugar Content

NUTRIENT VALUE

	PRODUCTS	SERVING SIZE	CALORIES	CARBO-HYDRATE (g.)	PROTEIN (g.)	FAT (g.)	SODIUM (mg.)	EXCHANGES
F	Shredded Beef Taquitos with Guacamole	8 oz.	490	45	15	25	990	3 starch, 1 meat, 4 fat
	Sirloin Burrito Grande	11 oz.	440	45	25	15	1120	3 starch, 2 meat, 1 fat

VELVEETA® (Kraft, Inc.)

	PRODUCTS	SERVING SIZE	CALORIES	CARBO-HYDRATE (g.)	PROTEIN (g.)	FAT (g.)	SODIUM (mg.)	EXCHANGES
	Shells and Cheese	¾ cup	260	32	12	10	720-860	2 starch, 1 meat, ½ fat

WEIGHT WATCHERS® (Foodways National, Inc.)

Entrees

	PRODUCTS	SERVING SIZE	CALORIES	CARBO-HYDRATE (g.)	PROTEIN (g.)	FAT (g.)	SODIUM (mg.)	EXCHANGES
	Baked Cheese Ravioli	9 oz.	320	37	17	12	760	2 starch, 1 veg., 1½ meat, ½ fat
	Beef Enchiladas Ranchero	8½ oz.	310	26	21	14	1230	2 starch, 2 meat, ½ fat
	Beef Salisbury Steak Romana	8¾ oz.	300	24	25	12	1010	1 starch, 1 veg., 3 lean meat, ½ fat
	Beef Stroganoff with Parsley Noodles	9 oz.	300	24	24	12	1050	1½ starch, 3 lean meat, ½ fat
	Beefsteak Burritos	1 burrito (5 oz.)	300	34	14	12	940	2 starch, 1 veg., 1 meat, 1 fat
F	Cheese Enchiladas Ranchero	8⅞ oz.	360	28	16	21	1070	2 starch, 1½ meat, 2½ fat
	Cheese Manicotti	9¼ oz.	320	30	18	14	860	2 starch, 2 meat, ½ fat
	Chicken Ala King	9 oz.	230	15	26	7	1030	1 starch, 3 lean meat
	Chicken Burritos	1 burrito (5 oz.)	280	31	15	10	820	2 starch, 1½ meat
	Chicken Cacciatore	10½ oz.	280	28	25	8	610	2 starch, 2½ lean meat
	Chicken Enchiladas Suiza	9⁵/₁₆ oz.	330	28	22	14	950	2 starch, 2 meat, ½ fat
	Chicken Nuggets	4 nuggets (3 oz.)	190	9	14	10	335	½ starch, 2 meat
	Chicken Patty Parmigiana	8¹/₁₆ oz.	290	14	18	18	960	½ starch, 1 veg., 2 meat, 1½ fat

†For Occasional Use   **Not Recommended For Use   *Not Available   F More Than 2 Fat Exchanges   S Moderate To High Sugar Content

NUTRIENT VALUE

PRODUCTS	SERVING SIZE	CALORIES	CARBO-HYDRATE (g.)	PROTEIN (g.)	FAT (g.)	SODIUM (mg.)	EXCHANGES
Chopped Beef Steak in Green Pepper and Mushroom Sauce	9 oz.	290	13	19	18	980	½ starch, 1 veg., 2 meat, 1½ fat
Fillet of Fish Au Gratin	9.25 oz.	210	12	25	7	910	½ starch, 1 veg., 3 lean meat
Imperial Chicken	9¼ oz.	240	29	22	4	820	2 starch, 2 lean meat
Italian Cheese Lasagna	12 oz.	360	35	19	16	1420	2 starch, 1 veg., 1½ meat, 1½ fat
Lasagna with Meat	12 oz.	360	40	24	11	1200	2 starch, 2 veg., 2 meat
Oven Fried Fish in Seasoned Bread Crumbs	6.75 oz.	220	8	19	12	470	½ starch, 2½ lean meat, 1 fat
Southern Fried Chicken Patty	6.5 oz.	270	9	18	18	510	½ starch, 2 lean meat, 2 fat
Spaghetti with Meat Sauce	10½ oz.	280	36	16	8	920	2 starch, 1 veg., 1 meat
Stuffed Pepper with Veal and Tomato Sauce	11¾ oz.	300	28	25	10	1270	1½ starch, 1 veg., 3 lean meat
Stuffed Turkey Breast	8½ oz.	260	21	22	10	980	1 starch, 1 veg., 2½ lean meat
Ⓢ Sweet 'n Sour Chicken Tenders	10³/₁₆ oz.	240	42	16	2	656	1½ starch, 1 veg., 1 lean meat, 1 fruit†
Veal Patty Parmigiana	8⁷/₁₆ oz.	220	10	23	10	750	2 veg., 3 lean meat
Ziti Macaroni	11¼ oz.	290	32	21	9	810	2 starch, 1 veg., 2 lean meat

WOLF'S® (Quaker Oats Co.)

PRODUCTS	SERVING SIZE	CALORIES	CARBO-HYDRATE (g.)	PROTEIN (g.)	FAT (g.)	SODIUM (mg.)	EXCHANGES
Beef Stew	scant cup	180	18	10	8	1040	1 starch, 1 high fat meat
Ⓕ Chili Mac	scant cup	320	23	12	20	850	1½ starch, 1 meat, 3 fat
Chili with Beans	1 cup	350	22	15	22	1010	1½ starch, 1½ high fat meat, 2 fat

†For Occasional Use   **Not Recommended For Use   *Not Available   Ⓕ More Than 2 Fat Exchanges   Ⓢ Moderate To High Sugar Content

NUTRIENT VALUE

PRODUCTS	SERVING SIZE	CALORIES	CARBO-HYDRATE (g.)	PROTEIN (g.)	FAT (g.)	SODIUM (mg.)	EXCHANGES
Chili without Beans	1 cup	390	16	21	27	1040	1 starch, 2½ high fat meat, 1 fat

FISH
BOOTH® (Booth Fisheries Corp.)

Cod, Light and Tender

PRODUCTS	SERVING SIZE	CALORIES	CARBO-HYDRATE (g.)	PROTEIN (g.)	FAT (g.)	SODIUM (mg.)	EXCHANGES
Mildly Seasoned	1 fillet (3 oz.)	150	18	11	4	310	1 starch, 1 lean meat
Sherry Flavored	1 fillet (3 oz.)	190	8	9	13	330	½ starch, 1 lean meat, 2 fat
Fishburger Sandwich Rounds	1 fishburger (3 oz.)	137	12	11	5	*	1 starch, 1 lean meat, ½ fat
Fish Fillets, Breaded							
F Beer Batter, French Fried	1 fillet (3 oz.)	249	11	8	19	*	1 starch, 1 lean meat, 3 fat
F Extra Crunchy, Beer Battered	1 fillet (3 oz.)	230	14	9	15	300	1 starch, 1 lean meat, 2½ fat
F Extra Crunchy Breaded, Original Flavor	1 fillet (3 oz.)	233	17	9	15	370	1 starch, 1 lean meat, 2½ fat
Fish Sticks, Breaded							
F Beer Batter, French Fried	3 sticks (3 oz.)	263	13	8	20	351	1 starch, 1 lean meat, 3 fat
Extra Crunchy Breaded, Original Flavor	3 sticks (3 oz.)	224	15	9	14	294	1 starch, 1 lean meat, 2 fat
Fish Sticks	4 sticks (4 oz.)	230	26	13	8	650	1 starch, 1 lean meat, ½ fat
Flounder, Light and Tender with Lemon and Herb	1 fillet (3 oz.)	170	12	10	9	290	1 starch, 1 lean meat, 1 fat
Haddock, Light and Tender, with Romano Cheese	1 fillet (3 oz.)	190	12	12	10	380	1 starch, 1 lean meat, 1 fat
Ocean Perch, Light and Tender, Cajun flavored	1 fillet (3 oz.)	160	11	10	8	380	1 starch, 1 lean meat, 1 fat

†For Occasional Use   **Not Recommended For Use   *Not Available   F More Than 2 Fat Exchanges   S Moderate To High Sugar Content

NUTRIENT VALUE

PRODUCTS	SERVING SIZE	CALORIES	CARBO-HYDRATE (g.)	PROTEIN (g.)	FAT (g.)	SODIUM (mg.)	EXCHANGES
Shrimp, Breaded, Gourmet Breaded or Oriental Breaded, ready to fry	4 oz.	160	23	14	1	*	1½ starch, 1 lean meat (add fats for frying)
Sole, Light and Tender, New England Style	1 fillet (3 oz.)	160	18	10	6	430	1 starch, 1 lean meat, ½ fat
FEATHERWEIGHT® (Sandoz Nutrition)							
Salmon-Pink, Low Sodium, canned	3 oz.	120	0	17	6	60	2½ lean meat
Sardines, Low Sodium, oil or water packed, canned	1⅞ oz.	109	0	13	6	65	2 lean meat
Tuna, Low Sodium, canned	3 oz.	97	0	20	2	44	3 lean meat
GORTON'S® (The Gorton Group, Division of General Mills, Inc.)							
F Clam Strips, Crunchy Fried	½ package	240	20	7	15	460	1 starch, ½ lean meat, 2½ fat
Fish Fillets							
F Crispy Batter Dipped	1 fillet	250	18	8	16	440	1 starch, ½ lean meat, 3 fat
F Crunchy	2 fillets	350	19	10	26	440	1 starch, 1 lean meat, 4½ fat
F Potato Crisp™	2 fillets	340	20	10	24	460	1 starch, 1 lean meat, 4 fat
Fish Sticks							
Crispy Batter Dipped	4 sticks	230	18	9	14	560	1 starch, 1 lean meat, 2 fat
F Crunchy	4 sticks	220	15	7	15	370	1 starch, ½ lean meat, 2½ fat
with Breading	4 sticks	210	24	8	9	480	1½ starch, ½ lean meat, 1½ fat
F Potato Crisp™	4 sticks	280	17	8	20	400	1 starch, ½ lean meat, 3 fat
F Fishniks 'N Chips	⅓ package	450	44	14	24	460	3 starch, 1 lean meat, 4 fat

†For Occasional Use   **Not Recommended For Use   *Not Available   F More Than 2 Fat Exchanges   S Moderate To High Sugar Content

NUTRIENT VALUE

PRODUCTS	SERVING SIZE	CALORIES	CARBO-HYDRATE (g.)	PROTEIN (g.)	FAT (g.)	SODIUM (mg.)	EXCHANGES
GORTON'S® LIGHT RECIPE™ (The Gorton Group, Division of General Mills, Inc.)							
Crab							
Crab Au Gratin	1 package	280	18	22	13	810	1 starch, 2½ lean meat, 1 fat
F Stuffed Crabs Imperial	1 package	360	29	16	20	670	2 starch, 1½ lean meat, 3 fat
Fish Fillets							
Lightly Breaded	1 fillet	170	16	11	7	380	1 starch, 1 lean meat, 1 fat
Tempura Batter	1 fillet	190	10	10	12	400	½ starch, 1½ lean meat, 1½ fat
Flounder							
Entree Size Fish Fillet	1 fillet	260	23	18	11	710	1½ starch, 2 lean meat, 1 fat
Stuffed Flounder	1 package	260	11	22	14	880	1 starch, 3 lean meat, 1 fat
Haddock							
Entree Size Fish Fillet	1 fillet	260	23	19	10	570	1½ starch, 2 lean meat, ½ fat
Fillet with Lemon Butter Sauce	1 package	240	8	26	11	570	½ starch, 3½ lean meat
Scrod							
Baked Stuffed	1 package	260	4	26	15	490	4 lean meat, ½ fat
Shrimp							
Baked Stuffed	1 package	340	36	15	15	950	2½ starch, 1 lean meat, 2 fat
Oriental	1 package	350	72	11	2	740	4½ starch, ½ lean meat
Pasta Medley	1 package	370	30	19	19	550	2 starch, 2 lean meat, 2 fat
F Scampi	1 package	350	15	19	24	420	1 starch, 2½ lean meat, 3 fat
Sole							
Fillet with Lemon Butter Sauce	1 package	250	8	24	13	730	½ starch, 3 lean meat, 1 fat

†For Occasional Use   **Not Recommended For Use   *Not Available   F More Than 2 Fat Exchanges   S Moderate To High Sugar Content

NUTRIENT VALUE

PRODUCTS	SERVING SIZE	CALORIES	CARBO-HYDRATE (g.)	PROTEIN (g.)	FAT (g.)	SODIUM (mg.)	EXCHANGES
MRS. PAUL'S® (Campbell Soup Co.)							
Catfish							
Fillets, Breaded	1 fillet (3⅝ oz.)	220	20	12	10	300	1 starch, 1½ lean meat, 1 fat
Strips, Breaded	4 oz.	240	21	10	13	290	1½ starch, 1 lean meat, 1½ fat
Clams							
Fried Clams in Light Batter	2½ oz.	240	22	8	13	380	1½ starch, ½ lean meat, 2 fat
Ⓕ Combination Seafood Platter	9 oz.	590	58	20	31	1220	4 starch, 1 lean meat, 5 fat
Crab							
Deviled Crabs	1 piece (3 oz.)	190	21	8	8	370	1½ starch, ½ lean meat, ½ fat
Deviled Crab Miniatures	3½ oz.	250	29	8	12	480	2 starch, ½ lean meat, 1½ fat
Fish Cakes							
Fish Cakes	2 cakes (4 oz.)	250	27	11	11	840	2 starch, 1 lean meat, 1½ fat
Fish Cake Thins	2 cakes (5 oz.)	290	29	15	13	1210	2 starch, 1½ lean meat, 1½ fat
Fish Fillets							
Ⓕ Batter Dipped	2 fillets (6 oz.)	390	31	17	25	610	2 starch, 1½ lean meat, 4 fat
Buttered	2 fillets (5 oz.)	170	4	20	9	390	3 lean meat
Crispy Crunchy	2 fillets (4¼ oz.)	280	26	11	16	550	2 starch, 1 lean meat, 2 fat
Ⓕ Crunchy Light Batter	2 fillets (4½ oz.)	310	28	11	17	810	2 starch, 1 lean meat, 2½ fat
Light Breaded	1 fillet (6 oz.)	290	21	22	13	770	1½ starch, 2½ lean meat, 1 fat
Supreme Light Batter	1 fillet (3⅝ oz.)	210	21	9	12	540	1½ starch, ½ lean meat, 2 fat

†For Occasional Use   **Not Recommended For Use   *Not Available   Ⓕ More Than 2 Fat Exchanges   Ⓢ Moderate To High Sugar Content

NUTRIENT VALUE

PRODUCTS	SERVING SIZE	CALORIES	CARBO-HYDRATE (g.)	PROTEIN (g.)	FAT (g.)	SODIUM (mg.)	EXCHANGES
Fish Parmesan	5 oz.	220	16	15	11	540	1 starch, 2 lean meat, 1 fat
Fish Sticks							
Crispy Crunchy	4 sticks (2½ oz.)	200	19	9	10	350	1 starch, 1 lean meat, 1 fat
Crunchy Light Batter	4 sticks (3½ oz.)	240	23	8	13	590	1½ starch, ½ lean meat, 2 fat
Flounder Fillets							
Crispy Crunchy	2 fillets (4 oz.)	270	23	11	15	500	1½ starch, 1 lean meat, 2 fat
F Crunchy Light Batter	2 fillets (4½ oz.)	310	29	10	16	790	2 starch, ½ lean meat, 2½ fat
Light Breaded	1 fillet (6 oz.)	280	19	21	13	700	1 starch, 2½ lean meat, 1 fat
Haddock Fillets							
Crispy Crunchy	2 fillets (4 oz.)	270	21	15	12	485	1½ starch, 1½ lean meat, 2 fat
F Crunchy Light Batter	2 fillets (4½ oz.)	330	35	9	17	670	2 starch, ½ lean meat, 2½ fat
Light Breaded	1 fillet (6 oz.)	290	21	23	13	960	1½ starch, 2½ lean meat, 1 fat
Light Seafood Entrees							
Crown of Flounder Divan	9 oz.	200	10	20	9	1090	½ starch, 2½ lean meat
Crown of Sole Divan	9 oz.	200	10	20	9	1090	½ starch, 2½ lean meat
Fillet of Flounder with Shrimp Souffle	9 oz.	200	7	24	8	970	½ starch, 3 lean meat
Fillet of Sole with Shrimp Souffle	9 oz.	230	10	24	10	1100	½ starch, 3 lean meat
Fish and Pasta Florentine	9½ oz.	240	19	21	9	710	1 starch, 1 veg., 2 lean meat, ½ fat

†For Occasional Use   **Not Recommended For Use   *Not Available   F More Than 2 Fat Exchanges   S Moderate To High Sugar Content

NUTRIENT VALUE

PRODUCTS	SERVING SIZE	CALORIES	CARBO-HYDRATE (g.)	PROTEIN (g.)	FAT (g.)	SODIUM (mg.)	EXCHANGES
Fish Dijon	8½ oz.	260	13	21	17	690	1 starch, 2½ lean meat, 2 fat
Fish Florentine	9 oz.	280	12	25	14	750	1 starch, 3 lean meat, 1 fat
Fish Mornay	10 oz.	280	17	23	14	700	1 starch, 3 lean meat, 1 fat
Scallops Mediterranean	11 oz.	250	36	17	5	775	2½ starch, 1 lean meat
Seafood Newburg	8½ oz.	270	35	14	9	920	2 starch, 1 lean meat, 1 fat
Shrimp Oriental	11 oz.	280	46	12	5	880	2½ starch, 1 veg., ½ lean meat, ½ fat
Shrimp Primavera	11 oz.	290	38	15	8	860	2½ starch, 1 lean meat, 1 fat
F Perch Fillets, Crispy Crunchy	2 fillets (4 oz.)	320	25	13	19	460	1½ starch, 1 lean meat, 3 fat
Scallops, French Fried	3½ oz.	230	26	11	9	480	2 starch, 1 lean meat, 1 fat
Shrimp, Fried	3 oz.	200	16	9	11	430	1 starch, 1 lean meat, 1 fat
Sole Fillets, Light Breaded	1 fillet (6 oz.)	280	19	21	13	700	1 starch, 2½ lean meat, 1 fat

NUTRADIET® (S and W Fine Foods)

PRODUCTS	SERVING SIZE	CALORIES	CARBO-HYDRATE (g.)	PROTEIN (g.)	FAT (g.)	SODIUM (mg.)	EXCHANGES
Salmon, Low Sodium	½ cup	188	0	22	11	45	3 lean meat

SEAPAK® (Rich-SeaPak Corp.)

PRODUCTS	SERVING SIZE	CALORIES	CARBO-HYDRATE (g.)	PROTEIN (g.)	FAT (g.)	SODIUM (mg.)	EXCHANGES
Breaded Round Butterfly Shrimp	4 oz.	150	20	14	1	*	1 starch, 1½ lean meat
Shrimp 'n Batter	4 oz.	260	26	9	13	520	2 starch, ½ lean meat, 2 fat

VAN DE KAMP'S® (Van de Kamp's® Frozen Foods)
Cod

PRODUCTS	SERVING SIZE	CALORIES	CARBO-HYDRATE (g.)	PROTEIN (g.)	FAT (g.)	SODIUM (mg.)	EXCHANGES
F Lightly Breaded	1 piece (5 oz.)	290	10	20	20	370	½ starch, 2½ lean meat, 2½ fat
F Fish and Chips Batter-Dipped (½ fish/½ fries)	7 oz.	440	35	20	25	640	2 starch, 2 lean meat, 3½ fat

†For Occasional Use   **Not Recommended For Use   *Not Available   F More Than 2 Fat Exchanges   S Moderate To High Sugar Content

NUTRIENT VALUE

	PRODUCTS	SERVING SIZE	CALORIES	CARBO-HYDRATE (g.)	PROTEIN (g.)	FAT (g.)	SODIUM (mg.)	EXCHANGES
	Fish Fillets							
	Batter-Dipped	1 piece (3 oz.)	180	15	10	10	230	1 starch, 1 lean meat, 1 fat
Ⓕ	Breaded	1 piece (2 oz.)	180	10	5	15	175	½ starch, ½ lean meat, 2½ fat
	Country Seasoned	1 piece (2 oz.)	200	10	10	10	335	½ starch, 1 lean meat, 1 fat
	Fish Kabobs							
	Batter-Dipped	4 oz.	240	15	10	15	430	1 starch, 1 lean meat, 2 fat
	Fish Nuggets							
	Breaded	2 oz.	130	10	10	10	160	½ starch, 1 lean meat, 1 fat
	Fish Sticks							
	Batter-Dipped	4 pieces (4 oz.)	220	15	10	15	330	1 starch, 1 lean meat, 2 fat
Ⓕ	Breaded	4 pieces (3¾ oz.)	270	15	10	20	300	1 starch, 1 lean meat, 3 fat
	Flounder							
	Lightly Breaded	1 piece (5 oz.)	300	15	15	15	410	1 starch, 2 lean meat, 2 fat
	Haddock							
	Batter-Dipped	2 pieces (4 oz.)	240	20	10	10	430	1 starch, 1 lean meat, 1 fat
Ⓕ	Breaded Fillets	1 piece (2 oz.)	180	10	5	15	160	½ starch, ½ lean meat, 2½ fat
Ⓕ	Lightly Breaded	1 piece (5 oz.)	300	15	15	20	310	1 starch, 1½ lean meat, 3 fat
	Halibut							
	Batter-Dipped	3 pieces (4 oz.)	260	15	10	15	440	1 starch, 1 lean meat, 2 fat
	Lightly Breaded	1 piece	220	15	15	10	520	1 starch, 2 lean meat, ½ fat
	Perch							
	Batter-Dipped	2 pieces (4 oz.)	270	20	10	15	510	1 starch, 1 lean meat, 2 fat
	Breaded Fillets	1 piece (2 oz.)	170	10	5	10	115	½ starch, ½ lean meat, 1½ fat

†For Occasional Use   **Not Recommended For Use   *Not Available   Ⓕ More Than 2 Fat Exchanges   Ⓢ Moderate To High Sugar Content

PRODUCTS	SERVING SIZE	CALORIES	CARBO-HYDRATE (g.)	PROTEIN (g.)	FAT (g.)	SODIUM (mg.)	EXCHANGES
Sole							
Batter-Dipped	2 pieces (4 oz.)	280	25	15	15	575	1½ starch, 1½ lean meat, 2 fat
Lightly Breaded	1 piece (5 oz.)	300	15	15	15	410	1 starch, 2 lean meat, 2 fat

MEATS, PROCESSED (Cold Cuts, Wieners, etc.)
ARMOUR® (Armour-Dial, Inc.)
Canned Meats

PRODUCTS	SERVING SIZE	CALORIES	CARBO-HYDRATE (g.)	PROTEIN (g.)	FAT (g.)	SODIUM (mg.)	EXCHANGES
F Chopped Beef	3 oz.	280	3	11	24	1250	1½ high fat meat, 2½ fat
Chopped Ham	3 oz.	240	2	13	20	1280	2 high fat meat, 1 fat
Dried Beef, Sliced	1 oz.	45	1	5	1	1220	1 lean meat
Lunch Tongue	3 oz.	200	1	15	14	1400	2 high fat meat
Pork Brains in Milk Gravy	2¾ oz.	100	1	7	7	410	1 high fat meat
F Treet	3 oz.	290	4	9	26	1190	1½ high fat meat, 3 fat
Tripe, Beef	6 oz.	210	1	29	9	280	4 lean meat
Deviled/Potted Meats							
Deviled Ham	1½ oz.	120	0	6	9	380	1 high fat meat
Deviled Treet	1½ oz.	120	1	6	10	390	1 high fat meat
Potted Meats, all varieties (average)	1½ oz.	80	0	5	6	460-490	½ high fat meat, ½ fat
Sausage							
Banner Sausage	2.6 oz.	160	2	10	12	560	1½ high fat meat
Vienna Sausage, all varieties (average)	2 oz.	185	1	6	17	390-750	1 high fat meat, 2 fat

CARNATION® (Calreco®, Inc.)
The Spreadables - Sandwich Spreads

PRODUCTS	SERVING SIZE	CALORIES	CARBO-HYDRATE (g.)	PROTEIN (g.)	FAT (g.)	SODIUM (mg.)	EXCHANGES
Chicken Salad	1⅞ oz. (¼ container)	100	2	6	6	200	1 lean meat, ½ fat

†For Occasional Use   **Not Recommended For Use   *Not Available   F More Than 2 Fat Exchanges   S Moderate To High Sugar Content

NUTRIENT VALUE

PRODUCTS	SERVING SIZE	CALORIES	CARBO-HYDRATE (g.)	PROTEIN (g.)	FAT (g.)	SODIUM (mg.)	EXCHANGES
Ham Salad	1⅞ oz. (¼ container)	100	4	5	6	350	½ lean meat, 1 fat
Tuna Salad	1⅞ oz. (¼ container)	90	2	6	6	370	1 lean meat, ½ fat
Turkey Salad	1⅞ oz. (¼ container)	100	2	6	6	190	1 lean meat, ½ fat

DINTY MOORE® (George A. Hormel and Co.)

Corned Beef	2 oz.	130	0	15	8	*	2 lean meat

HILLSHIRE FARM® (Hillshire Farm Co.)

PRODUCTS	SERVING SIZE	CALORIES	CARBO-HYDRATE (g.)	PROTEIN (g.)	FAT (g.)	SODIUM (mg.)	EXCHANGES
F Beef Smoked Sausage	3½ oz.	331	3	13	30	985	2 high fat meat, 3 fat
F Bratwurst	3½ oz.	326	1	13	30	816	2 high fat meat, 3 fat
F Cheddarwurst	3½ oz.	343	1	15	31	908	2 high fat meat, 3 fat
F Polska Kielbasa	3½ oz.	336	4	13	30	903	2 high fat meat, 3 fat
F Smoked Sausage	3½ oz.	334	3	13	30	905	2 high fat meat, 3 fat
F Wieners, Natural Casing	3½ oz.	330	2	11	31	842	1½ high fat meat, 4 fat

HORMEL® (George A. Hormel and Co.)

Frozen Products

PRODUCTS	SERVING SIZE	CALORIES	CARBO-HYDRATE (g.)	PROTEIN (g.)	FAT (g.)	SODIUM (mg.)	EXCHANGES
F Beef Steaks, breaded	4 oz.	370	13	14	30	*	1 starch, 2 meat, 4 fat
Pork Steaks, breaded	3 oz.	220	11	12	15	*	1 starch, 1 meat, 1½ fat
Veal Steaks	4 oz.	130	2	22	4	*	3 lean meat
Veal Steaks, breaded	4 oz.	240	13	17	13	*	1 starch, 2 meat, ½ fat
Vienna Sausage, canned	3 sausages	150	1	5	14	360	1 high fat meat, 1 fat
Wieners, Batter Wrapped Corn Dogs	1	220	21	7	12	656	1½ starch, ½ high fat meat, 1½ fat
Tater Dogs	1	210	15	6	14	*	1 starch, ½ high fat meat, 2 fat

†For Occasional Use   **Not Recommended For Use   *Not Available   F More Than 2 Fat Exchanges   S Moderate To High Sugar Content

NUTRIENT VALUE

PRODUCTS	SERVING SIZE	CALORIES	CARBO-HYDRATE (g.)	PROTEIN (g.)	FAT (g.)	SODIUM (mg.)	EXCHANGES
Lunch Meats							
Bologna	2 slices	170	1	6	16	592	1 high fat meat, 1½ fat
Beef Salami	2 slices	50	0	3	5	219	½ high fat meat
Breast of Turkey	2 slices	60	0	9	2	484	1 lean meat
Chopped Ham	2 slices	88	0	11	5	685	1½ lean meat
Ham and Cheese Loaf	2 slices	110	0	11	7	668	1½ meat
Pepperoni	2 slices	80	0	3	7	281	½ high fat meat, ½ fat
Spiced Luncheon Meat	2 slices	118	1	9	9	702	1 high fat meat
Summer Sausage	2 slices	140	0	10	11	706	1½ high fat meat
Meat Patties, Canned							
Ham Patties	1 patty	180	0	7	16	456	1 meat, 2 fat
F Ham and Cheese Patties	1 patty	190	0	7	18	468	1 meat, 2½ fat
Sausage Patties, all varieties (average)	1 patty	150	0	17	13	541-549	1 high fat meat, 1 fat
Meat Spreads							
Chicken Spreads	1 oz.	60	0	4	4	*	½ meat, ½ fat
Corned Beef Spread	1 oz.	70	0	4	6	*	½ meat, ½ fat
Liverwurst Spread	1 oz.	70	0	4	6	*	½ meat, ½ fat
Roast Beef Spread	1 oz.	62	0	4	4	*	½ meat, ½ fat
Sausage, Dry Products							
Beefy Summer Sausage	1 oz.	100	0	5	9	313	½ high fat meat, 1 fat
Cotto Salami	1 oz.	100	0	5	9	385	½ high fat meat, 1 fat
Hard Salami	1 oz.	110	0	7	10	468	1 high fat meat
Pepperoni	1 oz.	140	0	6	13	462	1 high fat meat, 1 fat
Thuringer Summer Sausage	1 oz.	90	0	4	9	332	½ high fat meat, 1 fat
Viking Cervalat	1 oz.	90	0	5	8	325	½ high fat meat, 1 fat

†For Occasional Use   **Not Recommended For Use   *Not Available   F More Than 2 Fat Exchanges   S Moderate To High Sugar Content

NUTRIENT VALUE

PRODUCTS	SERVING SIZE	CALORIES	CARBO-HYDRATE (g.)	PROTEIN (g.)	FAT (g.)	SODIUM (mg.)	EXCHANGES
Sausage, Prepared Items							
Braunschweiger (Liverwurst)	1 oz.	80	0	4	7	322	½ high fat meat, ½ fat
Brown 'N Serve Sausage, cooked	2 sausage	140	0	6	13	430	1 high fat meat, 1 fat
Bologna, all varieties (average)	2 oz.	160	1	8	14	576-596	1 high fat meat, 1 fat
Polish Sausage	2 sausages	170	0	9	14	574	1 high fat meat, 1 fat
Wieners, Beef (12 oz. package)	1 wiener	100	1	4	10	362	½ high fat meat, 1 fat
Wieners, Meat (12 oz. package)	1 wiener	110	1	4	10	378	½ high fat meat, 1 fat

HORMEL® GREAT BEGINNINGS® (George A. Hormel and Co.)

Great Beginnings®, Canned

PRODUCTS	SERVING SIZE	CALORIES	CARBO-HYDRATE (g.)	PROTEIN (g.)	FAT (g.)	SODIUM (mg.)	EXCHANGES
with Chunky Beef	5 oz.	136	7	12	7	904	1 veg., 1½ meat
with Chunky Chicken	5 oz.	147	5	14	8	567	1 veg., 2 lean meat
with Chunky Pork	5 oz.	140	5	14	8	567	1 veg., 2 lean meat
with Chunky Turkey	5 oz.	138	7	11	8	585	1 veg., 1½ meat

HORMEL® LIGHT AND LEAN® (George A. Hormel and Co.)

Lunch Meat

PRODUCTS	SERVING SIZE	CALORIES	CARBO-HYDRATE (g.)	PROTEIN (g.)	FAT (g.)	SODIUM (mg.)	EXCHANGES
BBQ Ham	2 slices	50	0	8	2	*	1 lean meat
Bologna	2 slices	140	2	6	12	*	1 high fat meat, 1 fat
Breast of Turkey	2 slices	60	0	8	2	*	1 lean meat
Cotto Salami	2 slices	80	0	6	6	*	1 meat
Ham and Cheese Loaf	2 slices	90	0	8	6	*	1 meat
New England Brand Luncheon Meat	2 slices	90	0	10	6	*	1½ lean meat
Spiced Luncheon Meat	2 slices	120	1	8	9	*	1 high fat meat
Summer Sausage	2 slices	100	0	6	8	*	1 high fat meat

†For Occasional Use   **Not Recommended For Use   *Not Available   Ⓕ More Than 2 Fat Exchanges   Ⓢ Moderate To High Sugar Content

NUTRIENT VALUE

PRODUCTS	SERVING SIZE	CALORIES	CARBO-HYDRATE (g.)	PROTEIN (g.)	FAT (g.)	SODIUM (mg.)	EXCHANGES
HORMEL® WRANGLERS® (George A. Hormel and Co.)							
Smoked Franks, all varieties (average)	1 frank	175	1	7	16	546-619	1 high fat meat, 1½ fat
JONES DAIRY FARM® (Jones Dairy Farm)							
Beef Roll Sausage (as purchased)	1 oz.	110-115	0	4	11	177	½ high fat meat, 1½ fat
Brown and Serve (as purchased)	1 oz.	125-130	0	3	13	189	½ high fat meat, 2 fat
Italian Links (as purchased)	1 oz.	90-95	0	4	8	222	½ high fat meat, 1 fat
Light Breakfast Links (as purchased)	1 oz.	70	1	4	6	220	½ high fat meat, ½ fat
Light Breakfast Roll (as purchased)	1 oz.	70	1	4	6	220	½ high fat meat, ½ fat
Liver Sausage (as purchased)	1 oz.	85-90	0	4	8	222	½ high fat meat, 1 fat
Pork Roll Sausage (as purchased)	1 oz.	90-95	0	4	8	222	½ high fat meat, 1 fat
Pork Sausage Links (as purchased)	1 oz.	130-135	0	3	13	177	½ high fat meat, 2 fat
Scrapple (as purchased)	1 oz.	50-55	3	3	4	144	½ high fat meat
LAND O' FROST® (Land O' Frost, Inc.)							
Thin Sliced Meat Products, all varieties (average)	1¼ oz.	50	1	7	3	463-538	1 lean meat
OSCAR MAYER® (Oscar Mayer and Co.)							
Bacon (22-26 slices/ 1 lb.)	3 slices, cooked	105	0	3	9	345	½ high fat meat, 1 fat
Bacon Bits (real bacon)	1 Tbsp.	20	0	2	1	190	Free
Beef Franks (10/1 lb.)	1	145	1	5	13	460	½ high fat meat, 2 fat
Braunschweiger, (liver sausage) all varieties (average)	2 oz.	190	2	6	18	650-710	1 high fat meat, 2 fat

†For Occasional Use   **Not Recommended For Use   *Not Available   Ⓕ More Than 2 Fat Exchanges   Ⓢ Moderate To High Sugar Content

NUTRIENT VALUE

PRODUCTS	SERVING SIZE	CALORIES	CARBO-HYDRATE (g.)	PROTEIN (g.)	FAT (g.)	SODIUM (mg.)	EXCHANGES
Canadian Style Bacon	1 oz.	40	0	6	2	415	1 lean meat
Cooked Ham (95% fat free)	1½ oz.	50	1	8	2	570	1 lean meat
Head Cheese	2 slices (2 oz.)	110	1	8	8	700	1 high fat meat
Hot Dogs, all varieties (10/1 lb.) (average)	1	145	1	5	13	430-480	1 high fat meat, 1 fat
Lean 'n Tasty™ Breakfast Strips, Beef or Pork (average)	2 strips	80	1	4	6	400	½ high fat meat, ½ fat
Liver Cheese (pork fat wrapped)	1 slice	115	1	5	10	455	1 meat, 1 fat
Luncheon Meats, Sliced							
Bar-B-Q Loaf (90% fat free)	2 slices (2 oz.)	100	4	8	6	720	1 meat
Bologna, all varieties (average)	2 slices (2 oz.)	150	1	4	14	480-590	½ high fat meat, 2 fat
Cotto Salami	2 slices	100	1	6	8	490	1 high fat meat
Loaf Luncheon Meats, all varieties (average)	2 slices	130	4	7	9	640-790	1 high fat meat
Luncheon Meat	2 slices	200	2	6	18	710	1 high fat meat, 2 fat
92% Fat Free Sausage Products (average)	2 slices	70	1-2	8	4	570-620	1 meat
93%-95% Fat Free Loaf Luncheon Meats (average)	2 slices	80-90	0-3	10	4	560-740	1½ lean meat
Meat Spreads							
Cheese and Bacon	1 oz.	70	1	4	5	325	½ meat, ½ fat
Cheese and Salami	1 oz.	65	1	4	5	350	½ meat, ½ fat
Ham and Cheese	1 oz.	70	1	4	5	335	½ meat, ½ fat

†For Occasional Use   **Not Recommended For Use   *Not Available   F More Than 2 Fat Exchanges   S Moderate To High Sugar Content

NUTRIENT VALUE

PRODUCTS	SERVING SIZE	CALORIES	CARBO-HYDRATE (g.)	PROTEIN (g.)	FAT (g.)	SODIUM (mg.)	EXCHANGES
Ham Salad	2 oz.	120	6	4	8	540	½ starch, ½ meat, 1 fat
Sandwich	2 oz.	130	8	4	9	540	½ starch, ½ meat, 1 fat
Salami for Beer	2 slices	110	1	6	8	560	1 high fat meat
Sausage Links							
Beef Smokies	1 link	130	1	6	12	450	1 high fat meat, ½ fat
Cheese Smokies	1 link	145	1	6	13	460	1 high fat meat, 1 fat
Little Friers Pork Sausage	2 links	160	1	6	14	430	1 high fat meat, 1 fat
Little Smokies	3 links	90	1	3	9	255	½ high fat meat, 1 fat
Wieners	1	145	1	5	13	430	½ high fat meat, 2 fat
Wieners, Jumbo	1	185	1	6	17	545	1 high fat meat, 2 fat
F Wieners, "The Big One"™	1	365	3	12	34	1080	2 high fat meat, 3½ fat

SCHWEIGERT® (Lea Foods)

PRODUCTS	SERVING SIZE	CALORIES	CARBO-HYDRATE (g.)	PROTEIN (g.)	FAT (g.)	SODIUM (mg.)	EXCHANGES
Tenderbite Weiners	1	150	2	5	13	*	1 high fat meat, 1 fat

SPAM® (George A. Hormel and Co.)

PRODUCTS	SERVING SIZE	CALORIES	CARBO-HYDRATE (g.)	PROTEIN (g.)	FAT (g.)	SODIUM (mg.)	EXCHANGES
Spam®	1 oz.	85	0	4	8	862	½ high fat meat, ½ fat
Spam® with Cheese Chunks	1 oz.	85	0	4	8	811	½ high fat meat, ½ fat
Spam®, Deviled	2 Tbsp.	70	0	4	6	250	½ high fat meat, ½ fat

WILSON® (Wilson Foods Corp.)

PRODUCTS	SERVING SIZE	CALORIES	CARBO-HYDRATE (g.)	PROTEIN (g.)	FAT (g.)	SODIUM (mg.)	EXCHANGES
Bacon	3 slices	130	1	6	12	*	1 high fat meat, 1 fat
Bacon, Hearty Cut	2 slices	130	1	5	12	*	½ high fat meat, 1 fat
Canadian Bacon	1 oz.	40	1	5	2	*	1 lean meat
Ham, canned	3 oz.	120	1	15	6	*	2 lean meat

†For Occasional Use   **Not Recommended For Use   *Not Available   F More Than 2 Fat Exchanges   S Moderate To High Sugar Content

NUTRIENT VALUE

PRODUCTS	SERVING SIZE	CALORIES	CARBO-HYDRATE (g.)	PROTEIN (g.)	FAT (g.)	SODIUM (mg.)	EXCHANGES
Ham, Masterpiece, canned, all varieties (average)	4 oz.	140	1	20	6	*	3 lean meat
Ham Patties, canned	2 oz.	190	1	7	18	*	1 high fat meat, 2 fat
Ham, boneless smoked	3 oz.	110	1	13	6	*	2 lean meat
Jalapeno Loaf	2 slices	180	2	6	17	*	1 high fat meat, 2 fat
Pork Chops, smoked	4 oz.	220	1	16	17	*	2 high fat meat
Sausage, Beef, smoked	2 oz.	190	1	8	17	*	1 high fat meat, 2 fat
Sausage, Pork	1 oz.	170	1	6	14	*	1 high fat meat, 1 fat
Variety Pack (average)	2 slices	130	3	5	11	*	1 high fat meat, ½ fat

PIZZA, PIZZA MIX
APPIAN WAY® (Armour-Dial, Inc.)

PRODUCTS	SERVING SIZE	CALORIES	CARBO-HYDRATE (g.)	PROTEIN (g.)	FAT (g.)	SODIUM (mg.)	EXCHANGES
Regular	¼ of 12½ oz. pizza	190	36	5	4	510	2 starch, ½ fat
Thick Crust	¼ of 21 oz. pizza	370	65	13	8	980	4 starch, 1 fat

CELESTE® (Quaker Oats Co.)

PRODUCTS	SERVING SIZE	CALORIES	CARBO-HYDRATE (g.)	PROTEIN (g.)	FAT (g.)	SODIUM (mg.)	EXCHANGES
Canadian Style Bacon Pizza	½ of 7¾ oz. pizza	275	26	14	13	875	2 starch, 1 meat, 1½ fat
Canadian Style Bacon Pizza	¼ of 19 oz. pizza	340	29	17	17	1030	2 starch, 1½ meat, 1½ fat
Cheese Pizza	½ of 6½ oz. pizza	250	24	11	12	460	1½ starch, 1 meat, 1 fat
Cheese Pizza	¼ of 17¾ oz. pizza	330	28	14	17	*	2 starch, 1 meat, 2 fat
Deluxe Pizza	½ of 8¼ oz. pizza	300	27	11	16	750	2 starch, 1 meat, 2 fat

†For Occasional Use   **Not Recommended For Use   *Not Available   F More Than 2 Fat Exchanges   S Moderate To High Sugar Content

NUTRIENT VALUE

	PRODUCTS	SERVING SIZE	CALORIES	CARBO-HYDRATE (g.)	PROTEIN (g.)	FAT (g.)	SODIUM (mg.)	EXCHANGES
F	Deluxe Pizza	¼ of 22¼ oz. pizza	390	32	15	22	1050	2 starch, 1½ meat, 2½ fat
	Pepperoni Pizza	½ of 6¾ oz. pizza	270	25	10	15	780	1½ starch, 1 high fat meat, 1 fat
F	Pepperoni Pizza	¼ of 19 oz. pizza	370	30	15	21	1170	2 starch, 1 high fat meat, 2½ fat
	Sausage Pizza	½ of 7½ oz. pizza	290	25	12	16	705	1½ starch, 1 high fat meat, 1½ fat
	Sausage Pizza	¼ of 20 oz. pizza	390	31	16	22	1080	2 starch, 1½ high fat meat, 2 fat
	Sausage and Mushroom Pizza	½ of 8½ oz. pizza	300	27	12	16	745	2 starch, 1 high fat meat, 1 fat
	Sausage and Mushroom Pizza	¼ of 22½ oz. pizza	410	32	17	23	1140	2 starch, 1½ high fat meat, 2 fat
	Supreme	½ of 9 oz. pizza	345	29	13	20	930	2 starch, 1 high fat meat, 2 fat
	Supreme	¼ of 23 oz. pizza	410	31	16	24	1140	2 starch, 1½ high fat meat, 2 fat
	CHEF BOY-AR-DEE® (American Home Foods)							
	Pizza Mix (as prepared)							
	Cheese	¼ of 15⅜ oz. pizza	230	36	9	6	740	2 starch, 1½ meat, ½ fat
	Cheese	⅛ of 28⅞ oz. pizza	210	31	10	5	650	2 starch, ½ meat
	Hamburger	¼ of 16⅞ oz. pizza	300	42	13	9	775	3 starch, 1 meat, ½ fat
	Pepperoni	¼ of 16⅝ oz. pizza	250	31	13	9	870	2 starch, 1 meat, ½ fat

†For Occasional Use **Not Recommended For Use *Not Available F More Than 2 Fat Exchanges S Moderate To High Sugar Content

NUTRIENT VALUE

PRODUCTS	SERVING SIZE	CALORIES	CARBO-HYDRATE (g.)	PROTEIN (g.)	FAT (g.)	SODIUM (mg.)	EXCHANGES
Pepperoni	⅛ of 30 oz. pizza	210	31	10	7	595	2 starch, ½ meat, ½ fat
Plain	¼ of 14 oz. pizza	180	32	6	3	640	2 starch, ½ fat
Sausage	¼ of 16⅞ oz. pizza	270	34	14	10	930	2 starch, 1 meat, 1 fat

CONTADINA® (Calreco®, Inc.)
Pizzeria Kit, (as prepared)

PRODUCTS	SERVING SIZE	CALORIES	CARBO-HYDRATE (g.)	PROTEIN (g.)	FAT (g.)	SODIUM (mg.)	EXCHANGES
Thick Crust	¼ pizza	295	56	9	4	820	3 starch, 1 veg., ½ fat
Thin Crust	¼ pizza	209	39	6	3	650	2 starch, 1 veg., ½ fat

FOX DELUXE® (The Pillsbury Co.)

PRODUCTS	SERVING SIZE	CALORIES	CARBO-HYDRATE (g.)	PROTEIN (g.)	FAT (g.)	SODIUM (mg.)	EXCHANGES
Cheese Pizza	⅓ pizza	170	22	7	6	520	1½ starch, ½ meat, ½ fat
Hamburger Pizza	⅓ pizza	180	23	8	6	470	1½ starch, ½ meat, ½ fat
Pepperoni Pizza	⅓ pizza	170	23	7	6	520	1½ starch, ½ meat, ½ fat
Sausage Pizza	⅓ pizza	180	23	7	7	530	1½ starch, ½ meat, ½ fat
Sausage/Pepperoni Combination Pizza	⅓ pizza	170	23	7	6	530	1½ starch, ½ meat, ½ fat

PILLSBURY® (The Pillsbury Co.)
Heat 'n Eat™ Microwave Pizza

PRODUCTS	SERVING SIZE	CALORIES	CARBO-HYDRATE (g.)	PROTEIN (g.)	FAT (g.)	SODIUM (mg.)	EXCHANGES
Cheese	4.1 oz.	270	31	13	11	670	2 starch, 1 meat, 1 fat
Ⓕ Combination	4.9 oz.	380	31	14	21	1190	2 starch, 1 meat, 3 fat
Ⓕ Pepperoni	4.6 oz.	350	31	13	18	1070	2 starch, 1 meat, 2½ fat
Ⓕ Sausage	4.8 oz.	360	31	13	20	1130	2 starch, 1 meat, 3 fat

Microwave French Bread Pizza

PRODUCTS	SERVING SIZE	CALORIES	CARBO-HYDRATE (g.)	PROTEIN (g.)	FAT (g.)	SODIUM (mg.)	EXCHANGES
Cheese	1 piece	340	40	14	14	570	2½ starch, 1 meat, 1½ fat

†For Occasional Use   **Not Recommended For Use   *Not Available   Ⓕ More Than 2 Fat Exchanges   Ⓢ Moderate To High Sugar Content

NUTRIENT VALUE

PRODUCTS	SERVING SIZE	CALORIES	CARBO-HYDRATE (g.)	PROTEIN (g.)	FAT (g.)	SODIUM (mg.)	EXCHANGES
Pepperoni	1 piece	410	40	17	20	1160	2½ starch, 1½ meat, 2 fat
Sausage	1 piece	410	40	18	19	1020	2½ starch, 1½ meat, 2 fat
Sausage and Pepperoni Combination	1 piece	430	41	18	21	1140	3 starch, 1½ meat, 2 fat
Microwave Pizza Cheese	7.1 oz.	480	56	21	19	1190	4 starch, 1½ meat, 2 fat
F Combination	9 oz.	670	60	27	36	1550	4 starch, 2 meat, 5 fat
F Pepperoni	8.5 oz.	590	59	27	28	1560	4 starch, 2 meat, 3 fat
F Sausage	8.75 oz.	650	59	25	34	1420	4 starch, 2 meat, 4 fat

STOUFFER'S® (Stouffer Foods Corp.)
French Bread Pizzas

PRODUCTS	SERVING SIZE	CALORIES	CARBO-HYDRATE (g.)	PROTEIN (g.)	FAT (g.)	SODIUM (mg.)	EXCHANGES
Cheese	½ of 10⅜ oz. pizza	340	41	15	13	840	3 starch, 1 meat, 1½ fat
Deluxe	½ of 12⅜ oz. pizza	430	41	18	21	1130	3 starch, 1 high fat meat, 2 fat
Hamburger	½ of 12¼ oz. pizza	410	40	21	18	1040	2½ starch, 2 meat, 1½ fat
Pepperoni	½ of 11¼ oz. pizza	390	41	17	18	1040	3 starch, 1 high fat meat, 2 fat
Sausage	½ of 12 oz. pizza	420	42	18	20	1080	3 starch, 1 high fat meat, 2 fat
Sausage and Mushroom	½ of 12½ oz. pizza	400	44	18	17	1160	3 starch, 1 high fat meat, 1½ fat

TOMBSTONE® (Tombstone Pizza)

PRODUCTS	SERVING SIZE	CALORIES	CARBO-HYDRATE (g.)	PROTEIN (g.)	FAT (g.)	SODIUM (mg.)	EXCHANGES
Canadian Bacon Pizza	¼ of 22 oz. pizza	328	45	20	8	920	3 starch, 1½ lean meat
Cheese Pizza	¼ of 20 oz. pizza	327	42	19	9	737	3 starch, 1½ meat

†For Occasional Use   **Not Recommended For Use   *Not Available   F More Than 2 Fat Exchanges   S Moderate To High Sugar Content

NUTRIENT VALUE

PRODUCTS	SERVING SIZE	CALORIES	CARBO-HYDRATE (g.)	PROTEIN (g.)	FAT (g.)	SODIUM (mg.)	EXCHANGES
Cheese and Hamburger Pizza	¼ of 22 oz. pizza	358	43	21	12	873	3 starch, 1½ meat
Cheese and Sausage Pizza	¼ of 22 oz. pizza	357	41	22	12	670	3 starch, 2 meat
Cheese, Sausage, Mushroom Pizza	¼ of 24 oz. pizza	357	41	21	12	834	3 starch, 2 meat
Combination Sausage Pizza	¼ of 22½ oz. pizza	374	42	22	14	762	3 starch, 2 meat
Smoked Sausage with Pepperoni Seasoning Pizza	¼ of 22 oz. pizza	365	42	23	12	764	3 starch, 2 meat
Special Deluxe Pizza	¼ of 24 oz. pizza	365	43	22	12	834	3 starch, 2 meat

TOTINO'S® (The Pillsbury Co.)
Extra!™ Pizza

PRODUCTS	SERVING SIZE	CALORIES	CARBO-HYDRATE (g.)	PROTEIN (g.)	FAT (g.)	SODIUM (mg.)	EXCHANGES
Cheese	¼ pizza	250	24	11	12	450	1½ starch, 1 meat, 1 fat
Combination	¼ pizza	290	25	11	16	800	1½ starch, 1 meat, 2 fat
Pepperoni	¼ pizza	260	24	10	14	700	1½ starch, 1 meat, 1½ fat
Sausage	¼ pizza	280	24	10	16	770	1½ starch, 1 meat, 2 fat

Microwave Pizza

PRODUCTS	SERVING SIZE	CALORIES	CARBO-HYDRATE (g.)	PROTEIN (g.)	FAT (g.)	SODIUM (mg.)	EXCHANGES
Cheese	3.9 oz.	250	31	11	9	630	2 starch, ½ meat, 1 fat
Pepperoni	4 oz.	290	31	10	14	1270	2 starch, ½ meat, 2 fat
Sausage	4.2 oz.	300	31	10	15	920	2 starch, ½ meat, 2 fat
Sausage/Pepperoni Combination	4.2 oz.	310	31	11	15	1090	2 starch, ½ meat, 2 fat

My Classic™ Pizza

PRODUCTS	SERVING SIZE	CALORIES	CARBO-HYDRATE (g.)	PROTEIN (g.)	FAT (g.)	SODIUM (mg.)	EXCHANGES
Canadian Style Bacon	¼ pizza	320	38	16	12	830	2½ starch, 1 meat, 1 fat
Deluxe Cheese	¼ pizza	350	39	15	15	810	2½ starch, 1 meat, 1½ fat
F Deluxe Combination	¼ pizza	460	40	18	25	1040	2½ starch, 1½ meat, 3 fat
Deluxe Pepperoni	¼ pizza	410	40	17	20	1090	2½ starch, 1½ meat, 2 fat

†For Occasional Use   **Not Recommended For Use   *Not Available   F More Than 2 Fat Exchanges   S Moderate To High Sugar Content

NUTRIENT VALUE

	PRODUCTS	SERVING SIZE	CALORIES	CARBO-HYDRATE (g.)	PROTEIN (g.)	FAT (g.)	SODIUM (mg.)	EXCHANGES
F	Deluxe Sausage	¼ pizza	440	41	16	24	980	3 starch, 1 meat, 3½ fat
	Party Pizza							
	Bacon	⅓ pizza	270	29	8	12	710	2 starch, ½ meat, 2 fat
	Canadian Style Bacon	⅓ pizza	230	28	10	8	670	2 starch, ½ meat, 1 fat
	Cheese	⅓ pizza	250	27	9	12	650	2 starch, ½ meat, 2 fat
	Hamburger	⅓ pizza	280	28	12	13	650	2 starch, 1 meat, 1½ fat
	Mexican Style	⅓ pizza	240	21	8	14	600	1½ starch, ½ meat, 2 fat
	Nacho	⅓ pizza	230	20	9	12	480	1 starch, 1 meat, 1½ fat
	Pepperoni	⅓ pizza	260	28	10	12	720	2 starch, ½ meat, 2 fat
	Sausage	⅓ pizza	270	28	10	13	780	2 starch, ½ meat, 2 fat
	Sausage and Pepperoni Combination	⅓ pizza	270	28	10	13	770	2 starch, ½ meat, 2 fat
	Vegetable	⅓ pizza	220	29	8	8	630	2 starch, ½ meat, 1 fat
	Pizza Slices							
	Cheese	⅙ package	170	20	7	7	350	1 starch, ½ meat, 1 fat
	Combination	⅙ package	200	20	7	10	630	1 starch, ½ meat, 1½ fat
	Pepperoni	⅙ package	190	20	7	9	530	1 starch, ½ meat, 1½ fat
	Sausage	⅙ package	200	20	7	10	540	1 starch, ½ meat, 1½ fat

WEIGHT WATCHERS® (Foodways National, Inc.)

	PRODUCTS	SERVING SIZE	CALORIES	CARBO-HYDRATE (g.)	PROTEIN (g.)	FAT (g.)	SODIUM (mg.)	EXCHANGES
	Pizza							
	Cheese	6 oz.	350	37	20	14	670	2 starch, 1 veg., 2 meat, ½ fat
	Deluxe Combination	7¼ oz.	350	42	20	11	690	2½ starch, 1 veg., 1½ meat, ½ fat

†For Occasional Use   **Not Recommended For Use   *Not Available   F More Than 2 Fat Exchanges   S Moderate To High Sugar Content

NUTRIENT VALUE

PRODUCTS	SERVING SIZE	CALORIES	CARBO-HYDRATE (g.)	PROTEIN (g.)	FAT (g.)	SODIUM (mg.)	EXCHANGES
Pepperoni	6¼ oz.	340	39	20	12	610	2 starch, 1 veg., 2 meat
Veal Sausage	6¾ oz.	350	35	24	12	940	2 starch, 1 veg., 2 meat

QUICHE
MRS. SMITH'S® (Mrs. Smith's Frozen Foods, A Kellogg Company)

PRODUCTS	SERVING SIZE	CALORIES	CARBO-HYDRATE (g.)	PROTEIN (g.)	FAT (g.)	SODIUM (mg.)	EXCHANGES
Mushroom Quiche	9½ oz.	595	57	24	30	1565	3½ starch, 1 veg., 2 high fat meat, 2 fat
F Quiche Florentine	9½ oz.	625	53	27	34	1800	3 starch, 1 veg., 2 high fat meat, 3 fat
F Quiche Lorraine	9½ oz.	720	54	34	41	1965	3½ starch, 3 high fat meat, 3 fat

POUR-A-QUICHE® (Land O' Lakes, Inc.)

PRODUCTS	SERVING SIZE	CALORIES	CARBO-HYDRATE (g.)	PROTEIN (g.)	FAT (g.)	SODIUM (mg.)	EXCHANGES
Quiche, mix only, all varieties (average)	4⅓ oz.	230	5	13	18	360-385	1 veg., 1½ high fat meat, 1 fat

TURKEY
LAND O'LAKES® (Land O'Lakes, Inc.)

PRODUCTS	SERVING SIZE	CALORIES	CARBO-HYDRATE (g.)	PROTEIN (g.)	FAT (g.)	SODIUM (mg.)	EXCHANGES
Turkey Breast Fillets with Cheese	5 oz.	300	16	25	16	835	1 starch, 3 lean meat, 1 fat
Turkey Ham	3 oz.	100	2	18	2	845	2½ lean meat
Turkey Patties	2¼ oz.	170	10	8	11	330	½ starch, 1 lean meat, 1½ fat
Turkey Rolls (average)	3 oz.	110	2	14	5	510-560	2 lean meat
Turkey Sticks	2 sticks (2 oz.)	150	9	7	10	295	½ starch, 1 lean meat, 1½ fat

LOUIS RICH™ (Oscar Mayer and Co.)

PRODUCTS	SERVING SIZE	CALORIES	CARBO-HYDRATE (g.)	PROTEIN (g.)	FAT (g.)	SODIUM (mg.)	EXCHANGES
Breast of Turkey, barbecued, roasted, or smoked (average)	2 oz.	75	1	12	2	460-630	2 lean meat
Turkey Franks (10/1 lb.)	1 frank	105	1	6	9	480	1 high fat meat

†For Occasional Use   **Not Recommended For Use   *Not Available   F More Than 2 Fat Exchanges   S Moderate To High Sugar Content

NUTRIENT VALUE

PRODUCTS	SERVING SIZE	CALORIES	CARBO-HYDRATE (g.)	PROTEIN (g.)	FAT (g.)	SODIUM (mg.)	EXCHANGES
Turkey Cheese Franks	1 frank	110	2	6	9	510	1 high fat meat
Turkey Ham (average)	2 oz.	70	1	10	3	550-560	1½ lean meat
Luncheon Meats (average)							
Turkey Bologna	1 oz.	60	1	4	5	225	½ high fat meat
Turkey Luncheon Loaf	1 oz.	45	0	5	3	280	½ meat
Turkey Salami	1 oz.	50	0	5	4	245-255	½ lean meat, ½ fat
Sausage							
Turkey Breakfast Sausage	1 oz.	60	0	6	4	200	1 lean meat
Turkey Smoked Sausage	1 oz.	55	0	5	4	230	½ lean meat, ½ fat
Turkey Summer Sausage	1 oz.	50	0	5	4	310	½ lean meat, ½ fat
Turkey Pastrami	2 oz.	70	0	11	2	550	1½ lean meat

VEGETARIAN
LOMA LINDA® (Loma Linda Foods)
Canned Products

PRODUCTS	SERVING SIZE	CALORIES	CARBO-HYDRATE (g.)	PROTEIN (g.)	FAT (g.)	SODIUM (mg.)	EXCHANGES
Dinner Cuts, 145 & 150	2 cuts (3.5 oz.)	110	4	21	1	550	3 lean meat
Dinner Cuts, 154	1½ cuts (3.5 oz.)	110	4	21	1	550	3 lean meat
Dinner Cuts, 151, No Salt Added	2 cuts (3.5 oz.)	110	4	21	1	30	3 lean meat
Linketts	2 links (2.6 oz.)	150	5	15	8	340	2 meat
Little Links	2 links (1.6 oz.)	80	2	8	5	210	1 meat
Meatless Big Franks	1 frank (1.8 oz.)	100	4	10	5	220	1½ lean meat
Meatless Fried Chicken with Gravy	2 pieces (3 oz.)	140	4	9	10	340	1 meat, 1 fat
Meatless Redi Burger	½" slice (2.4 oz.)	130	5	14	6	370	2 lean meat

†For Occasional Use   **Not Recommended For Use   *Not Available   Ⓕ More Than 2 Fat Exchanges   Ⓢ Moderate To High Sugar Content

NUTRIENT VALUE

PRODUCTS	SERVING SIZE	CALORIES	CARBO-HYDRATE (g.)	PROTEIN (g.)	FAT (g.)	SODIUM (mg.)	EXCHANGES
Meatless Sizzle Franks	2 franks (2.4 oz.)	170	3	10	13	340	1½ meat, 1 fat
Meatless Swiss Steak with Gravy	1 steak (2.6 oz.)	140	8	9	8	350	½ starch, 1 lean meat, 1 fat
Nuteena 090, 095	½" slice (2.4 oz.)	160	5	8	12	120	1 high fat meat, 1 fat
Proteena 110	½" slice (2.5 oz.)	140	5	17	6	460	2½ lean meat
Sandwich Spread	3 Tbsp.	70	4	4	4	300	1 veg., 1 fat
Stew Pac	2 oz.	70	4	10	2	220	1½ lean meat
Tastee Cuts	2 cuts (2.5 oz.)	70	2	12	1	230	2 lean meat
Tender Bits	4 pieces (2 oz.)	80	4	8	3	340	1 lean meat
Tender Rounds with Gravy	6 meatballs	120	7	15	4	310	½ starch, 2 lean meat
Vege-Burger	½ cup (3.8 oz.)	110	4	22	1	190	2 lean meat
Vege-Burger, No Salt Added	½ cup (3.8 oz.)	140	4	27	2	55	4 lean meat
Vege-Scallops	6 pieces (2.75 oz.)	70	2	14	1	180	1½ lean meat
Dry Pack Products Meatless Chicken Supreme (dry mix)	¼ cup	50	4	9	1	450	1 lean meat
Meatless Vita-burger Chunks (dry mix)	¼ cup	70	7	10	<1	150	½ starch, 1 lean meat
Meatless Vita-burger Granules (dry mix)	3 Tbsp.	70	7	10	<1	150	½ starch, 1 lean meat
Ocean Platter (dry mix)	¼ cup	50	5	8	<1	260	1 lean meat
Patty Mix (dry mix)	¼ cup	50	4	9	<1	320	1 lean meat
Savory Dinner Loaf (dry mix)	¼ cup	50	4	9	<1	380	1 lean meat

†For Occasional Use   **Not Recommended For Use   *Not Available   F More Than 2 Fat Exchanges   S Moderate To High Sugar Content

NUTRIENT VALUE

PRODUCTS	SERVING SIZE	CALORIES	CARBO-HYDRATE (g.)	PROTEIN (g.)	FAT (g.)	SODIUM (mg.)	EXCHANGES
Frozen Products							
Chik-Nuggets	5 pieces (3 oz.)	230	15	14	13	640	1 starch, 1½ meat, 1 fat
Chik-Patties	1 patty (3 oz.)	230	15	14	13	640	1 starch, 1½ meat, 1 fat
Corn Dogs	1 dog (2.5 oz.)	200	21	7	10	620	1½ starch, ½ high fat meat, 1 fat
Meatless Bologna	2 slices (20 oz.)	150	5	14	9	490	2 meat
Meatless Chicken	2 slices (2 oz.)	160	1	10	13	330	1½ meat, 1 fat
Meatless Fried Chicken	1 piece (2 oz.)	180	2	13	14	510	2 meat, 1 fat
Meatless Roast Beef	2 slices (2 oz.)	150	2	11	11	670	1½ meat, ½ fat
Meatless Salami	2 slices (2 oz.)	130	2	13	7	640	2 lean meat
Meatless Sizzle Burger	1 burger (2.5 oz.)	210	13	15	11	320	1 starch, 2 meat
Meatless Swedish Meatballs	8 pieces (2.5 oz.)	190	7	22	8	420	½ starch, 3 lean meat
Meatless Turkey	¼" slice (2 oz.)	160	3	10	12	1350	1½ meat, 1 fat
Ocean Fillet	1 fillet (1.7 oz.)	130	4	11	8	230	2 meat

†For Occasional Use   **Not Recommended For Use   *Not Available   Ⓕ More Than 2 Fat Exchanges   Ⓢ Moderate To High Sugar Content

Fats

NUTRIENT VALUE

PRODUCTS	SERVING SIZE	CALORIES	CARBO-HYDRATE (g.)	PROTEIN (g.)	FAT (g.)	SODIUM (mg.)	EXCHANGES
BAC★OS® (General Mills, Inc.)							
Bac★Os®	2 tsp.	20	1	2	1	87	Free
BLUE BONNET® (Nabisco Brands, Inc.)							
Butter Blend, soft or stick	1½ tsp.	45	0	0	5	48	1 fat
Diet Margarine	1 Tbsp.	50	0	0	6	100	1 fat
Light Tasty Spread (52% Vegetable Oil)	2 tsp.	40	0	0	5	68	1 fat
Spread (52% fat)	2 tsp.	54	0	0	5	74	1 fat
Spread Stick (70-75% fat)	1½ tsp.	45	0	0	5	48	1 fat
Whipped Margarine	2 tsp.	47	0	0	5	47	1 fat
Whipped Spread (60% fat)	1 Tbsp.	50	0	0	6	55	1 fat
CARNATION® (Calreco®, Inc.)							
Coffee-Mate	1 packet	16	2	0	1	4	Free
CHIFFON® (Gaines Foods, Inc.)							
Soft Margarine	1 Tbsp.	90	0	0	10	105	2 fat
Soft Unsalted Margarine	1 Tbsp.	90	0	0	10	<10	2 fat
Soft Whipped Margarine	1 Tbsp.	70	0	0	8	80	1½ fat

†For Occasional Use   **Not Recommended For Use   *Not Available   Ⓕ More Than 2 Fat Exchanges   Ⓢ Moderate To High Sugar Content

NUTRIENT VALUE

PRODUCTS	SERVING SIZE	CALORIES	CARBO-HYDRATE (g.)	PROTEIN (g.)	FAT (g.)	SODIUM (mg.)	EXCHANGES
Stick Margarine	1 Tbsp.	100	0	0	11	110	2 fat
COUNTRY MORNING BLEND® (Land O'Lakes, Inc.)							
Margarine, all varieties (average)	1 Tbsp.	100	0	0	10	85-115	2 fat
DIA-MEL® (Estee Corp.)							
Mayonnaise, Dietetic	1 Tbsp.	106	0	0	11	22	2 fat
DURKEE® (Durkee Famous Foods)							
Bacon Chips	1 tsp.	15	1	1	1	93	Free
Imitation Bacon Bits	1 tsp.	8	1	1	0	229	Free
FLEISHMANN'S® (Nabisco Brands, Inc.)							
Light Corn Oil Spread	2 tsp.	54	0	0	5	47	1 fat
Liquid Corn Oil	1 tsp.	40	0	0	5	0	1 fat
Margarine							
Diet	1 Tbsp.	50	0	0	6	100	1 fat
Soft	1½ tsp.	50	0	0	6	48	1 fat
Squeeze	1½ tsp.	50	0	0	6	43	1 fat
Stick	1½ tsp.	50	0	0	6	48	1 fat
Whipped	2 tsp.	47	0	0	5	40	1 fat
HORMEL® (George A. Hormel and Co.)							
Bacon Bits	2 tsp.	20	0	2	1	210	Free
LAND O'LAKES® (Land O'Lakes, Inc.)							
Butter							
Sweet Cream	1 Tbsp.	100	0	0	11	115	2 fat
Whipped	1 Tbsp.	60	0	0	7	75	1½ fat
Lean Cream™	1 Tbsp.	20	2	1	1	20	Free
Margarine, all varieties (average)	1 Tbsp.	100	0	0	11	115	2 fat
MAZOLA® (Best Foods, CPC International)							
Diet Mazola, reduced calorie margarine	1 Tbsp.	50	0	0	6	130	1 fat
Margarine	1 Tbsp.	100	0	0	11	100	2 fat

†For Occasional Use   **Not Recommended For Use   *Not Available   Ⓕ More Than 2 Fat Exchanges   Ⓢ Moderate To High Sugar Content

NUTRIENT VALUE

PRODUCTS	SERVING SIZE	CALORIES	CARBO-HYDRATE (g.)	PROTEIN (g.)	FAT (g.)	SODIUM (mg.)	EXCHANGES
No-Stick vegetable spray coating	2.5 second spray	6	0	0	1	0	Free
MIRACLE® (Kraft, Inc.)							
Margarine	2 tsp.	40	0	0	5	50	1 fat
NUCOA® (Best Foods, CPC International)							
Margarine	1 Tbsp.	100	0	0	11	160	2 fat
Soft Margarine	1 Tbsp.	90	0	0	10	150	2 fat
OLD HOME® (Old Home® Foods, Inc.)							
Sour Cream	2 Tbsp.	60	2	2	4	16	1 fat
Sour Lean	1 Tbsp.	20	1	1	1	8	Free
PARKAY® (Kraft, Inc.)							
Corn Oil Margarine, stick or soft (average)	1 tsp.	34	0	0	4	39	1 fat
Light Corn Oil Spread	2 tsp.	47	0	0	5	74	1 fat
Light Spread (50% fat)	2 tsp.	40	0	0	5	74	1 fat
Margarine, stick or soft (average)	1 tsp.	34	0	0	4	39	1 fat
Soft Diet, Reduced Calorie Margarine	1 Tbsp.	50	0	0	6	110	1 fat
Squeeze® Margarine	1 tsp.	34	0	0	4	34	1 fat
Whipped Margarine (cup or stick)	2 tsp.	40	0	0	5	50	1 fat
PHILADELPHIA BRAND® (Kraft, Inc.)							
Cream Cheese, regular, whipped, or soft, all varieties (average)	1 oz.	90-100	2	2	9	75-160	2 fat

†For Occasional Use   **Not Recommended For Use   *Not Available   Ⓕ More Than 2 Fat Exchanges   Ⓢ Moderate To High Sugar Content

Jams, Jellies, Preserves

NUTRIENT VALUE

PRODUCTS	SERVING SIZE	CALORIES	CARBO-HYDRATE (g.)	PROTEIN (g.)	FAT (g.)	SODIUM (mg.)	EXCHANGES
DIA-MEL® (Estee Corp.)							
Preserves and Jellies, Dietetic, all varieties (average)	1 tsp.	2	0	0	0	<1	Free
FEATHERWEIGHT® (Sandoz Nutrition)							
Low Calorie Jellies and Preserves, artificially sweetened, all varieties (average)	1 Tbsp.	6	1	0	0	7-16	Free
Reduced Calorie Jellies and Preserves, saccharin free, all varieties (average)	1 Tbsp.	16	4	0	0	6-50	Free
KRAFT® (Kraft, Inc.)							
Jams, Jellies, Preserves, all varieties (average)	1 tsp.	16	4	0	0	0	Free
Reduced Calorie Grape Jelly	1 tsp.	6	2	0	0	5	Free
Reduced Calorie Strawberry Preserves	1 tsp.	8	2	0	0	5	Free

†For Occasional Use   **Not Recommended For Use   *Not Available   Ⓕ More Than 2 Fat Exchanges   Ⓢ Moderate To High Sugar Content

NUTRIENT VALUE

PRODUCTS	SERVING SIZE	CALORIES	CARBO-HYDRATE (g.)	PROTEIN (g.)	FAT (g.)	SODIUM (mg.)	EXCHANGES
NUTRADIET® (S and W Fine Foods)							
Reduced Calorie Jams, Jellies, Preserves, all varieties (average)	1 tsp.	4	1	0	0	*	Free
WELCH® (Welch Foods)							
Ⓢ Jam, Jellies, Preserves, all varieties (average)	2 tsp.	35	9	0	0	5	½ fruit†

†For Occasional Use   **Not Recommended For Use   *Not Available   Ⓕ More Than 2 Fat Exchanges   Ⓢ Moderate To High Sugar Content

Nuts, Seeds

NUTRIENT VALUE

PRODUCTS	SERVING SIZE	CALORIES	CARBO-HYDRATE (g.)	PROTEIN (g.)	FAT (g.)	SODIUM (mg.)	EXCHANGES
FISHER® (Fisher Nut Co.)							
Almonds, dry or oil roasted, salted (average)	1 oz.	175	5	5	16	45-56	1 meat, 2 fat
F Brazil Nuts, roasted, salted	1 oz.	195	3	4	25	57	½ meat, 4½ fat
F Cashews, dry or oil roasted, salted (average)	1 oz.	158	8	5	13	57	½ starch, ½ meat, 2½ fat
F Filberts, oil dipped, salted	1 oz.	180	5	4	18	57	½ meat, 3 fat
Peanuts, dry or oil roasted, salted (average)	1 oz.	165	5	7	14	100-120	1 meat, 2 fat
F Pecans, oil dipped or dry roasted, salted (average)	1 oz.	195	4	3	22	60-100	½ meat, 4 fat
F Pistachios, shelled, roasted, salted	1 oz.	174	5	6	20	100	1 meat, 3 fat
Pistachios in Shell, roasted, salted	1 oz.	84	3	3	8	50	½ meat, 1 fat

†For Occasional Use   **Not Recommended For Use   *Not Available   F More Than 2 Fat Exchanges   S Moderate To High Sugar Content

NUTRIENT VALUE

PRODUCTS	SERVING SIZE	CALORIES	CARBO-HYDRATE (g.)	PROTEIN (g.)	FAT (g.)	SODIUM (mg.)	EXCHANGES
Sunflower Seeds in Shell, roasted, salted	1 oz.	86	3	4	6	58	½ meat, ½ fat
Sunflower Seeds, shelled, dry or oil roasted, salted (average)	1 oz.	165	6	7	16	108	1 meat, 2 fat
Walnuts, Black or English, raw (average)	1 oz.	180	3	5	17	1	1 meat, 2 fat

PLANTERS® (Nabisco Brands, Inc.)

PRODUCTS	SERVING SIZE	CALORIES	CARBO-HYDRATE (g.)	PROTEIN (g.)	FAT (g.)	SODIUM (mg.)	EXCHANGES
Almonds							
Dry roasted	1 oz.	170	6	6	15	200	1 meat, 2 fat
Smoked	1 oz.	170	5	6	15	160	1 meat, 2 fat
Cashews							
Dry roasted	1 oz.	160	5	9	13	230	1 meat, 1½ fat
Honey roasted	1 oz.	170	11	4	12	170	½ fruit, ½ meat, 2 fat
Oil roasted	1 oz.	170	8	5	14	135	1 meat, 2 fat
Unsalted dry roasted	1 oz.	160	5	9	13	0	1 meat, 1½ fat
Fruit 'n Nut Mix	1 oz.	150	13	5	9	90	1 fruit, ½ meat, 1 fat
Mixed Nuts							
Dry roasted	1 oz.	160	7	5	14	270	1 meat, 2 fat
Oil roasted	1 oz.	180	5	6	16	130	1 meat, 2 fat
Peanuts							
Dry roasted	1 oz.	160	6	7	14	250	1 meat, 2 fat
Dry roasted lite	1 oz.	135	8	9	9	270	1 meat, 1 fat
Honey roasted	1 oz.	170	8	6	13	180	1 meat, 1½ fat
Oil roasted	1 oz.	170	5	7	15	160	1 meat, 2 fat
Red skin, oil roasted	1 oz.	170	5	7	15	150	1 meat, 2 fat
Spanish, dry roasted	1 oz.	160	6	7	14	200	1 meat, 2 fat
Spanish, oil roasted	1 oz.	170	5	7	15	150	1 meat, 2 fat
Pistachios							
Dry roasted	1 oz.	170	6	5	15	250	1 meat, 2 fat

†For Occasional Use **Not Recommended For Use *Not Available F More Than 2 Fat Exchanges S Moderate To High Sugar Content

NUTRIENT VALUE

PRODUCTS	SERVING SIZE	CALORIES	CARBO-HYDRATE (g.)	PROTEIN (g.)	FAT (g.)	SODIUM (mg.)	EXCHANGES
Sesame Nut Mix							
Dry roasted	1 oz.	160	8	5	12	330	1 meat, 1½ fat
Oil roasted	1 oz.	160	8	5	13	220	1 meat, 2 fat
Sunflower Nuts							
Dry roasted	1 oz.	160	5	7	14	260	1 meat, 2 fat
Oil roasted	1 oz.	170	5	6	15	190	1 meat, 2 fat
Sunflower Seeds	1 oz.	160	5	7	14	30	1 meat, 2 fat

†For Occasional Use   **Not Recommended For Use   *Not Available   Ⓕ More Than 2 Fat Exchanges   Ⓢ Moderate To High Sugar Content

Salad Dressings, Sauces, Gravies

NUTRIENT VALUE

PRODUCTS	SERVING SIZE	CALORIES	CARBO-HYDRATE (g.)	PROTEIN (g.)	FAT (g.)	SODIUM (mg.)	EXCHANGES
DRESSINGS, SANDWICH SPREADS							
CATALINA® (Kraft, Inc.)							
French Dressing	2 tsp.	47	3	0	4	121	1 fat
Reduced Calorie Dressing	1 Tbsp.	16	3	0	0	125	Free
DIA-MEL® (Estee Corp.)							
Salad Dressings, Dietetic, all varieties (average)	1 Tbsp.	1-2	<1	0	0	5-35	Free
DURKEE WEIGHT WATCHER® (Durkee Famous Foods)							
Salad Dressing Mixes, all varieties (as prepared) (average)	1 Tbsp.	2-6	0-1	0	0	110-270	Free
ESTEE® (Estee Corp.)							
Salad Dressings, Dietetic, all varieties (average)	1 Tbsp.	4-6	1-2	0	0	80-150	Free
FEATHERWEIGHT® (Sandoz Nutrition)							
Soyamaise, Low Sodium	1 Tbsp.	60	0	0	11	3	2 fat

†For Occasional Use   **Not Recommended For Use   *Not Available   F More Than 2 Fat Exchanges   S Moderate To High Sugar Content

NUTRIENT VALUE

PRODUCTS	SERVING SIZE	CALORIES	CARBO-HYDRATE (g.)	PROTEIN (g.)	FAT (g.)	SODIUM (mg.)	EXCHANGES
Low Calorie Dressings (average) 2 Calorie, Low Sodium Herb, Low Sodium Italian New Bleu Red Wine/Vinegar Russian	1 Tbsp.	2-6	1-2	0	0	5-134	Free
Creamy Caesar, Low Sodium Creamy Cucumber/Onion, Low Sodium French Style Thousand Island	1 Tbsp.	12-18	2-3	0	0-1	12-70	Free

GOOD SEASONS® (General Foods Corp.)

PRODUCTS	SERVING SIZE	CALORIES	CARBO-HYDRATE (g.)	PROTEIN (g.)	FAT (g.)	SODIUM (mg.)	EXCHANGES
Salad Dressing Mix, all varieties except Lite Italian (as prepared) (average)	1 Tbsp.	80	1	0	9	135-190	2 fat
Salad Dressing Mix, Lite Italian, all varieties (average)	2 Tbsp.	50	2	0	6	360	1 fat
Salad Dressing Mix, No Oil Italian (as prepared)	2 Tbsp.	12	4	0	0	60	Free

HEALTH VALLEY® (Health Valley Foods)

PRODUCTS	SERVING SIZE	CALORIES	CARBO-HYDRATE (g.)	PROTEIN (g.)	FAT (g.)	SODIUM (mg.)	EXCHANGES
Soy Mayonnaise	1 Tbsp.	99	0	0	11	78	2 fat

HELLMAN'S® (Best Foods, CPC International, Inc.)

PRODUCTS	SERVING SIZE	CALORIES	CARBO-HYDRATE (g.)	PROTEIN (g.)	FAT (g.)	SODIUM (mg.)	EXCHANGES
Real Mayonnaise	1 tsp.	35	0	0	4	27	1 fat
Sandwich Spred	1 Tbsp.	50	2	0	5	170	1 fat

HENRI'S® (Henri's Food Products Company, Inc.)

PRODUCTS	SERVING SIZE	CALORIES	CARBO-HYDRATE (g.)	PROTEIN (g.)	FAT (g.)	SODIUM (mg.)	EXCHANGES
Salad Dressings Blue Cheese	1 Tbsp.	60	3	0	5	*	1 fat
Buttermilk Farm	1 Tbsp.	80	2	0	8	*	1½ fat
Creamy Italian	1 Tbsp.	50	3	0	5	*	1 fat
Cucumber 'n Onion	1 Tbsp.	35	4	0	2	*	1 veg.
French	1 Tbsp.	60	3	0	6	*	1 fat
Frontier French	1 Tbsp.	70	5	0	6	*	1 fat

†For Occasional Use   **Not Recommended For Use   *Not Available   F More Than 2 Fat Exchanges   S Moderate To High Sugar Content

NUTRIENT VALUE

PRODUCTS	SERVING SIZE	CALORIES	CARBO-HYDRATE (g.)	PROTEIN (g.)	FAT (g.)	SODIUM (mg.)	EXCHANGES
Sweet 'n Tart	1 Tbsp.	30	6	0	1	*	½ fruit
Tas-tee	1 Tbsp.	50	4	0	4	*	1 fat
Yogo Blue Cheese, reduced calorie	1 Tbsp.	30	4	0	2	*	1 veg.
Yogo French Style, reduced calorie	1 Tbsp.	40	6	0	2	*	½ fruit

HIDDEN VALLEY RANCH® (The Clorox Company)

PRODUCTS	SERVING SIZE	CALORIES	CARBO-HYDRATE (g.)	PROTEIN (g.)	FAT (g.)	SODIUM (mg.)	EXCHANGES
Bottled Salad Dressings, all varieties (average)	1 Tbsp. **or** 2 tsp.	80 / 53	0 / 0	0 / 0	8 / 5	115-160 / 76-106	1½ fat / 1 fat
Salad Dressing Mixes, all varieties (as prepared with milk and mayonnaise) (average)	1 Tbsp.	55	1	0	6	97-117	1 fat
Salad Dressing Mixes, all varieties (as prepared with milk and salad dressing) (average)	1 Tbsp.	36	2	0	3	99-119	½ fat

KRAFT® (Kraft, Inc.)

PRODUCTS	SERVING SIZE	CALORIES	CARBO-HYDRATE (g.)	PROTEIN (g.)	FAT (g.)	SODIUM (mg.)	EXCHANGES
Coleslaw Dressing	1 Tbsp.	70	4	0	6	200	1 fat
Mayonnaise	1 Tbsp.	100	0	0	11	70	2 fat
Mayonnaise, Light Reduced Calorie	1 Tbsp.	45	1	0	5	90	1 fat
Salad Dressings Reduced Calorie Dressings, all varieties (except Italian Reduced Calorie Dressing) (average)	1 Tbsp.	30	2	0	2	120-280	½ fat
Italian Reduced Calorie Dressing	1 Tbsp.	6	1	0	0	210	Free
Salad Dressings, all varieties (except Oil-Free Italian) (average)	2 tsp.	50	1	0	5	63-188	1 fat
Oil-Free Italian Dressing	1 Tbsp.	4	1	0	0	210	Free

†For Occasional Use   **Not Recommended For Use   *Not Available   F More Than 2 Fat Exchanges   S Moderate To High Sugar Content

NUTRIENT VALUE

PRODUCTS	SERVING SIZE	CALORIES	CARBO-HYDRATE (g.)	PROTEIN (g.)	FAT (g.)	SODIUM (mg.)	EXCHANGES
Sandwich Spread	1 Tbsp.	50	3	0	5	95	1 fat
MIRACLE WHIP® (Kraft, Inc.)							
Light Reduced Calorie Salad Dressing	1 Tbsp.	45	2	0	4	95	1 fat
Salad Dressing	2 tsp.	46	1	0	5	57	1 fat
NUTRADIET® (S and W Fine Foods)							
Mayonnaise, reduced calorie	2 tsp.	17	1	0	2	75	Free
Salad Dressings, reduced calorie (average) Creamy Italian No-Oil Italian	1 Tbsp.	2-10	0-1	0	0-1	176-288	Free
1000 Island Blue Cheese Creamy Cucumber French Style Russian	2 tsp.	17	2-4	0	1-2	106-196	Free
PHILADELPHIA BRAND® (Kraft, Inc.)							
Salad Dressing, all varieties (average)	2 tsp.	46	1	0	5	77-107	1 fat
PRESTO® (Kraft, Inc.)							
Italian Dressing	2 tsp.	46	1	0	5	100	1 fat
RICHELIEU (Western Dressings, Inc.)							
Deluxe Coleslaw Dressing	1 Tbsp.	65	3	0	6	160	1 fat
Salad Dressings (average) 1000 Island, Whipped French Oil and Vinegar Russian Western	1 Tbsp.	60	3	0	5	50-165	1 fat
Salad Dressings, Creamy (average) Bacon Cucumber French Garlic Italian	1 Tbsp.	50-60	3	0	5-6	105-210	1 fat

†For Occasional Use   **Not Recommended For Use   *Not Available   Ⓕ More Than 2 Fat Exchanges   Ⓢ Moderate To High Sugar Content

NUTRIENT VALUE

PRODUCTS	SERVING SIZE	CALORIES	CARBO-HYDRATE (g.)	PROTEIN (g.)	FAT (g.)	SODIUM (mg.)	EXCHANGES
Salad Dressings, reduced calorie (average) 1000 Island Creamy Italian French Oil and Vinegar Western	1 Tbsp.	25	4	0	1	90-160	½ fat
ROKA (Kraft, Inc.) Blue Cheese Dressing	2 tsp.	40	1	1	4	114	1 fat
Blue Cheese Reduced Calorie Dressing	1 Tbsp.	14	1	1	1	280	Free
SEVEN SEAS® (Gaines Foods, Inc.) Salad Dressings (average) Buttermilk Recipe Capri Chunky Blue Cheese Creamy Bacon Creamy French Creamy Italian Creamy Parmesan Creamy Russian Green Goddess Herbs and Spices Mild Italian Red Wine Vinegar and Oil Thousand Island Viva Italian Viva Parmesan	1 Tbsp. **or** 2 tsp.	70 46	1 0	0 0	7 5	Varies Varies	1½ fat 1 fat
WEIGHT WATCHERS® (Nutrition Industries Corp.) Reduced Calorie Mayonnaise	1 Tbsp.	40	1	0	4	80	1 fat
Reduced Calorie Salad Dressing	1 Tbsp.	35	3	0	3	80	½ fat
Salad Dressings Creamy Italian	1 Tbsp.	50	2	0	5	80	1 fat
French Style	1 Tbsp.	10	2	0	0	170	Free
Thousand Island	1 Tbsp.	50	2	0	5	80	1 fat
Tomato Vinaigrette	1 Tbsp.	8	2	0	0	180	Free

†For Occasional Use   **Not Recommended For Use   *Not Available   Ⓕ More Than 2 Fat Exchanges   Ⓢ Moderate To High Sugar Content

PRODUCTS	SERVING SIZE	CALORIES	CARBO-HYDRATE (g.)	PROTEIN (g.)	FAT (g.)	SODIUM (mg.)	EXCHANGES
WISH-BONE® (Thomas J. Lipton, Inc.)							
Dressings, all varieties except Deluxe, French, and Russian (average)	2 tsp.	50	1	0	5	*	1 fat
Deluxe, French, and Russian Dressings	1 Tbsp.	50	2	0	5	80-140	1 fat
Lite Dressings, reduced calorie (average)							
Russian	2 tsp.	17	3	0	<1	94	Free

Creamy Italian
  French Style
  Italian
  Sweet 'n Spicy
	1 Tbsp.	30	2	0	3	70-210	½ fat

Buttermilk
  Chunky Blue Cheese
  Creamy Cucumber
  Onion 'n Chive
  Thousand Island
	1 Tbsp.	40	2	0	4	110-190	1 fat

PIZZA SAUCES AND SPAGHETTI SAUCES

PRODUCTS	SERVING SIZE	CALORIES	CARBO-HYDRATE (g.)	PROTEIN (g.)	FAT (g.)	SODIUM (mg.)	EXCHANGES
APPIAN WAY® (Armour-Dial, Inc.)							
Pizza Topping	3 oz.	50	8	0	4	370	½ fruit, 1 fat
CHEF BOY-AR-DEE® (American Home Foods)							
Pizza Sauce with Cheese	2½ oz.	70	7	1	4	385	½ starch, 1 fat
Pizza Sauce with Sausage **or** Pepperoni Slices (average)	2½ oz.	100	6	3	7	510-600	1 veg., 1½ fat
Portovista Sauce, Regular	3½ oz.	60	11	1	1	720	2 veg.
Portovista Sauce with Meat	3½ oz.	60	10	1	2	715	2 veg.
Portovista Sauce with Mushrooms	3½ oz.	60	11	1	1	760	2 veg.
Spaghetti Sauce, Meatless	½ cup	60	12	1	1	660	1 starch
Spaghetti Sauce with Ground Beef	½ cup	90	14	2	3	605	1 starch, ½ fat

†For Occasional Use   **Not Recommended For Use   *Not Available   Ⓕ More Than 2 Fat Exchanges   Ⓢ Moderate To High Sugar Content

NUTRIENT VALUE

PRODUCTS	SERVING SIZE	CALORIES	CARBO-HYDRATE (g.)	PROTEIN (g.)	FAT (g.)	SODIUM (mg.)	EXCHANGES
Spaghetti Sauce with Meat	½ cup	80	11	2	3	755	2 veg., ½ fat
Spaghetti Sauce with Mushrooms	½ cup	70	14	1	1	650	1 starch
DIA-MEL® (Estee Corp.) Spaghetti Sauce, Dietetic	½ cup	70	13	2	2	30	1 starch
DURKEE® (Durkee Famous Foods) Spaghetti Sauce Dry Mix (as prepared)	½ cup	45	10	1	0	787	2 veg. **or** ½ starch
Spaghetti Sauce with Mushrooms (as prepared)	½ cup	40	10	1	0	620	2 veg. **or** ½ starch
Extra Thick and Rich Spaghetti Sauce Mix (as prepared)	½ cup	48	11	2	0	416	2 veg. **or** ½ starch
FEATHERWEIGHT® (Sandoz Nutrition) Spaghetti Sauce, Low Sodium	⅓ cup	50	9	1	1	44	2 veg. **or** ½ starch
NUTRADIET® (S and W Fine Foods) Spaghetti Sauce, Low Sodium	½ cup	50	9	2	2	30	½ starch **or** 2 veg.
PREGO® (Campbell Soup Co.) Spaghetti Sauce, Plain, Meat Flavor, or with Mushrooms (average)	½ cup	140	21	2	5	640-680	1½ starch, 1 fat
Spaghetti Sauce, No Salt Added	½ cup	100	10	2	6	25	½ starch, 1 fat
Prego Plus, all varieties (average)	½ cup	160	20	4	7	380-480	1 starch, 1 veg., 1 fat
RAGÚ® (Chesebrough-Ponds, Inc.) Marinara Sauce (spaghetti sauce)	4 oz.	90	12	2	4	740	2 veg., 1 fat **or** 1 starch, ½ fat
Pizza Quick Sauce (average) Regular, all varieties	¼ cup	55	5	2	3	400-440	1 veg., ½ fat

†For Occasional Use   **Not Recommended For Use   *Not Available   Ⓕ More Than 2 Fat Exchanges   Ⓢ Moderate To High Sugar Content

NUTRIENT VALUE

PRODUCTS	SERVING SIZE	CALORIES	CARBO-HYDRATE (g.)	PROTEIN (g.)	FAT (g.)	SODIUM (mg.)	EXCHANGES
Chunky, all varieties	¼ cup	60	8	1	3	426	½ starch, ½ fat
Spaghetti Sauce Plain	½ cup	80	11	2	3	740	2 veg., ½ fat
Flavored with Meat	½ cup	80	11	2	2	740	2 veg., ½ fat
With Mushrooms	½ cup	90	9	2	4	740	2 veg., 1 fat
With Extra Cheese	½ cup	80	11	2	3	570	2 veg., ½ fat
Chunky Gardenstyle, all varieties (average)	½ cup	80	14	2	2	400	1 starch
Extra Thick and Zesty Plain	½ cup	100	15	2	4	740	1 starch, ½ fat
Extra Thick and Zesty, Flavored with Meat	½ cup	100	14	2	4	740	1 starch, ½ fat
Extra Thick and Zesty with Mushrooms	½ cup	110	13	2	5	740	1 starch, 1 fat
Homestyle, Plain and with Mushrooms	½ cup	70	12	2	2	400	1 starch
Homestyle, Flavored with Meat	½ cup	80	12	3	2	400	1 starch

SPATINI® (Thomas J. Lipton, Inc.)

Spaghetti Sauce Mix (as prepared)	½ cup (4 oz.)	80	16	4	0	520	1 starch

SAUCES, SEASONINGS, GRAVY MIXES

CHEF BOY-AR-DEE® (American Home Foods)

Chili Hotdog Sauce with Beef	2 Tbsp.	30	4	1	1	140	1 veg.

CONTADINA® (Calreco®, Inc.)

S Sweet 'n Sour Sauce	4 oz.	150	30	0	3	430	**

DIA-MEL® (Estee Corp.)

Barbecue Sauce, Dietetic	1 Tbsp.	18	3	<1	<1	0	Free

†For Occasional Use   **Not Recommended For Use   *Not Available   F More Than 2 Fat Exchanges   S Moderate To High Sugar Content

NUTRIENT VALUE

PRODUCTS	SERVING SIZE	CALORIES	CARBO-HYDRATE (g.)	PROTEIN (g.)	FAT (g.)	SODIUM (mg.)	EXCHANGES
Cocktail Sauce, Dietetic	1 Tbsp.	10	2	<1	<1	35	Free
Picante Sauce, Dietetic	2 Tbsp.	8	2	<1	0	60	Free
Steak Sauce, Dietetic	½ oz.	15	3	<1	<1	10	Free
Taco Sauce, Dietetic	2 Tbsp.	14	3	<1	0	25	Free

DURKEE® (Durkee Famous Foods)

PRODUCTS	SERVING SIZE	CALORIES	CARBO-HYDRATE (g.)	PROTEIN (g.)	FAT (g.)	SODIUM (mg.)	EXCHANGES
Chris' and Pitt's Barbeque Sauce	1 Tbsp.	15	4	0	0	141	Free
Famous Sauce	1 Tbsp.	69	2	1	7	67	1½ fat
Gravy Mix (as prepared) (average) Au Jus Mix	1 cup	31	7	2	0	913	1 veg. **or** ½ starch
Brown Brown with Mushrooms Brown with Onions Homestyle Mushroom Pork	½ cup	32	5	1	1	415-1085	1 veg.
Chicken Onion Turkey	½ cup	44	7	2	1	476-855	½ starch
Creamy Chicken	½ cup	78	7	1	5	764	½ starch, 1 fat
Swiss Steak	½ cup	23	5	1	0	740	1 veg.
Weight Watcher Gravy Mix, Brown or Chicken	2 Tbsp.	12-20	2-4	2	0-1	240-1040	Free
Sauce Mixes (as prepared) A-la-King	1 cup	133	14	1	8	1384	1 starch, 1½ fat
Cheese	1 cup	316	25	16	17	1098	1½ starch, 2 meat, 1 fat
Enchilada	1 cup	57	12	2	1	96	2 veg. **or** 1 starch

†For Occasional Use   **Not Recommended For Use   *Not Available   Ⓕ More Than 2 Fat Exchanges   Ⓢ Moderate To High Sugar Content

		NUTRIENT VALUE					
PRODUCTS	SERVING SIZE	CALORIES	CARBO-HYDRATE (g.)	PROTEIN (g.)	FAT (g.)	SODIUM (mg.)	EXCHANGES
Hollandaise	¾ cup	173	11	9	14	548	1 starch, 1 meat, 1½ fat
Lemon Butter	1 Tbsp.	6	1	0	1	120	Free
[S] Sweet and Sour	½ cup	115	23	1	3	527	1½ fruit, ½ fat†
[F] White Sauce	1 cup	317	23	11	20	799	1 starch, 1 skim milk, 3½ fat
FEATHERWEIGHT® (Sandoz Nutrition)							
Barbecue Sauce, Low Calorie, Low Sodium	2 Tbsp.	14	4	0	0	38	Free
Chili Sauce, Low Sodium	1 Tbsp.	8	2	0	0	10	Free
FRENCH'S® (The R. T. French Co.)							
Gravy Mixes, all varieties (as prepared) (average)	¼ cup	25	4	1	1	250-290	1 veg.
Sauce Mixes (as prepared)							
Cheese	¼ cup	80	7	3	4	425	½ skim milk, 1 fat
Hollandaise	3 Tbsp.	45	2	1	4	290	1 fat
Sour Cream	2½ Tbsp.	60	5	2	5	130	¼ skim milk, 1 fat
Stroganoff	⅓ cup	110	11	5	5	490	1 skim milk, 1 fat **or** 1 starch, 1 fat
[S] Sweet 'n Sour	½ cup	55	14	0	0	150	1 fruit†
Teriyaki Sauce	2 Tbsp.	35	7	1	0	1200	½ fruit **or** ½ starch
HEALTH VALLEY® (Health Valley Foods)							
"Tamari-Ya" Soy Sauce	1 Tbsp.	1	0	0	0	429	Free
HEINZ® (H.J. Heinz Co.)							
Barbecue Sauce, all varieties (average)	3 Tbsp.	60	15	0	0	200-230	1 fruit
Chili Sauce	1 Tbsp.	17	4	0	0	190	Free

†For Occasional Use **Not Recommended For Use *Not Available [F] More Than 2 Fat Exchanges [S] Moderate To High Sugar Content

NUTRIENT VALUE

PRODUCTS	SERVING SIZE	CALORIES	CARBO-HYDRATE (g.)	PROTEIN (g.)	FAT (g.)	SODIUM (mg.)	EXCHANGES
57 Sauce	1 Tbsp.	15	3	0	0	270	Free
Home Style Gravies, all varieties (average)	2 Tbsp. (1 oz.)	14	2	0	1	110-200	Free
Seafood Cocktail Sauce	1 Tbsp.	20	*	*	*	160	Free
Taco Sauce, all varieties (average)	2 Tbsp.	12	2	0	0	*	Free
HELLMAN'S® BIG H (Best Foods, CPC International, Inc.)							
Tartar Sauce	2 tsp.	47	0	0	5	147	1 fat
KRAFT® (Kraft, Inc.)							
Barbecue Sauce, all varieties (except Thick 'n Spicy) (average)	2 Tbsp.	40	9	0	1	420-630	½ fruit
[S] Barbecue Sauce, Thick 'n Spicy all varieties (average)	2 Tbsp.	60	12	0	1	380-510	1 fruit†
Horseradish Sauce	1 Tbsp.	50	2	0	5	100	1 fat
Tartar Sauce	2 tsp.	50	1	0	5	107	1 fat
MAGGIE GIN'S® (The Clorox Company)							
Sauces							
5-Spice Chicken Sauce	1 Tbsp.	56	4	3	4	401	1 fat
Hot and Spicy Sauce	1 Tbsp.	26	2	2	1	342	1 veg.
Pork and Rib Sauce	1 Tbsp.	40	7	2	0	248	½ starch
Seafood Sauce	1 Tbsp.	40	5	2	3	310	1 veg., ½ fat
Stir Fry Sauce	1 Tbsp.	27	4	2	0	304	1 veg.
Sweet and Sour Plum Sauce	1 Tbsp.	22	6	0	0	59	½ fruit
OCEAN SPRAY® (Ocean Spray Cranberries, Inc.)							
[S] Cranberry Sauce, Jellied	2 oz.	90	22	0	0	17	1½ fruit†
[S] Cranberry Sauce, Whole	2 oz.	90	22	0	0	16	1½ fruit†
[S] Cran-Orange Sauce	2 oz.	100	26	0	0	18	2 fruit†

†For Occasional Use **Not Recommended For Use *Not Available [F] More Than 2 Fat Exchanges [S] Moderate To High Sugar Content

NUTRIENT VALUE

PRODUCTS	SERVING SIZE	CALORIES	CARBO-HYDRATE (g.)	PROTEIN (g.)	FAT (g.)	SODIUM (mg.)	EXCHANGES
Ⓢ Cran-Raspberry Sauce, Jellied	2 oz.	90	21	0	0	14	1½ fruit†
OPEN PIT® (General Foods Corp.)							
Ⓢ Barbecue Sauce, all flavors (average)	2 Tbsp.	50	12	0	0	190-250	1 fruit†
PILLSBURY® (The Pillsbury Co.)							
Gravy Mixes (as prepared)							
Brown	¼ cup	15	3	<1	0	300	Free
Chicken	2 Tbsp.	13	2	<1	0	115	Free
Home Style	¼ cup	15	3	<1	0	300	Free
RAGÚ® (Chesebrough-Ponds, Inc.)							
Joe Sauce for Sloppy Joes	3½ oz.	50	11	1	0	645	1 starch **or** 2 veg.
RICHELIEU® (Western Dressings, Inc.)							
Barbecue Sauce	1 Tbsp.	20	5	0	0	7	Free
Ham Glaze	2 Tbsp.	50	12	0	0	15	1 fruit
Shrimp Sauce	3 Tbsp.	45	9	0	0	195	½ fruit
Smoked BBQ Sauce	1 Tbsp.	15	3	0	0	110	Free
Tartar Sauce	1 Tbsp.	35	3	0	3	115-120	½ fat
Vegetable Marinade	1 Tbsp.	20	5	0	0	240	Free
SAUCEWORKS® (Kraft, Inc.)							
Cocktail Sauce	1 Tbsp.	12	3	0	0	190	Free
Horseradish Sauce	1 Tbsp.	50	2	0	5	110	1 fat
Hot Mustard Sauce	1 Tbsp.	35	4	0	2	90	½ fat
Sweet 'N Sour Sauce	1 Tbsp.	20	5	0	0	50	Free
Tartar Sauce	2 tsp.	50	1	0	5	107	1 fat
Western BBQ Sauce	2 Tbsp.	50	11	0	1	510	1 fruit
SPATINI® (Thomas J. Lipton, Inc.)							
Family Style Brown Gravy Mix (as prepared)	1 oz.	8	2	0	0	205	Free

†For Occasional Use　　**Not Recommended For Use　　*Not Available　　Ⓕ More Than 2 Fat Exchanges　　Ⓢ Moderate To High Sugar Content

Snack Foods

NUTRIENT VALUE

PRODUCTS	SERVING SIZE	CALORIES	CARBO-HYDRATE (g.)	PROTEIN (g.)	FAT (g.)	SODIUM (mg.)	EXCHANGES
CHICO SAN® (H.J. Heinz Company)							
Rice Cakes, all varieties (average)	1 cake	35	8	0	0	0-10	½ starch
DURKEE (Durkee Famous Foods)							
O & C Potato Sticks	1 oz.	154	15	2	10	256	1 starch, 2 fat
ESTEE® (Estee Corp.)							
Pretzels, unsalted	15	75	15	1-2	1-2	<15	1 starch
FEATHERWEIGHT® (Sandoz Nutrition)							
Cheese Curls, Low Sodium	1 oz.	150	16	2	9	81	1 starch, 1½ fat
Corn Chips, Low Sodium	1 oz.	170	15	2	11	3	1 starch, 2 fat
Potato Chips, Low Sodium	1 oz.	160	14	2	11	10	1 starch, 2 fat
Pretzels, Low Sodium	12 pretzels	80	16	4	0	20	1 starch
FLAVOR TREE® (Thomas J. Lipton, Inc.)							
Cheddar Sticks	1 oz.	160	12	3	11	445	1 starch, 2 fat
Corn Chips	1 oz.	150	17	2	8	260	1 starch, 1½ fat
Corn Sticks, buttered and popped	1 oz.	160	15	2	10	220	1 starch, 2 fat
Fruit Rolls, all varieties (average)	1 roll (¾ oz.)	80	18	0	<1	15	1 fruit
Party Mix	1 oz.	160	11	4	11	400	1 starch, 2 fat
Party Mix, No Salt Added	1 oz.	160	11	4	11	10	1 starch, 2 fat

†For Occasional Use   **Not Recommended For Use   *Not Available   Ⓕ More Than 2 Fat Exchanges   Ⓢ Moderate To High Sugar Content

NUTRIENT VALUE

PRODUCTS	SERVING SIZE	CALORIES	CARBO-HYDRATE (g.)	PROTEIN (g.)	FAT (g.)	SODIUM (mg.)	EXCHANGES
Sesame Chips	1 oz.	150	13	3	10	410	1 starch, 2 fat
Sesame Crunch	1 oz.	150	10	5	10	70	½ starch, ½ meat, 1½ fat
Sesame Sticks	1 oz.	150	13	3	10	405	1 starch, 2 fat
Sesame Sticks, No Salt Added	1 oz.	160	12	3	11	10	1 starch, 2 fat
Sesame Sticks with Bran	1 oz.	160	11	4	11	370	1 starch, 2 fat
Sour Cream and Onion Sticks	1 oz.	150	13	3	10	415	1 starch, 2 fat
F Wheat Nuts	1 oz.	200	5	4	18	185	½ meat, 3 fat

FRITO-LAY® (Frito-Lay, Inc.)

PRODUCTS	SERVING SIZE	CALORIES	CARBO-HYDRATE (g.)	PROTEIN (g.)	FAT (g.)	SODIUM (mg.)	EXCHANGES
Baken-ets® Fried Pork Rind	1 oz.	150	1	17	9	570	2 meat
Cheese Flavored Popcorn	1 oz.	150	14	3	9	185	1 starch, 1½ fat
Chee●tos®, all varieties (average)	1 oz.	160	15	2	10	260-350	1 starch, 2 fat
Delta Gold™ Potato Chips, all varieties (average)	1 oz.	150	15	2	10	200	1 starch, 2 fat
Doritos® Tortilla Chips, all varieties (average)	1 oz.	140	18	2	7	190-250	1 starch, 1 fat
Fritos® Corn Chips, all varieties (average)	1 oz.	160	16	2	10	190-320	1 starch, 2 fat
Funyuns® Onion Flavored Snack	1 oz.	140	18	2	6	260	1 starch, 1 fat
Lay's® Potato Chips, all varieties (average)	1 oz.	150	14	2	10	260-325	1 starch, 2 fat
Munchos® Potato Crisps	1 oz.	150	16	1	9	290	1 starch, 1½ fat
O'Grady's® Potato Chips, all varieties (average)	1 oz.	150	16	2	9	160-390	1 starch, 1½ fat

†For Occasional Use   **Not Recommended For Use   *Not Available   F More Than 2 Fat Exchanges   S Moderate To High Sugar Content

NUTRIENT VALUE

PRODUCTS	SERVING SIZE	CALORIES	CARBO-HYDRATE (g.)	PROTEIN (g.)	FAT (g.)	SODIUM (mg.)	EXCHANGES
Rold Gold®							
Pretzel Rods	¾ oz.	80	16	2	1	375	1 starch
Pretzel Sticks	¾ oz.	80	16	2	1	500	1 starch
Pretzel Twists	¾ oz.	80	16	2	1	300	1 starch
Ruffles® Potato Chips, all varieties (average)	1 oz.	150	15	2	10	260-325	1 starch, 2 fat
Rumbles™ Granola Nuggets, all varieties (average)	1 oz.	140	20	2	6	70-100	1 starch, 1 fat
Santitas® Corn Tortilla Chips	1 oz.	140	20	2	6	80	1 starch, 1 fat
Smoked Beef Sticks	½ oz.	80	0	3	7	215	½ meat, 1 fat
Toppels® Flavored Snack Thins, all varieties (average)	1 oz.	130	19	2	5	370-610	1 starch, 1 fat
Tostitos® Round Chips, all varieties (average)	1 oz.	150	17	2	8	180-220	1 starch, 1½ fat
FRUIT CORNERS™ (General Mills, Inc.)							
Chewy Fruit Bars, all varieties (average)	1 bar	90	18	<1	2	10	1 fruit, ½ fat
Fruit Roll-ups®, all varieties (average)	1 roll (½ oz.)	50	12	0	<1	5-10	1 fruit
Fruit Wrinkles	1 pouch	100	21	<1	2	50-140	1½ fruit
GENERAL MILLS (General Mills, Inc.)							
Bugles®, all varieties (average)	1 oz.	150	18	2	8	270-290	1 starch 1½ fat
HEALTH VALLEY® (Health Valley Foods)							
Cheese Puffs	½ oz.	80	8	2	4	70	½ starch, 1 fat
Cheese Puffs, No Salt	½ oz.	80	8	2	4	20	½ starch, 1 fat
Corn Chips, all varieties (average)	1 oz.	160	15	2	11	90-115	1 starch, 2 fat

†For Occasional Use   **Not Recommended For Use   *Not Available   F More Than 2 Fat Exchanges   S Moderate To High Sugar Content

NUTRIENT VALUE

PRODUCTS	SERVING SIZE	CALORIES	CARBO-HYDRATE (g.)	PROTEIN (g.)	FAT (g.)	SODIUM (mg.)	EXCHANGES
Corn Chips, No Salt, all varieties (average)	1 oz.	160	15	2	10	1-34	1 starch, 2 fat
Fruit Bakes, all varieties (average)	1½ oz.	180	33	3	4	35-45	1 starch, 1 fruit, 1 fat
Potato Chips, all varieties (average)	1 oz.	160	14	2	11	60	1 starch, 2 fat
Potato Chips, No Salt, all varieties (average)	1 oz.	160	14	2	11	1	1 starch, 2 fat
Pretzels	¾ oz.	90	15	3	2	200	1 starch
Pretzels, No Salt	¾ oz.	90	15	3	2	10	1 starch
Tortilla Chips/ Buenitos, all varieties (average)	1 oz.	150	17	2	8	60-100	1 starch, 1½ fat
Tortilla Chips/ Buenitos, No Salt, all varieties (average)	1 oz.	150	17	2	8	5	1 starch, 1½ fat
JIFFY POP® (American Home Foods)							
Popcorn, regular (as prepared)	⅓ package	180	21	4	9	680	1½ starch, 1½ fat
Popcorn, butter flavor (as prepared)	⅓ package	210	24	4	11	640	1½ starch, 2 fat
KRAFT® HANDI-SNACKS® (Kraft, Inc.)							
Cheez 'n Crackers	1 package	130	8	4	9	440	½ starch, ½ meat, 1 fat
Peanut Butter 'n Cheez Crackers	1 package	190	11	6	13	250	1 starch, ½ meat, 2 fat
LITE MUNCHIES® (Superior Protein Products Co.)							
Lite Munchies®, all varieties (average)	½ oz.	60	6	4	2	60-130	½ skim milk, ½ fat

†For Occasional Use   **Not Recommended For Use   *Not Available   F More Than 2 Fat Exchanges   S Moderate To High Sugar Content

NUTRIENT VALUE

PRODUCTS	SERVING SIZE	CALORIES	CARBO-HYDRATE (g.)	PROTEIN (g.)	FAT (g.)	SODIUM (mg.)	EXCHANGES
MISTER SALTY® (Nabisco Brands, Inc.)							
Dutch Pretzels	2 (1 oz.)	110	22	3	1	440	1½ starch
Pretzel Juniors, plain or butter flavored	22 (¾ oz.)	83	16	2	1	383	1 starch
Pretzel Logs	7 (¾ oz.)	83	16	2	1	383	1 starch
Pretzel Mini	12 (¾ oz.)	83	16	2	1	338	1 starch
Pretzel Nuggets	16 (¾ oz.)	83	16	2	1	413	1 starch
Pretzel Rings, plain or butter flavor	17 (¾ oz.)	83	16	2	2	383-428	1 starch
Pretzel Rods	2 (1 oz.)	110	21	3	1	500	1½ starch
Pretzel Sticks, plain or butter flavor	68 (¾ oz.)	83	17	2	1	465	1 starch
Pretzel Twists, plain or butter flavor	4 (0.8 oz.)	88	17	2	2	408-472	1 starch
Veri-Thin Pretzel Sticks	34 (¾ oz.)	83	17	2	1	578	1 starch
NABISCO® (Nabisco Brands, Inc.)							
Cheese 'n Crunch Cheese Flavored Snack	41 (1 oz.)	160	15	2	11	190	1 starch, 2 fat
Chipsters® Light 'n Crisp Potato Snacks	57 (1 oz.)	120	19	1	5	580	1 starch, 1 fat
Corn and Sesame Chips	16 (1 oz.)	160	15	3	10	*	1 bread, 2 fat
Diggers®	36 (1 oz.)	150	17	2	8	260	1 starch, 1½ fat
DooDads Snacks, all varieties (average)	1 oz.	140	18	3	6	350-420	1 starch, 1 fat

†For Occasional Use   **Not Recommended For Use   *Not Available   F More Than 2 Fat Exchanges   S Moderate To High Sugar Content

PRODUCTS	SERVING SIZE	CALORIES	CARBO-HYDRATE (g.)	PROTEIN (g.)	FAT (g.)	SODIUM (mg.)	EXCHANGES
		NUTRIENT VALUE					
NATURE VALLEY® (General Mills, Inc.)							
[S] Dandy Bars™	1 bar	160	23	2	7	105-110	1 starch, ½ fruit, 1 fat†
[S] Granola Bars, all varieties (average)	1 bar	120	17	2	5	65-85	1 starch, 1 fat†
[S] Peanut Butter Boppers™	1 bar	170	15	4	10	100-125	1 starch, 2 fat†
NEW TRAIL® (Hershey Foods Corp.)							
[S] Granola Snack Bars, all varieties (average)	1.4 oz. bar	200	23	4	10	100-110	1½ starch, 2 fat†
PILLSBURY (The Pillsbury Co.)							
Microwave Popcorn, frozen							
Original or Butter flavored (average)	3 cups, popped	190	19	3	11	270	1 starch, 2 fat
Salt Free	3 cups, popped	140	19	3	6	5	1 starch, 1 fat
PLANTERS® (Nabisco Brands, Inc.)							
Cheese Curls	1 oz.	160	14	2	11	290	1 starch, 2 fat
Cheez Balls	1 oz.	160	14	2	11	270	1 starch, 2 fat
Corn Chips	1 oz.	160	15	2	10	160	1 starch, 2 fat
Crackers, Round Toast or Square Cheese	1 oz.	140	15	4	7	270	1 starch, 1 fat
Naturally Nut 'n Fruit Bars, all varieties (average)	1 oz.	140	17	3	7	70-90	1 starch, 1 fat
Pizza Crunchies	1 oz.	160	15	2	10	160	1 starch, 2 fat
Pretzels	¾ oz.	83	16	2	1	525	1 starch
Sour Cream and Onion Puffs	1 oz.	160	16	1	10	300	1 starch, 2 fat
Tortilla Chips, all varieties (average)	1 oz.	150	18	2	8	150-160	1 starch, 1½ fat

†For Occasional Use **Not Recommended For Use *Not Available [F] More Than 2 Fat Exchanges [S] Moderate To High Sugar Content

NUTRIENT VALUE

PRODUCTS	SERVING SIZE	CALORIES	CARBO-HYDRATE (g.)	PROTEIN (g.)	FAT (g.)	SODIUM (mg.)	EXCHANGES
POP SECRET® (General Mills, Inc.)							
Popcorn, all varieties (average)	2 cups	120	14	2	7	210-220	1 starch, 1 fat
QUAKER® (Quaker Oats Company)							
Ⓢ Chewy® Granola Bars, all varieties (average)	1 bar	130	18	3	5	95-130	1 starch, 1 fat†
Ⓢ Granola Dipps® Bars, all varieties (average)	1 bar	140	18	2	6	70-105	1 starch, 1 fat†
SKINNY CRUNCHY™ (Skinny Haven, Inc.)							
Carob and Rice, plain or mint flavored	1 package (⅞ oz.)	125	15	2	6	*	1 starch, 1 fat
SKINNY MUNCHIES® (Skinny Haven, Inc.)							
Chocolate Fudge	1 package (½ oz.)	66	9	1	2	30	½ starch, ½ fat
Nacho Cheese	1 package (½ oz.)	59	7	2	2	110	½ starch, ½ fat
Smoky Bar-B-Q	1 package (½ oz.)	59	7	2	2	150	½ starch, ½ fat
Toasted Onion	1 package (½ oz.)	59	7	2	2	120	½ starch, ½ fat
SUNKIST® (Thomas J. Lipton, Inc.)							
Fruit Rolls, all flavors (average)	1 roll (½ oz.)	50	12	0	<1	10	1 fruit
SUN●MAID® (Sun●Maid Growers of California)							
Apple Chunks (dried apples)	1 oz.	75	21	1	0	<40	1½ fruit
Fruit Bits	1 oz.	75	20	1	0	<50	1½ fruit
Mixed Fruit	1 oz.	75	20	1	0	<20	1½ fruit
WEIGHT WATCHERS® (Nutrition Industries Corp.)							
Fruit Snacks, all varieties (average)	1 package (½ oz.)	50	13	<1	<1	75	1 fruit

†For Occasional Use   **Not Recommended For Use   *Not Available   Ⓕ More Than 2 Fat Exchanges   Ⓢ Moderate To High Sugar Content

Soups

NUTRIENT VALUE

PRODUCTS	SERVING SIZE	CALORIES	CARBO-HYDRATE (g.)	PROTEIN (g.)	FAT (g.)	SODIUM (mg.)	EXCHANGES
CAMPBELL'S® (Campbell Soup Co.)							
Chunky Soups, Ready to Serve, Individual Serving							
Chunky Beef	1 can (10¾ oz.)	190	23	14	5	1110	1½ starch, 1 meat
Chunky Stroganoff Style Beef	1 can (10¾ oz.)	300	28	15	15	1290	2 starch, 1 meat, 2 fat
Chunky Chicken Noodle with Mushrooms	1 can (10¾ oz.)	200	20	14	7	1190	1 starch, 1 veg., 1 lean meat, 1 fat
Chunky Old Fashioned Bean 'n Ham	1 can (11 oz.)	290	37	14	9	1150	2½ starch, 1 meat, ½ fat
Chunky Old Fashioned Chicken	1 can (10¾ oz.)	170	21	12	5	1340	1½ starch, 1 lean meat
Chunky Old Fashioned Vegetable Beef	1 can (10¾ oz.)	180	20	12	5	1210	1 starch, 1 veg., 1 meat
Chunky Sirloin Burger	1 can (10¾ oz.)	220	23	12	9	1285	1½ starch, 1 meat, ½ fat
Chunky Split Pea with Ham	1 can (10¾ oz.)	230	33	12	6	1070	2 starch, 1 meat
Chunky Soups, Ready to Serve 19 oz. size							
Chunky Chicken Rice	½ can (9½ oz.)	140	15	10	4	1080	1 starch, 1 meat

†For Occasional Use   **Not Recommended For Use   *Not Available   Ⓕ More Than 2 Fat Exchanges   Ⓢ Moderate To High Sugar Content

NUTRIENT VALUE

PRODUCTS	SERVING SIZE	CALORIES	CARBO-HYDRATE (g.)	PROTEIN (g.)	FAT (g.)	SODIUM (mg.)	EXCHANGES
Chunky Chicken Vegetable	½ can (9½ oz.)	170	19	10	6	1110	1 starch, 1 veg., 1 meat
Chunky Chili Beef	½ can (9¾ oz.)	260	33	19	6	1020	2 starch, 2 lean meat
Chunky Clam Chowder (Manhattan Style)	½ can (9½ oz.)	150	22	6	4	1080	1½ starch, ½ fat
Chunky Mediterranean Vegetable	½ can (9½ oz.)	160	24	4	5	1020	1½ starch, 1 fat
Chunky Minestrone	½ can (9½ oz.)	140	21	4	5	940	1 starch, 1 veg., 1 fat
Chunky Steak 'n Potato	½ can (9½ oz.)	170	21	12	4	1110	1½ starch, 1 meat
Chunky Turkey Vegetable	½ can (9⅜ oz.)	150	16	9	6	1080	1 starch, 1 lean meat, ½ fat
Chunky Vegetable	½ can (9½ oz.)	130	21	3	4	970	1 starch, 1 veg., ½ fat
Condensed, Canned (as prepared)							
Asparagus, Cream of	1 cup	90	11	2	4	900	1 starch, ½ fat
Bean with Bacon	1 cup	150	21	6	5	860	1½ starch, 1 fat
Beef	1 cup	80	10	6	2	855	½ starch, ½ meat **or** 1 starch
Beef Noodle	1 cup	70	7	4	3	870	½ starch, ½ fat
Celery, Cream of	1 cup	100	8	1	7	860	½ starch, 1 fat
Cheddar Cheese	1 cup	130	10	3	8	800	½ starch, 1½ fat
Chicken Noodle	1 cup	70	8	3	2	920	½ starch, ½ fat
Chicken Vegetable	1 cup	70	8	3	3	870	½ starch, ½ fat
Chili Beef	1 cup	130	17	5	5	900	1 starch, 1 fat
Clam Chowder, New England (with water)	1 cup	80	11	3	3	880	1 starch, ½ fat

†For Occasional Use   **Not Recommended For Use   *Not Available   Ⓕ More Than 2 Fat Exchanges   Ⓢ Moderate To High Sugar Content

NUTRIENT VALUE

PRODUCTS	SERVING SIZE	CALORIES	CARBO-HYDRATE (g.)	PROTEIN (g.)	FAT (g.)	SODIUM (mg.)	EXCHANGES
Green Pea	1 cup	160	25	8	3	840	1½ starch, ½ lean meat
Minestrone	1 cup	80	12	4	2	930	1 starch
Mushroom, Cream of	1 cup	100	9	1	7	820	½ starch, 1 fat
Mushroom, Golden	1 cup	80	10	2	3	900	½ starch, ½ fat **or** 1 starch
Oyster Stew (with water)	1 cup	80	5	3	5	850	½ starch, 1 fat
Potato, Cream of	1 cup	70	11	1	3	930	½ starch, ½ fat
Split Pea with Ham and Bacon	1 cup	160	24	8	4	800	1½ starch, ½ fat
Tomato (with water)	1 cup	90	17	1	2	720	1 starch
Vegetable	1 cup	80	13	3	2	770	1 starch
Vegetable, Old Fashioned	1 cup	60	9	2	2	910	2 veg. **or** ½ starch, ½ fat
Vegetarian Vegetable	1 cup	80	13	2	2	770	1 starch
Won Ton	1 cup	40	5	3	1	870	½ starch
Home Style Soups, Condensed (as prepared)							
Beef Noodle	1 cup	80	8	6	3	810	½ starch, ½ meat
Chicken Noodle	1 cup	70	8	3	3	920	½ starch, ½ fat
Tomato, Cream of (with water)	1 cup	110	20	1	3	830	1 starch, ½ fat
Vegetable	1 cup	80	13	3	2	770	1 starch
Ready to Serve, Low Sodium							
Chicken with Noodles	10¾ oz.	160	15	14	5	85	1 starch, 1½ lean meat
Chunky Beef and Mushroom	10¾ oz.	210	23	13	7	65	1 starch, 1 veg., 1 meat
Chunky Chicken Vegetable	10¾ oz.	240	20	15	11	95	1 starch, 1 veg., 1½ meat, ½ fat
F Cream of Mushroom	10½ oz.	200	17	3	14	55	1 starch, 2½ fat

†For Occasional Use   **Not Recommended For Use   *Not Available   F More Than 2 Fat Exchanges   S Moderate To High Sugar Content

NUTRIENT VALUE

PRODUCTS	SERVING SIZE	CALORIES	CARBO-HYDRATE (g.)	PROTEIN (g.)	FAT (g.)	SODIUM (mg.)	EXCHANGES
French Onion	10½ oz.	80	8	2	4	50	½ starch, 1 fat
Split Pea	10¾ oz.	240	38	11	5	25	2½ starch, ½ meat
Tomato with Tomato Pieces	10½ oz.	180	29	3	5	40	2 starch, 1 fat
Semi-Condensed Soup for One (as prepared)							
Bean with Ham, Old Fashioned	11 oz.	220	30	8	7	1400	2 starch, 1 fat
Burly Vegetable Beef and Bacon	11 oz.	160	20	8	5	1480	1 starch, 1 veg., 1 fat
Clam Chowder, New England (with water)	11 oz.	130	19	6	4	1360	1 starch, ½ meat
Chicken Vegetable, Full Flavored	11 oz.	120	13	4	6	1500	1 starch, 1 fat
Golden Chicken and Noodles	11 oz.	120	14	6	4	1450	1 starch, ½ meat
F Savory Cream of Mushroom	11 oz.	180	14	3	13	1500	1 starch, 2½ fat
Tomato Royale	11 oz.	180	35	3	3	1080	2 starch, 1 veg.

DIA-MEL® (Estee Corp.)
Soups, Dietetic

PRODUCTS	SERVING SIZE	CALORIES	CARBO-HYDRATE (g.)	PROTEIN (g.)	FAT (g.)	SODIUM (mg.)	EXCHANGES
Chicken Noodle	8 oz.	50	7	3	1	20	½ starch
Cream of Mushroom	8 oz.	85	9	2	5	30	½ starch, 1 fat
Tomato	8 oz.	50	11	1	<1	15	2 veg. or 1 starch
Vegetable Beef	8 oz.	70	12	3	2	20	1 starch

ESTEE® (Estee Corp.)
Soup Mixes, Dietetic (as prepared)

PRODUCTS	SERVING SIZE	CALORIES	CARBO-HYDRATE (g.)	PROTEIN (g.)	FAT (g.)	SODIUM (mg.)	EXCHANGES
Beef Vegetable	6 oz.	30	3	2	<1	115	1 veg.
Chicken Noodle	6 oz.	35	2	2	1	140	1 veg.
Manhattan Clam Chowder	6 oz.	30	3	2	0	130	1 veg.
Mushroom	6 oz.	30	2	2	1	140	1 veg.
Tomato	6 oz.	40	5	1	<1	55	1 veg.

†For Occasional Use   **Not Recommended For Use   *Not Available   F More Than 2 Fat Exchanges   S Moderate To High Sugar Content

NUTRIENT VALUE

PRODUCTS	SERVING SIZE	CALORIES	CARBO-HYDRATE (g.)	PROTEIN (g.)	FAT (g.)	SODIUM (mg.)	EXCHANGES
FEATHERWEIGHT® (Sandoz Nutrition)							
Beef or Chicken Instant Bouillon, Low Sodium	1 tsp.	18	2	0	1	5-10	Free
Soups, Low Sodium, (as prepared)							
Chicken Noodle	1 cup	60	8	4	2	40	½ starch ½ lean meat
Mushroom	1 cup	50	9	1	2	15	½ starch
Tomato	1 cup	60	15	2	0	10	1 starch
Vegetable Beef	1 cup	80	12	4	3	20	1 starch, ½ fat
HEALTH VALLEY® (Health Valley Foods)							
Bean	4 oz.	115	16	5	3	640	1 starch, ½ fat
Clam Chowder	8 oz.	160	16	8	6	780	1 starch, 1 meat
Green Split Pea	4 oz.	80	13	6	1	680	1 starch
Lentil	8 oz.	160	12	10	8	940	1 starch, 1 lean meat, 1 fat
Minestrone	8 oz.	180	20	6	8	780	1 starch, ½ meat, 1 fat
Mushroom	8 oz.	140	16	6	6	700	1 starch, 1 fat
Potato	8 oz.	140	20	6	4	1080	1 starch, 1 fat
Tomato	8 oz.	120	16	4	4	740	1 starch, 1 fat
Vegetable	8 oz.	160	18	4	8	1160	1 starch, 1½ fat
Chunky Soups							
Bean	4 oz.	100	14	4	4	310	1 starch, ½ fat
Clam Chowder	8 oz.	160	16	8	6	720	1 starch, 1 lean meat, ½ fat
Minestrone	4 oz.	70	12	3	1	295	1 starch
Split Pea	8 oz.	140	20	10	2	610	1 starch, 1 lean meat
Vegetable	8 oz.	140	20	6	4	800	1 starch, 1 veg., 1 fat
Vegetable Beef	8 oz.	170	16	8	8	560	1 starch, 1 meat, ½ fat
Vegetable Chicken	4 oz.	120	10	3	7	240	½ starch, 1½ fat

†For Occasional Use   **Not Recommended For Use   *Not Available   F More Than 2 Fat Exchanges   S Moderate To High Sugar Content

NUTRIENT VALUE

PRODUCTS	SERVING SIZE	CALORIES	CARBO-HYDRATE (g.)	PROTEIN (g.)	FAT (g.)	SODIUM (mg.)	EXCHANGES
LIPTON® (Thomas J. Lipton, Inc.)							
Cup-A-Soup® (as prepared)							
Chicken (Cup-A-Broth)	6 oz.	25	4	1	<1	780	1 veg.
Cream of Mushroom Cream of Chicken	6 oz.	80	9	2	4	830-890	½ starch, 1 fat
Green Pea	6 oz.	120	16	4	4	710	1 starch, 1 fat
Tomato	6 oz.	100	20	3	1	570	1 starch
Onion	6 oz.	30	5	1	1	870	1 veg.
Seafood Flavor Bisque	6 oz.	160	20	3	8	820	1 starch, 1½ fat
Beef Flavored Noodle Chicken Noodle with Meat Chicken Rice Chicken Vegetable Ring Noodle Spring Vegetable Vegetable Beef	6 oz.	45	8	2	1	570-865	½ starch
Cup-A-Soup®, Country Style (as prepared)							
Chicken Flavor and Sweet Corn	6 oz.	130	17	3	6	700	1 starch, 1 fat
Chicken Supreme	6 oz.	100	11	3	5	870	1 starch, 1 fat
Cream of Tomato	6 oz.	100	21	2	1	850	1½ starch
Harvest Vegetable	6 oz.	80	16	2	1	590	1 starch
Hearty Chicken	6 oz.	70	10	4	1	970	1 starch
Shrimp Bisque	6 oz.	180	17	4	11	970	1 starch, 2 fat
Tomato Noodle with Meatballs and Vegetables	6 oz.	100	15	5	2	770	1 starch
Virginia Pea	6 oz.	140	18	5	5	870	1 starch, ½ meat, ½ fat
Cup-A-Soup®, Lots-A-Noodles® (as prepared)							
Beef Flavor Chicken Flavor Garden Vegetable Oriental Style	7 oz.	120	22	5	2	745-940	1½ starch

†For Occasional Use   **Not Recommended For Use   *Not Available   Ⓕ More Than 2 Fat Exchanges   Ⓢ Moderate To High Sugar Content

NUTRIENT VALUE

PRODUCTS	SERVING SIZE	CALORIES	CARBO-HYDRATE (g.)	PROTEIN (g.)	FAT (g.)	SODIUM (mg.)	EXCHANGES
Cream of Chicken	7 oz.	150	22	5	5	755	1½ starch, 1 fat
Tomato Vegetable	7 oz.	110	21	4	1	855	1½ starch
Cup-A-Soup® Trim, all varieties (as prepared) (average)	6 oz.	10	1	1	0	440-695	Free
Hearty Soup, all varieties, except Cream of Chicken, (as prepared) (average)	8 oz.	80	14	3	1-2	680-930	1 starch
Hearty Cream of Chicken Vegetable Soup Mix (as prepared)	8 oz.	110	12	2	4	760	1 starch, ½ fat
International Soup Classics California Cream of Broccoli (as prepared)	9 oz.	170	17	7	7	920	1 starch, ½ meat, 1 fat
Soup, Dry Mix (as prepared) (average) Beef Flavored Mushroom Beefy Onion Onion Onion Mushroom	8 oz.	35-45	5-7	1	1	640-995	½ starch **or** 1 veg.
Cream of Asparagus Parisienne Golden Mushroom Chicken Broth Golden Onion Vegetable Beef	8 oz.	60	8	3	1	900-995	½ starch **or** 2 veg.
Chicken and Mushroom Royale	8 oz.	150	9	7	9	880	½ starch, 1 meat, 1 fat
Country Vegetable	8 oz.	80	14	3	1	995	1 starch
Cream of Mushroom a La Reine	9 oz.	180	19	8	7	1030	1 starch, ½ meat, 1 fat
Nacho Cheese Soup and Recipe Mix	8 oz.	120	13	6	5	910	1 starch, ½ meat, ½ fat
New England Clam Chowder	9 oz.	120	19	5	2	920	1 starch, ½ meat

†For Occasional Use   **Not Recommended For Use   *Not Available   Ⓕ More Than 2 Fat Exchanges   Ⓢ Moderate To High Sugar Content

NUTRIENT VALUE

PRODUCTS	SERVING SIZE	CALORIES	CARBO-HYDRATE (g.)	PROTEIN (g.)	FAT (g.)	SODIUM (mg.)	EXCHANGES
Noodle, all varieties (average)	8 oz.	70	10	3	2	785-925	1 starch
Soup, Frozen Chicken Noodle	8 oz.	100	12	6	3	810	1 starch, ½ fat
Homestyle Beef with Rotini	8 oz.	130	14	8	4	1110	1 starch, ½ meat
Creamy Harvest Broccoli	8 oz.	140	13	5	7	1130	1 starch, 1 fat
Old Country Creamy Mushroom	8 oz.	150	13	5	9	1010	1 starch, 1½ fat
Old Fashioned Minestrone	8 oz.	190	24	8	7	800	1½ starch, ½ meat, ½ fat

STOUFFER'S® (Stouffer Foods Corp.)

PRODUCTS	SERVING SIZE	CALORIES	CARBO-HYDRATE (g.)	PROTEIN (g.)	FAT (g.)	SODIUM (mg.)	EXCHANGES
F Cream of Spinach	8 oz.	220	16	7	14	1020	1 starch, ½ meat, 2½ fat
New England Clam Chowder	8 oz.	200	16	8	11	790	1 starch, 1 meat, 1 fat
Split Pea with Ham	8¼ oz.	200	30	12	3	1130	2 starch, 1 lean meat

†For Occasional Use   **Not Recommended For Use   *Not Available   F More Than 2 Fat Exchanges   S Moderate To High Sugar Content

Vegetables

NUTRIENT VALUE

PRODUCTS	SERVING SIZE	CALORIES	CARBO-HYDRATE (g.)	PROTEIN (g.)	FAT (g.)	SODIUM (mg.)	EXCHANGES
CONTADINA® (Calreco®, Inc.)							
Multipurpose Sauces							
Tomato Puree	¼ cup	24	5	1	0	*	1 veg.
Tomato Sauce	¼ cup	24	5	1	0	*	1 veg.
DURKEE® (Durkee Famous Foods)							
F French Fried Onions	1 oz.	175	9	2	15	178	½ starch, 3 fat **or** 2 veg., 3 fat
MOORE'S® (The Clorox Company)							
Onion Rings, fried	2½ oz.	200	25	3	9	190	1 starch, 1 veg., 2 fat
MRS. PAUL'S® (Campbell Soup Co.)							
S Candied Yams	4 oz.	200	48	0	1	125	**
S Candied Yams n' Apples	4 oz.	160	39	0	0	70	1 starch, 1½ fruit†
Crispy Onion Rings	2½ oz.	180	20	2	10	270	1 starch, 1 veg., 2 fat
F Eggplant Parmigiana	5½ oz.	270	20	8	17	905	1 starch, 1 veg., ½ meat, 3 fat
Light Batter Zucchini Sticks	3 oz.	200	21	2	12	440	1 starch, 1 veg., 2 fat
ORE-IDA® (Ore-Ida Foods, Inc.)							
Onion Ringers®	2 oz.	130	18	2	7	190	1 starch, 1 fat
PEPPERIDGE FARM® (Campbell Soup Co.)							
Vegetables in Pastry							
F Asparagus with Mornay Sauce	1 pastry	240	19	5	16	250	1 starch, 1 veg., 3 fat
F Broccoli with Cheese	1 pastry	230	18	5	16	380	1 starch, 1 veg., 3 fat

†For Occasional Use   **Not Recommended For Use   *Not Available   F More Than 2 Fat Exchanges   S Moderate To High Sugar Content

NUTRIENT VALUE

	PRODUCTS	SERVING SIZE	CALORIES	CARBO-HYDRATE (g.)	PROTEIN (g.)	FAT (g.)	SODIUM (mg.)	EXCHANGES
F	Cauliflower and Cheese Sauce	1 pastry	210	19	5	13	450	1 starch, 1 veg., 2½ fat
F	Green Beans with Mushroom Sauce	1 pastry	250	20	4	17	270	1 starch, 1 veg., 3 fat
F	Mushroom Dijon	1 pastry	220	19	4	15	340	1 starch, 1 veg., 3 fat

STOUFFER'S® (Stouffer Foods Corp.)

	PRODUCTS	SERVING SIZE	CALORIES	CARBO-HYDRATE (g.)	PROTEIN (g.)	FAT (g.)	SODIUM (mg.)	EXCHANGES
	Broccoli in Cheddar Cheese Sauce	½ of 9 oz. package	150	7	8	10	480	1 veg., 1 meat, 1 fat
F	Creamed Spinach	½ of 9 oz. package	190	9	4	15	440	2 veg., 3 fat
	Corn Souffle	⅓ of 12 oz. package	150	16	5	7	540	1 starch, 1½ fat
F	Green Bean Mushroom Casserole	½ of 9½ oz. package	170	12	3	12	640	2 veg., 2½ fat
	Ratatouille	½ of 10 oz. package	80	8	2	4	800	1½ veg., 1 fat
	Spinach Souffle	⅓ of 12 oz. package	140	10	5	9	560	2 veg., 2 fat
	Yams and Apples	½ of 10 oz. package	160	33	1	3	200	1 starch, 1 fruit, ½ fat

VAN CAMP'S® (Quaker Oats Co.)

	PRODUCTS	SERVING SIZE	CALORIES	CARBO-HYDRATE (g.)	PROTEIN (g.)	FAT (g.)	SODIUM (mg.)	EXCHANGES
	Golden Hominy	½ cup	65	15	2	1	350	1 starch
	White Hominy	½ cup	70	15	2	1	355	1 starch

†For Occasional Use   **Not Recommended For Use   *Not Available   F More Than 2 Fat Exchanges   S Moderate To High Sugar Content

Index

If you found this book helpful and would like more information on this and other related subjects you may be interested in one or more of the following titles from our *Wellness and Nutrition Library*.

BOOKS:
The Joy of Snacks—Good Nutrition for People Who Like to Snack (270 pages)
The Physician Within (176 pages)
Pass The Pepper Please (90 pages)
Fast Food Facts (60 pages)
Convenience Food Facts (210 pages)
Opening The Door To Good Nutrition (186 pages)
Learning To Live Well With Diabetes (392 pages)
Exchanges For All Occasions (210 pages)
A Guide To Healthy Eating (60 pages)

BOOKLETS & PAMPHLETS
Diabetes & Alcohol (4 pages)
Diabetes & Exercise (20 pages)
Emotional Adjustment to Diabetes (16 pages)
Healthy Footsteps For People With Diabetes (13 pages)
Diabetes Record Book (68 pages)
Diabetes & Brief Illness (8 pages)
Diabetes & Impotence: A Concern for Couples (6 pages)
Adding Fiber To Your Diet (10 pages)
Gestational Diabetes: Guidelines for A Safe Pregnancy and Healthy Baby (24 pages)
Recognizing and Treating Insulin Reactions (4 pages)
Hypoglycemia (functional) (4 pages)

The *Wellness and Nutrition Library* is published by Diabetes Center, Inc. in Minneapolis, Minnesota, publishers of quality educational materials dealing with health, wellness, nutrition, diabetes and other chronic illnesses. All our books and materials are available nationwide and in Canada through leading bookstores. If you are unable to find our books at your favorite bookstore contact us directly for a free catalog:

Diabetes Center, Inc.
P.O. Box 739
Wayzata, MN 55391